Borders and Brethren

Iran and the Challenge of Azerbaijani Identity

Brenda Shaffer

BCSIA Studies in International Security

The MIT Press
Cambridge, Massachusetts
London, England

Library of Congress Cataloging-in-Publication Data

Shaffer, Brenda.
Borders and brethren : Iran and the challenge of Azerbaijani identity /
Brenda Shaffer.
p.   cm. — (BCSIA studies in international security)
Includes bibliographical references and index.
ISBN 0-262-19477-5 (hc. : alk. paper) — ISBN 0-262-69277-5 (pbk. : alk. paper)
1. Nationalism — Azerbaijan — History — 20th century. 2. Azerbaijanis —
Iran — Ethnic identity. I. Title. II. Series.

DK697.3 .S49   2002
305.8'009553 — dc21   2001054651

On the cover: The Astara border crossing between Azerbaijan and Iran. Astara is a divided city. Photo by Rahim Gadimov. Design assistance from Donna Whipple.

In memory of Melanie Rose Silverman and Edward Silverman

Contents

Acknowledgments

Many people have been generous with their time, ideas, and materials and have contributed to this research. I would like to express my special gratitude to Professor David Menashri and Professor Yaacov Ro'i, who served as my advisers in the doctoral dissertation at Tel-Aviv University that formed the basis for this book. I am also indebted to Professor Ronald Grigor Suny, Professor Tadeusz Swietochowski and Professor Ervand Abrahamian, whose comments were essential to this book. Professor Abrahamian also shared many materials with me, such as his collection of the Khalq-e Musulman newspapers. Professor Nasib Nasibli served as an excellent teacher and shared essential documents with me. Dr. Alireza Asgharzade, Amir, Habib Azarsina, Dr. Hasan Shariatmadari and others whose names cannot be explicitly mentioned, taught me a lot about the Azerbaijanis in Iran and events there. Professor Hamlet Isaxanli, President of Khazar University in Baku, who made extensive comments on this manuscript and provided important insights. At the Belfer Center for Science and International Affairs, Graham Allison, Steven Miller and Melissa Carr provided outstanding support and I am grateful to them. Tom de Waal gave insightful comments, as did Professor Gabriel Sheffer, Professor Nikki Keddie, Professor Gerard Libaridian, and Professor Azade-Ayşe Rorlich. Azerbaijan's Ambassador to the United States, Hafiz Pashayev, encouraged me to publish this book and conducted lively and interesting debate with me on various aspects of Azerbaijani history and culture. I am grateful to Miriam Avins who was an outstanding editor; BCSIA Executive Editor Karen Motley, Sean Lynn-Jones, Emily Goodhue, Arman Grigorian, and Saba Mwine; a special debt of gratitude goes to John Grennan, researcher, editor, and indexer *extraordinaire*. The Harry S. Truman Research Institute for the Advancement of Peace at the Hebrew University of Jerusalem and the Raymond and Jenine Bollag Fund generously supported my research. A number of people referred me to important materials and gave assistance in translation: Evan Siegal, Rovshan

Guseinov, Mirza Michaeli, Elshan Alekberov and Hasan Javadi. Gulbaniz, Javid and Zohrab Safraliyev shared their home in Baku with me, as did Jane Greenhood and Arthur Hughes in Cambridge. I especially thank Yehuda, Yael, and Omri Shaffer.

Brenda Shaffer
Jerusalem, Israel and
Cambridge, Massachusetts

Note on Transliteration and Terms

The research in this book is based on a number of primary sources, mostly in Azerbaijani, Persian, and Russian. The sources in Azerbaijani are written in three different alphabets: Latin, Cyrillic, and Arabic. In Soviet Azerbaijan, the Cyrillic alphabet was in use for Azerbaijani for most of the period under analysis. In the successor Republic of Azerbaijan, the Latin alphabet is officially in use. In Iran, Azerbaijanis use the Arabic alphabet to write the Azerbaijani language. To help researchers locate the original sources, separate transliteration systems have been used for each alphabet. As a result, in the notes some Azerbaijani words and names appear in different forms.

There are differences between the transliteration used within the text and in the footnotes. In the text, many non-English terms, names and writings are referred to phonetically, so that readers who are not familiar with Turkic languages can read the text freely. The notes have precise transliterations.

In the notes, the open pronounced ə in Azerbaijani is represented by ä. Many of the references to Azerbaijani texts written in the Arabic alphabet appear in the notes without precise vowel representation, since the original texts provide no vowel notation.

Some personal and place names that have a widely known spelling in English have not been transliterated from the Azerbaijani original, such as the name Aliyev and the city Baku. In Azerbaijani, the city is called Bakı. The spelling of the names of some major figures as they have appeared in other academic works has been retained, and this has caused some inconsistency in spelling in this work. For instance, in some cases there are two spellings for a name pronounced the same: For example, 'Ali bay Huseynzade, and Sheikh Husayn Najaf. Journals that are widely-known by certain transliterations, such as *Ädäbiyyat vä Injäsänät*, are referred to in the commonly known manner in the text and notes.

Most of the geographical place names in areas where Azerbaijanis live are spelled according to Azerbaijani pronunciations. The term Araz River is used, rather than the Persian Aras or the Russian Araxs; Ardebil is used and not the Persian version, Ardabil; Savalan Mountain and not Sabalan; and Shamakhi rather than the Russian pronunciation, Shemakha.

The names of some individuals mentioned in this work appear with varying name endings. For instance, the nineteenth-century writer and political thinker known as Mirza Fath 'Ali Akhundzade in Iran is often referred to in Azerbaijan as Akhundov, with a Russian name ending. Some individuals have changed their name endings as a conscious reflection of their identity. For instance, Nasib Nasibzade, a Baku scholar who served as the Republic of Azerbaijan's first ambassador to Iran, changed his last name to Nasibli, replacing the Persian name ending with a Turkic one.

Until the early 1990s, most Azerbaijanis in Iran referred to themselves as Turks. Some researchers and Azerbaijanis themselves refer to this group as the Azerbaijani Turks, emphasizing that the group is basically Turkic and that the Azerbaijani identity is as such a shade of Turkic identity. However, in conducting the research it became apparent that the term used in self-reference is not necessarily an expression of identity, except among highly educated and very politically conscious Azerbaijanis. I have used the term most commonly employed by the Azerbaijanis today, and which is considered most neutral. This is "Azerbaijani."

In this book, the terms north and south Azerbaijan are used without a political connotation and only to denote geographic areas north and south of the Araz River. Since the political division of Azerbaijan in 1828, the area north of the Araz River has been part of the Russian Empire; was the short lived Azerbaijan Democratic Republic (1918–1920); became Soviet Azerbaijan; and since 1991 has been independent again as the Republic of Azerbaijan. South of the Araz today is land within Iran. When Azerbaijanis use the terms north and south Azerbaijan, they do not always have a political intention either. For instance, Ayatollah Shariatmadari, who firmly defended the preservation of the territorial integrity of Iran, referred to the Azerbaijani provinces in Iran at times as "south Azerbaijan."

MAP | xiii

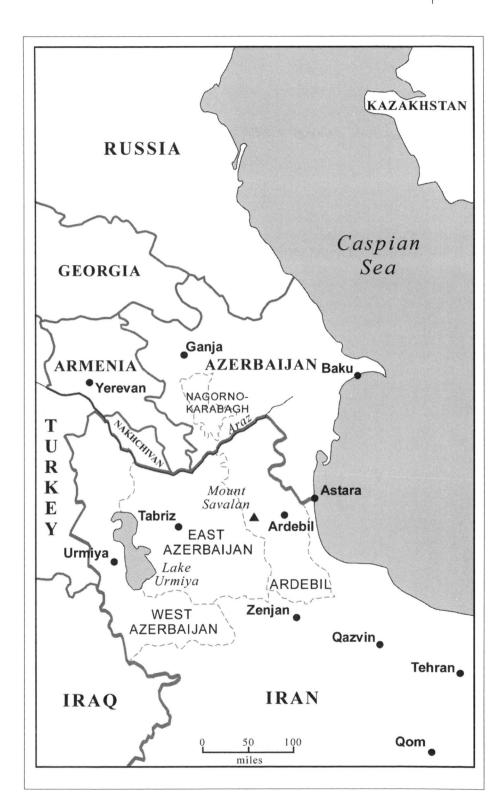

Introduction

Iran is a multi-ethnic society in which approximately 50 percent of its citizens are of non-Persian origin. The terms "Persians" and "Iranians," however, are often used interchangeably, just as once we called all the citizens of the Soviet Union "Russians." Among the ethnic minorities in Iran are large number of Azerbaijanis, Kurds, Turkmen, Arabs, and Baluch. Most of the non-Persians are concentrated in the frontier areas and have ties to large numbers of co-ethnics in adjoining states, such as Azerbaijan, Turkmenistan, Turkey, Pakistan, and Iraq. Ethnic politics in Iran is linked to events beyond Iran's borders.

Iran's ethnic minorities and especially the Azerbaijanis were strongly affected by the Soviet breakup and the ensuing renewal of ties with co-ethnics in the new states of the former Soviet Union. Approximately 7 million Azerbaijanis live in the Republic of Azerbaijan, which was established at the end of 1991, but the overwhelming majority of the Azerbaijanis live across the Araz River in neighboring Iran: approximately 20 million of Iran's population of 64 million are Azerbaijani.[1] Most of them live in three predominately Azerbaijani provinces (East Azerbaijan Province, West Azerbaijan Province, and Ardebil Province), and many Azerbaijanis refer to most of northwest Iran as "south Azerbaijan." A sizeable number of Azerbaijanis live in multi-ethnic Tehran.

The establishment of the Republic of Azerbaijan challenged the identity of co-ethnics beyond the borders of the new state and led many Azerbaijanis in Iran to identify with the Azerbaijani ethnic group, though

---

1. See Appendix for analysis of the number of Azerbaijanis and other ethnic groups in Iran.

not necessarily with the new state itself. Since the early 1990s, political expressions of Azerbaijani ethnic identity have increased. This rising Azerbaijani identity has generated few calls for the three Azerbaijani provinces to secede from Iran and join the new republic, but rather has focused on cultural rights within Iran.

This rising ethnic identity is affecting the character and the stability of the regime in multi-ethnic Iran. Indeed, Tehran's response to the Soviet breakup and the subsequent establishment of the new Muslim republics showed its awareness that the establishment of ethnic-based states on its north border could have ramifications for the ethnic groups in Iran. *Tehran Times* wrote:

The first ground for concern from the point of view in Tehran is the lack of political stability in the newly independent republics. The unstable conditions in those republics could be serious causes of insecurity along the lengthy borders (over 2000 kilometers) Iran shares with those countries. Already foreign hands can be felt at work in those republics, specially in Azerbaijan and Turkmenistan republics, with the ultimate objective of brewing discord among the Iranian Azeris and Turkmen by instigating ethnic and nationalistic sentiments.[2]

Despite Iran's multi-ethnic composition, few studies on ethnic identity or nationalism include the modern state of Iran as a case for analysis.[3] The lack of contemporary research on ethnic-based politics in Iran is difficult to fathom; if Iran actually has succeeded in preventing the cohesion of separate identities among its various ethnic minorities and fostering Iranian state identity as the primary identity of most of the residents of the state, Iran is an extraordinary case for study. However, if the contrary is true, and ethnic-based political activity is present in Iran, then it is also vital to study this large and influential state, especially in light of the security challenge that Iran poses in its region and beyond. The dissolution

---

2.   *Tehran Times*, December 30, 1991, p. 2.

3.   Examples include: Benedict Anderson, *Imagined Communities* (New York: Verso, 1991); Walker Connor, *Ethnonationalism: The Quest for Understanding* (Princeton, N.J.: Princeton University Press, 1994); Anthony D. Smith, *National Identity* (Reno: New York: University of Nevada Press, 1991). In Smith's *Theories of Nationalism* (New York: Holmes and Meier Publishers, 1983), he even gives "Persia" as an example of a case of "culturally homogenous group" that is "ethnically (almost) homogenous," p. 224. In contrast, Hugh Seton-Watson in *Nations and States: An Enquiry into the Origins of Nations and the Politics of Nationalism* (Boulder, Colo.: Westview Press, 1977), pp. 251–255, discusses the multi-ethnic character of Iran. Nevertheless, Seton-Watson concludes that except for the Arabs and possibly the Kurds, there is little evidence of ethnic assertion.

of dynastic empires and states is often regarded as a major catalyst for the fostering of separate, ethnic-based nationalisms or nation-states among their former subjects.[4] Moreover, ethnic-based nationalism is seen as a major factor contributing to the demise of many multi-ethnic states and empires.[5] The cases most often cited in discussing the connection between termination of dynastic empires and the emergence of nationalism are the Austro-Hungarian, Ottoman, and Russian Empires. Iran is rarely included in this list, despite the fact that two Iranian dynasties have been toppled in the last century.[6]

The vast majority of new states and sovereign political entities that have entered the international system in the last decade do not encompass large amounts of territories that the new states consider their historical lands. Moreover, significant numbers of co-ethnics reside outside the borders of the new states, which they nominally or otherwise claim to represent. In some cases, the overwhelming majority of the co-ethnics of a state's core ethnic group live beyond the borders of the states or political entities. In many cases, co-ethnics reside contingent to the new states. The establishment of an ethnic-based state adjacent to large number of members of that same ethnic group can impact and challenge the identity and political behavior of the co-ethnics abroad, and becomes an important factor in the bilateral relations of the neighboring states.[7] The behavior and response of contingent co-ethnics to the establishment of an ethnic-based state differs from that of non-contingent diaspora members.[8]

---

4. Anderson, *Imagined Communities*, p. 36; E.J. Hobsbawm, "The End of Empires," in Karen Barkey and Mark Von Hagen, eds., *After Empire: Multiethnic Societies and Nation-Building* (Boulder, Colo.: Westview Press, 1997), pp. 12–16.

5. Victor Zaslavsky, "The Soviet Union," in Barkey and Von Hagen, *After Empire*, p. 84.

6. These are the Qajar Dynasty in 1921 (officially in 1925) and the Pahlavi Dynasty in 1979.

7. For further discussion on the relationship between ethnic-based states, co-ethnics abroad and foreign policy, see Rogers Brubaker, *Nationalism Reframed: Nationhood and the National Question in the New Europe*, (Cambridge: Cambridge University Press, 1996); Charles King and Neil J. Melvin, eds., *Nations Abroad: Diaspora Politics and International Relations in the Former Soviet Union* (Boulder, Colo.: Westview Press, 1998); Charles King and Neil J. Melvin, "Diaspora Politics: Ethnic Linkages, Foreign Policy, and Security in Eurasia," *International Security*, Vol. 24, No. 3 (Winter 1999/2000), pp. 108–138.

8. In this book, a distinction is made between co-ethnics in territories contiguous to a state's borders which have been inhabited by that group for a significant period of time and is considered by them as part of their homeland, and a diaspora. Diaspora is used to refer to members of a group who have left or been forced to leave their traditional place of residence. The term diaspora is discussed in Gabriel Sheffer, "A New

Moreover, the existence of a sizeable community of co-ethnics beyond an ethnic-based state's borders obligates the state to create a policy toward them; and the question of co-ethnics abroad often becomes an integral part of the wider debate in a state on the question of state identity and on the relationship between ethnic identity in a state and the state itself. The Azerbaijanis are a particularly interesting case study of relations between ethnic-based states and their co-ethnics abroad, since most of the Azerbaijanis live beyond the borders of the Republic of Azerbaijan, and the majority of the territory considered by the Azerbaijanis as part of Azerbaijan is beyond the boundaries of the new state.[9]

The Azerbaijanis in Iran and in the Republic of Azerbaijan (and its predecessor states) provide almost laboratory conditions for studying ethnic identity. The populations have been split since 1828, when the Turkmenchay Treaty divided the Azerbaijani people and lands between the Russian Empire (and later the Soviet Union) and Iran. Most of the Azerbaijanis on both sides of the Araz are Shi'i Muslims, and most speak Azerbaijani Turkish as their native language.[10] Family ties have played an important role in maintaining a common identity between the people. Despite their separation under fundamentally different political and cultural systems and in spite of having undergone a different historical experience for over 150 years, the Azerbaijanis share a common ethnic identity. Yet, their more than 150 years of separation under very different regimes have created some differences—most notably, for political scientists, in the degree to which the two groups comfortably hold differing state and ethnic identities. This book examines trends in Azerbaijani collective identity from the period of the Islamic Revolution in Iran, through the Soviet breakup and most of the first decade of the Republic of Azerbaijan (1979–2000). It looks at both populations and at their connections and mutual influence. Few works have dealt comprehensively with the history and politics of both Azerbaijans.

This book shows that Azerbaijani identity has been the predominant form of collective identity of the Azerbaijani population in both Soviet

Field of Study: Modern Diasporas in International Politics," in Gabriel Sheffer, ed., *Modern Diasporas in International Politics* (London: Croom Helm, 1986), pp. 9–10.

9.   Examples of similar cases are the impact of the establishment of the Palestinian Authority (and subsequent Palestinian state) on Palestinians beyond its borders, and of the foundation of the Kurdish autonomy in Iraq on adjacent Kurdish communities in Iran, Turkey, and Syria.

10.   This language belongs to the Oghuz language group, which includes the Turkish predominantly spoken today in the Republic of Turkey, and the Turkmen language. Some linguists consider Azerbaijani Turkish a dialect of Turkish, while many think of it as a separate language.

Azerbaijan and its successor, the Republic of Azerbaijan. Few Azerbaijanis north of the Araz River became Soviets in terms of self-identity, and almost none considered themselves Russians, including those for whom Russian became their primary language. For most, Turkic identity forms a substantial and inseparable element of Azerbaijani identity, but rarely takes precedence over distinct Azerbaijani self-perception.

In Iran, Azerbaijani identity has remained a significant collective identity among most of the Azerbaijanis in Iran, and for many their primary collective identity. Each time central control over freedom of expression in Iran has diminished; for example, during the period of the Islamic Revolution, Azerbaijanis amplified their expressions of Azerbaijani identity and their demands for expanded cultural and language rights. In terms of primary identity, great diversity exists among the Azerbaijanis in Iran. Non-Persians in Iran separate between Iranian and Persian identity; they may strongly identify with the Iranian state and history, but do not define themselves as Persians. Some Azerbaijanis in Iran, such as those who form a significant portion of the ruling elite today, see their primary identity as Iranian, although many members of this group also express ties to Azerbaijani ethnic culture and language. Others, including many intellectuals during the period of the Islamic Revolution, maintain strong Azerbaijani identity, but strive to maintain state identity as Iranians in a future supra-ethnic Iran. Many see no contradiction in maintaining both Azerbaijani and Iranian identity. Others see their primary identity as Azerbaijani, though not all of them are actively pressing for a political manifestation of that identity. However, especially since the early 1990s, a small number of Azerbaijanis have become involved in political activity evincing their Azerbaijani primary identity. This political activity has emphasized many abstract demands, such as a change in the Azerbaijanis' image in the media, in addition to the concrete fulfillment of legal rights, such as the right to education in their language and use of Azerbaijani in the courts. This stress of abstract issues may emanate from the Azerbaijanis' perceived gap between their high economic and professional status, and their low social status in Iran.

The conclusion that a distinctive Azerbaijani identity exists on a meaningful level in Iran challenges the view of the mainstream of contemporary Iranian studies, which contend that Azerbaijanis in Iran are a "well-integrated minority," harbor little "sense of separate identity," and have assimilated into Iranian identity.[11] The Azerbaijani ethnic factor

11.   Patricia J. Higgins, "Minority-State Relations in Contemporary Iran," *Iranian Studies*, Vol. 17, No. 1 (Winter 1984), pp. 37–71; Hooshang Amirahmadi, "A Theory of Ethnic Collective Movements and its Application to Iran," *Ethnic and Racial Studies*

must be a part of studies on Iranian society and assessments of regime stability in Iran. This book also shows that Azerbaijani political activity was a facet of the Islamic Revolution in Iran, and that the failure of the revolution to meet many of the Azerbaijanis' expectations for language and cultural rights affected their ensuing support for the regime and their identity as Iranians.

Similarly, this book challenges the view of many articles on the Soviet period—that the ethnic Azerbaijani movements and activity in Iran were primarily a Soviet invention, and a mere instrument of Moscow's policies toward Iran.[12] In fact, wide-based Azerbaijani ethnic sentiments in Iran emerged many times in the twentieth century, often when the Soviet Union was not actively encouraging them. For example, in contrast to many of the Western depictions of the 1945–46 Provincial Government of Azerbaijan, this book shows that ethnic-based local Azerbaijani demands played a significant role in the emergence of the autonomy movement and were reflected in the policies of the short-lived autonomous government.

Many important works on the development of the Azerbaijani national movement in the Soviet Union claim that the Azerbaijanis began to assert their national identity in the late 1980s, and chiefly in response to challenges from Armenia and the struggle for control over the province of Nagorno-Karabagh.[13] However, expressions of Azerbaijani national identity were clearly present in the Soviet Union before the inauguration of glasnost in the mid-1980s.[14] While the Nagorno-Karabagh conflict had

---

Vol. 10 (1987), pp. 363–391; and Touraj Atabaki, *Azerbaijan: Ethnicity and Autonomy in Twentieth-Century Iran* (London: British Academic Press, 1993), p. 182.

12. For a comprehensive review of Soviet attempts to foster Azerbaijani ethnic sentiments in Iran, see David Nissman, *The Soviet Union and Iranian Azerbaijan: The Uses of Nationalism for Political Penetration* (Boulder, Colo.: Westview, 1987).

13. See, for instance, Mark Saroyan, "The Karabagh Syndrome and Azerbaijani Politics," *Problems of Communism*, Vol. 39, No. 5 (September/October 1990), pp. 14–29; and Helene Carrere d' Encausse, *The End of the Soviet Empire* (New York: Basic Books, 1993), p. 59.

14. In most of the central literature on collective identity, the role of the other, or the "you," is stressed in the formation of the "we." The most central aspect of construction of identities is the definition of borders between members of the collective and outsiders. Neighboring peoples and groups from which a collective emphasizes its differences often play an important role in the coalescence of a group's national identity. However, one must be careful not to overestimate the impact of the outsider, or to assume that the "other" was the main or only factor in the coalescence of national identity of a group of people. Even though one-time events and interactions, especially conflicts with another group, can have huge impact on the identity and formation of a nation, one should be careful not to apply that factor backwards, and assume that in

a significant impact on the activization of an Azerbaijani national political movement, it was far from its basis.

The fall of the Soviet Union has led to a dramatic change in the nature of the borders that now divide between the new states and their neighbors, such as Iran. Many of these borders have become hubs of exchange and cooperation, and epicenters of vibrant intellectual innovation. The independence of the Republic of Azerbaijan, for example, led to a dramatic increase in the importance of the Azerbaijani provinces in Iran. This new status has led to demands for greater resources from the central government. Most important, having conducted many of the cooperative endeavors directly with Baku, circumventing Tehran, they have acquired an appetite for increased unimpeded foreign ties and cooperation, affecting center-periphery relations in Iran. The center has traditionally been viewed as the place with the most access to resources and the nucleus of a state's activities. Peripheries are usually considered "cut off" or "dead-ends." However, the change in the nature of the border regions may have made being in the periphery an asset, and Iran's provinces, especially during difficult economic times in Iran, have attempted to transform their location into an advantage by strengthening their ties to the new state. This has had important political implications.

Chapters 1 and 2 provide historical background for this study, surveying the development of the Azerbaijani identity from the tenth century through the beginning of the twentieth century, and tracing developments during the Soviet and Pahlavi regimes. Chapter 3 examines the events of the Islamic Revolution, the role of the Azerbaijanis in the revolution, and its effect on the self-identity of the Azerbaijanis in Iran and in the Soviet Union. Chapter 4 focuses on 1983–1991. Chapter 5 examines the relationship between state and ethnic identity in the new Republic of Azerbaijan and how its independence affected co-ethnics beyond its borders, in Iran. Chapter 6 discusses the impact of Azerbaijan on the Iranian state, and draws theoretical conclusions on collective identity.

Nations, Ethnic Groups, Collective and National Identity

In political science, there is little consensus over the definition of the most widely used concepts for study and description of collective identity, such as nation, ethnic group, and nationalism. Many people use these terms interchangeably with each other and, at times, with the term

---

the past the "other" or the conflict was also a major force in the formation of a common identity of a group, or to presuppose that a national identity did not emerge prior to the significant interaction of the "other."

"state." In this book, I suggest three separate terms to describe three forms of identity: state identity, national identity, and ethnic identity. At times, some of these forms of identity are congruent, at times they are different and even competing and conflicting. Different members of a collective attach diversified feelings toward the group. Rarely is there complete consensus in a collective regarding feeling a sense of a nation. Often, different identities do not conflict and can be accommodating or compatible, and many individuals do not possess clear awareness of their primary identity. People possess different forms of communal identity concurrently. Since identities do not always conflict or demand prioritization, an individual may feel comfortable identifying with a number of collectives. Some members may view their ethnic identity as primary, while co-ethnics may feel primary attachment to their state identity. This diversity is common among the Azerbaijanis in Iran. The various self-perceptions within a people are the basis of interesting political interactions, and also fuel the claims of external opponents who deny the people the right to nationhood.

Since the French Revolution, much of mainstream western political thought has considered an individual's ethno-linguistic community as his or her primary collective identity, or nation. However, many people prefer units other than their ethno-linguistic community as their object of primary identity, particularly in non-European countries. For instance, in Tajikistan, regional groupings containing both Tajiks and Uzbeks often take priority for many over ethno-linguistic identity.[15] Furthermore, some individuals have joined supra-ethnic communist movements and worked against their own ethnic group's national movements, feeling greater allegiance to these non-ethnic-based ideological movements. Gender may be developing as a primary identity for some women, uniting them with other women more than ethno-linguistic bonds with males of their same ethnic group.

NATIONAL IDENTITY

National identity is one's primary collective identity, and the nation is the group to which one usually attributes one's primary political allegiance. A nation is based on some collective—such as an ethnic group, a tribe, a clan, a gender, common citizenship, an extended family grouping, inhab-

---

15. This is based on the author's 1986 conversations with Tajiks living in Samarkand in Uzbekistan. Some remarked that it was socially acceptable for Tajiks and Uzbeks to marry each other in Samarkand, which seems to indicate that their respective ethnic groups share another binding identity.

itants of a territorial unit, or holders of a value or ideological orientation. Thus, members of a nation usually have a number of tangible common or binding traits, and often elements of a common culture, beyond their political allegiance. These traits often make it difficult for researchers to differentiate between national identity and other collective identities, such as ethnic identity.

A nation, in contrast to the groups on which nations are based, implies an element of choice and preference. People possess a variety of identities—gender, family, tribe, clan, ethnic group, region, value system (liberal, communist, ecological). One's nation is the object of collective identity that one cherishes most. It is the collective element that, when push comes to shove, commands our greatest loyalty.

Single events can have a profound impact, and can determine the choice of primary identity. While historical ties often have important influence in determining the formation of a nation, national identity can and often does change. As Renan pointed out, "a nation is a daily plebiscite."[16] Researchers often point to the historic bonds and common nationhood as Iranians which is shared by Azerbaijanis and Persians to dismiss the existence of separate Azerbaijani national identity. Yet historical relationships only influence the present-day choice of a nation;[17] they do not dictate it, and new circumstances can give birth to new identity preferences. For example, Russians and Ukrainians speak a mutually understandable language, share a faith, and have been historically linked so much that the first Russian state was founded in Kiev in 860. Yet, by the nineteenth century and certainly under the Soviet system, separate Russian and Ukrainian national identities coalesced.

A nation is created by choice and should be defined accordingly. According to Hugh Seton-Watson:

a nation exists when a significant number of people in a community consider themselves to form a nation, or behave as if they formed one. It is not necessary that the whole of the population should so feel, or so behave, and it is not possible to lay down dogmatically a minimum percentage of a population which must be so affected. When a significant group holds this belief, it possesses 'national consciousness.'[18]

---

16.   Ernest Renan, "What Is a Nation?" in Omar Dahbour and Micheline R. Ishay, *The Nationalism Reader* (Atlantic Highlands, N.J.: Humanities Press, 1995), p. 154. Originally appeared in *Oeuvres Complètes* (Paris, 1947–1961), Vol. 1, pp. 887–907.

17.   Eric Hobsbawm, *Nations and Nationalism Since 1780* (Cambridge: Cambridge University Press, 1990), p. 73.

18.   Seton-Watson, *Nations and States*, p. 5.

A group, once it feels it is a nation, will act and make demands like one, so academic attempts to deny "nationhood" to a certain group by applying various criteria and definitions are superfluous. The fact that children of parents belonging to different nations can choose their own primary identity illustrates that national identity is selected.[19]

Size is also a factor in determining a group's status as a nation. In distinguishing between an ethnic group and a nation, Benjamin Akzin wrote,

The point at which the ethnic group enters our special field of interest is that at which it has both exceeded purely local dimensions and become of significance in the political sphere. It is at that point that the appellation of nation or nationality can be applied to it. Size is an important aspect of this phenomenon.[20]

People can lose the external symbols of the ethnic or other group upon which the nation is based, while retaining their national identification with it. For instance, many leaders of national movements are not native speakers of the language the activists are striving to preserve. It is precisely because national identity is a state of mind that it is so difficult to objectively assess, and so vulnerable to change.

Due to the fluctuating nature of national identity, all nations and states should be viewed as tentative and vulnerable to change. This change can lead to the dissolution of a nation; it may become a state or become assimilated into another grouping. A state's name and approximate borders may remain, but may undergo such fundamental change that it is questionable whether the same state still exists. Moreover, it seems that nations often become dormant. The British and French nations are widely recognized as nations but we know that the Scottish and Welsh, Corsican and Breton identities are looming in the background, and events can cause members of a people to revive a latent selfhood. Political movements often have an interest in activating seemingly lost identities as a rallying point against an existing political system. Even the United States, confident in its multi-ethnic national creed, seems alarmed by demands for bilingual education, illustrating awareness that it, too, is potentially vulnerable to change in national identity. Negative factors, such as attempted genocide, exile, discrimination, or competition over territory, can contribute to the emergence of a nation. National consolida-

---

19.   Hobsbawm, *Nations and Nationalism Since 1780* (1990), p. 45.

20.   Benjamin Akzin, *States and Nations* (Garden City, N.Y.: Anchor Books, 1964), p. 37.

tion as a result of negative factors does not make a nation any less a collective than one formed by positive factors. Some specialists have claimed that the Azerbaijanis have lost their identity as separate from Iranians.[21] However, determinations of this type are only valid for a specified point in time. Primary identity is the shifting result of a continual process.

ETHNICITY

In contrast to a nation, ethnicity seems to connote both inborn and inbred sets of characteristics. One cannot choose to be an ethnic Italian, but one can join the American nation. At the same time, ethnicity is beyond race. A child of one ethnic group adopted by a family that belongs to another ethnic group does not automatically acquire all of the elements of ethnicity of the adopting family. Nor will he or she have all the ethnic characteristics of the group of origin, since many, such as language and social mores, are learned. Ethnicity is also a set of behaviors and codes by which an individual measures reality and knows how he or she is expected to live.[22] A person may choose not to live by this code, but is raised to know how to. The ethnic group is a set of habits, while the nation is a set of choices. The ethnic group defines one's main food staple, how to mark the life cycle, which utensil one feels most comfortable eating with, how one's bed is arranged when growing up, and how one feels most comfortable washing. The ethnic group sets norms for parent-child relations, generation order (who waits on whom, who finances whom), and the proportion of resources invested by a society in education and social welfare. One often prefers or maybe even mandates the marriage of a child to a member of one's own ethnic group. As one Azerbaijani from Tehran stated, while trying to explain the difference between Azerbaijanis and Persians: "Of course, we are different from them, they eat rice and we eat vegetables. They write poetry and we sing songs."

STATES

States usually base their identity on that of an existing nation, or else foster a nation to support the state. Congruity of state, national, and ethnic identity seems to contribute to stability. We too frequently accept that the state's version of the identity of its citizens and the state identity that it is trying to promote accurately represents the identity of the residents of the

---

21.   For example, Atabaki, *Azerbaijan: Ethnicity and Autonomy in Twentieth-Century Iran*, p. 182.

22.   See Dusan Kecmanovic, *The Mass Psychology of Ethnonationalism* (New York: Plenum Press, 1996), p. 2.

state. Researchers of the Soviet Union, and Iran, have missed opportunities to understand many trends emerging in those societies in this way.

The extent to which the dominant community in a state permits assimilation of members of minority groups affects the collective identity of those minorities. In addition, the degree to which ethnic, national, and state identity are compatible is often determined by the ideologies each of these units adopts and the tolerance of each for the other identities. This is often true for multi-ethnic societies, such as the United States and Brazil, that base their identity on the value of being a community of tolerance of sub-national identities. In such societies, the state rarely tests the national identity of its citizens to see whether it is based on the ethnic group, for instance, or the state.

Some states may decide to base themselves on one or another of the ethnic or other groups that comprise the state, often forcing citizens to choose between their ethnic identity and their state identity. State identity and policy can also become more accommodating to alternative identities, but this will not always command the loyalty of the alternative groups, if they perceive the existence of a "score to be settled" with a community that treated the minority group inequitably in the past. This is illustrated by the desire of the Slovaks to leave Czechoslovakia, despite the Czechs' adoption of a policy of multi-ethnic accommodation in the post-communist period.

Events beyond the borders of a state, such as a war involving co-ethnics of some of its citizens, or the establishment of an independent state or other political unit based on ethnic or other collective identity, can also challenge the relationship or harmony between various identities and lead people to determine a primary identity.

Democracy and democratization in a state can have varying impacts on the collective identity of members of groups within a state. At times, democratization and pluralism in the society provide for accommodation of the members of various collectives, strengthening their attachment to and identification with it. Under other circumstances, democracy leads to increased demands by the members of collectives within the state and increases their feeling of legitimacy in demanding self-rule, thus weakening the ties to the existing state.

Members of a nation do not always actively seek to establish a state.[23] A nation may choose to be a part of a supra-national political community that does not conflict with the components' national affiliation. On the other hand, members of a nation sometimes prefer to have an independ-

23. Smith, *National Identity*, p. 74.

ent national state, but view the chances of achieving it as meager, or consider the price of attaining it (war, economic isolation, etc.) as too high. A nation is often activated to achieve statehood during historical "earthquakes"—when borders and state structures are reshuffled significantly and opportunity for statehood emerges.

History and Identity Formation

A group's version of its prior history is an important vehicle for expressing current national or ethnic identity. Groups generally seek to show that they possess primordial ties and are not new nations. In part, this is because nations today are generally born under conditions of resource shortages and competition and look for justification for the possession of disputed territories and symbols. A newly asserted national identity, especially if it manifests itself through nationalism, usually challenges adjacent nations for resources considered by both nations as their own national possession, such as territory, revered landmarks, etc. These properties are often claimed by more than one nation. Members of other nations often try to deny the rights of challengers to their nationhood in an attempt to undermine their claims to these resources. Thus, the rhetoric of two conflicting groups is often a dispute over the extent of each other's primordial ties. In the current international system, respect and support is given for preserving existing nations, rather than for creating newer ones. This process compounds a nation's desire to look into its past to justify its right to be a nation. In addition, nationalist activists often use a sense of common history and primordial ties dating back to antiquity to foster national identity among a group of people. Hence, as Azerbaijanis have become more national, they have expressed heightened interest in their past—by means of archaeology and historical research, for example—and have stressed a view of possessing an ancient common origin.

Yet the impact of historical facts on the formation of identity should not be overestimated. The identity of any people is influenced by its historical myths more than by concrete facts; the uncovering of new archives does not usually alter group identity.[24] The significance of historical events is generally measured by their impact on future developments. When examining the ethnic and national identity of a group, we must look at their perceived view of history to understand history's impact.

---

24. For the role of the myth of common descent in shaping national identity, see Connor, "Ethnonationalism: Looking Backward," pp. 205–206.

Chapter 1

The Azerbaijanis until 1920

The Azerbaijanis live in an area that has been a center of ideological activity, confrontation, and accommodation between different cultures. Until the second half of the nineteenth century, the delineation between their identities as Turks, Azerbaijanis, Iranians, and Muslims was not clear, and Azerbaijanis rarely referred to themselves as "Azerbaijani." The development of the Azerbaijanis' collective identity intensified and became a struggle toward the end of the nineteenth century, when a distinctive Azerbaijani national identity emerged as a political force. The polemics and competition over the identity of the Azerbaijanis were stimulated by revolutionary changes occurring in all the empires surrounding the Azerbaijanis, their increased exposure to the growing nationalism of the peoples around them, the idea of modern nationalism, and the political activities of various ideological movements that competed in the region at that time: Pan-Islam, Pan-Turkism, Iranian nationalism, and communism.

The competition between these rival ideologies further intensified in the first quarter of the twentieth century after the fall of the Ottoman Empire and the subsequent disengagement of Muslim and Ottoman identities, and the division between Turkic cultural identity and Turkish state identity that occurred with the establishment of the Republic of Turkey.

The change in the state identity of Iran also intensified the struggle over the identity of the Azerbaijanis. Until the establishment of the Pahlavi regime in the twentieth century, the identity of Iran was not exclusively Persian, but supra-ethnic. From the eleventh century until the founding of the Pahlavi regime, the political leadership of Iran was mostly Turkic, and both Turkic and Persian cultural elements influenced the ethnic character of the regime and the culture of the country. The various Iranian empires were distinguished by cultural diversity.[1] Throughout much of this period, the capital cities of Iran were in Azerbaijan, and from the eleventh century until the 1920s, Tabriz was Iran's major commercial center. Once the Pahlavi regime began its policy of emphasizing exclusively the Persian character and composition of Iran—a policy that has been partly continued under the Islamic Republic—Azerbaijani or Turkic identity came into clear conflict with Iranian identity; this intensified the struggle over Azerbaijani national identity in Iran.

Advances in technology in the second half of the nineteenth century and the beginning of the twentieth century also made the question of national identity more pressing. Vast improvements in infrastructure in both Russia and Iran increased the centralization of the empires and their ability to touch the lives of populations that had previously been virtually autonomous. In many cases, interaction between the center and the periphery created an awareness of differences and also contributed to the development of a sense of common identity among co-ethnics from adjoining areas, thus forming the basis for the development of a common identity separate from the identity of the state. In other cases, exposure to the center spurred the assimilation of some of the minority members into Persian culture in Iran.

This chapter and the next survey the historical events leading up to 1979–2000. This chapter covers the major waves of Turkic immigration into Azerbaijan in the tenth century, the establishment of the Safavid regime in 1501, and the first decades of Qajar rule in the late eighteenth century; the split of Azerbaijan in 1828, after the Russian conquest of north Azerbaijan, until 1905, the period when a separate Azerbaijani national identity began to emerge as a political force and in literature; and the period from 1905 until the establishment of the Pahlavi regime in Iran and the establishment of Soviet rule in north Azerbaijan. Chapter 2 looks at the period of Pahlavi rule in Iran, and Soviet rule through the late 1970s.

THE PERCEIVED ROOTS OF THE AZERBAIJANIS

Historians debate the ethnic-linguistic composition of the areas north and south of the Araz River and the historical borders of Azerbaijan before the major waves of Turkic migration in the tenth and eleventh cen-

---

1. Many historians see Turkic-Persian tension as a constant factor in the history of Iran. According to E.G. Browne, the history of Persia: "from the legendary wars between the Kiyanian kings and Afrasiyab down to the present day, is the story of a struggle between the Turkish races . . . and the Persians." See *A Year Amongst the Persians* (London: Adam and Charles Black, 1959) pp. 109–110.

turies. Many Azerbaijani sources claim that much of the population was Turkic, or of other non-Persian origin; Persian sources generally maintain that prior to the tenth century the people were predominantly Persian.

This debate has been confounded by supporters of various ideologies—Iranian nationalism, Turkism, and Azerbaijani nationalism—who have attempted to manipulate historical materials to justify or deny the Azerbaijanis' "right" to certain identities, or courses of action, and as a basis for the claim that those living in the north and those living in Iran are not the same nation. In addition, many researchers base their claims on the works of the historian Ahmad Kasravi, whose ideological convictions and political goals tainted his research on Azerbaijan.[2] Some researchers have attempted to dismiss the idea that the populations on both sides of the Araz belong to the same people, claiming that the area north of the Araz River was not part of the historical territory of what has been called for many centuries "Azerbaijan," and that the people inhabiting this area are not part of the same people as those in Iranian Azerbaijan. In the pre-Islamic period the area in the north was known as Albania or Caucasian Albania, and after the Islamic conquest (639–643) as Arran. However, whether Arran was a separate entity from Azerbaijan or a subentity, it seems that they often interacted culturally as one region. In addition, at least since the Muslim conquest, the areas were administered together within most of the various empires that ruled the area, and were subject to similar influences until the division of the territory in 1828.[3] Finally, territorial borders in the region were quite fluid, especially before the establishment of the Safavid regime in 1501.

The Islamization of Azerbaijan took place during the Arab conquest under 'Omar's caliphate sometime between 639 and 643.[4] Zoroastrianism was prominent in both north and south Azerbaijan at the time of the Is-

---

2.   Along with his own strong Iranian identity, Kasravi's unwavering commitment to eradicate any subidentities to Iranian identity calls into question his ability to conduct objective research on Azerbaijan. As Ernest Renan wrote: "Getting its history wrong is part of being a nation" (Renan, "What is A Nation?" p. 145). Kasravi himself claimed that historical materials on the origins of the Azerbaijanis in Iran were often manipulated to suit interested parties' needs in the political polemics raging in the area. (See Ahmed Kasravi, al-'Irfan, Tishrin I, 1922, pp. 121–123, Evan Siegal translation).

3.   C.E. Bosworth, "Azerbaijan," in Encyclopedia Iranica (London and New York: Routledge and Kegan Paul, 1989) p. 224; and Audrey Alstadt, The Azerbaijani Turks (Stanford: Hoover Institute, 1992), p. 9. On the common administration of the territories in the Safavid period, see Javad Heyat, "Origins of the Name and Boundaries of Azerbaijan," Reform, Vol. 1, No. 1 (March 1995), p. 24.

4.   Bosworth, "Azerbaijan," Encyclopedia Iranica, p. 225.

lamic conquest, and one of the Azerbaijani terms of capitulation was Arab agreement to respect the sanctity of the fire temples there.[5]

The conquest of Azerbaijan did not instill any universal Muslim identity. The region served as the base of the socially motivated revolt of Babak that began in 816–17 and lasted over twenty years. To Azerbaijanis, Babak and the revolt he led still symbolize resistance to foreign rule.[6] His rebellion was glorified in the national museums of both Soviet Azerbaijan and the Republic of Azerbaijan, and the name Babak is common in north Azerbaijan and Iran.

Under Seljuk rule in the tenth and eleventh centuries, major waves of immigration of Oghuz Turks into Azerbaijan created a clear Turkic majority and unified the ethnic basis of both north and south Azerbaijan. More Turks came during Mongol Ilkhanid rule from the thirteenth through the fourteenth centuries, and during the Qara Qoyunlu and Aq Qoyunlu Turkmen dynasties in the fifteenth century, which had their capital in south Azerbaijan, at Tabriz. In north Azerbaijan, a native Shirvanshah dynasty ruled through the sixteenth century. Historians give varying dates for the establishment of this dynasty, beginning with the ninth century.

In this period, Turkic and Persian cultural elements were quite fluid. Until the nineteenth century, Azerbaijani cultural figures wrote in both Persian and Azerbaijani, and throughout most of this period there was no formal separation between the Azerbaijani and Turkish languages. During the twelfth century, the most prominent Azerbaijani poet, Nizami Ganjevi, wrote in Persian. His epic work *Khamsa*, a collection of five poems including the classic love story of "Khosrow and Shirin," is highly esteemed by Azerbaijanis. Hassan-oglu Izzeddin, wrote in both Azerbaijani and Persian.[7] Nasimi Imadeddin, a fourteenth century author, wrote in Azerbaijani, as well as Arabic and Persian.[8] Azerbaijanis attach special meaning to the works of Muhammed Suleiman-Oglu Fizuli, and his poem, "Leyli and Majnun," written in Azerbaijani in the sixteenth

---

5. Urmiya (in southern Azerbaijan) is considered to be the birthplace of Zaratushta. Christianity was also present, especially in Nakhchivan and Tabriz.

6. Gholam-Reza Sabri Tabrizi, *Iran: A Child's Story, a Man's Experience* (Edinburgh: Mainstream, Ltd., 1989), pp. 143–144.

7. Nizami (1141–1209) was a native and resident of Ganja, today in the Republic of Azerbaijan. Izzeddin lived at the end of the thirteenth century and the beginning of the fourteenth century, in Asfarain, a town near Khorasan.

8. Imadeddin was born in 1369 or 1370. According to some sources, he was born in Shamakhi, which is in the Republic of Azerbaijan.

century, is especially revered in the contemporary national culture of Azerbaijan.[9]

AZERBAIJAN-BASED RULE IN IRAN: SHI'A IMPOSED ON THE PEOPLES OF IRAN

The establishment of the Safavid regime in Tabriz in 1501 had a major impact on the development of the identity of the peoples of the region and the events of the time. Under the Safavids, Iran returned to local rule and to its larger pre-Islamic borders, and regained its position as a major regional power. The Safavids united the peoples of Iran under the ideology of Shi'i Islam, which they established as the state religion of Iran, forcibly imposing it on its peoples, who were predominantly Sunni.[10] While the ethnic roots of the Safavid dynasty's founder, Shah Isma'il, are under debate,[11] he was raised in Ardebil and was a native Turkic-speaker,[12] as attested to by his poetry written in Azerbaijani under the pen-name of Khata'i.[13] Shah Isma'il's poetry set a precedent in the development of Azerbaijani literature because he was one of the first major writers to use the colloquial language, and generally avoided the Perso-Arabic vocabulary.[14] He based his regime on the power of the *Qizilbash* Turkic tribes, who shared his language. Indeed, these linguistic ties formed one of the main bases for unity between them. At the Safavid court, Azerbaijani Turkish was predominant, especially among the early rulers of the dynasty, and during this period Turkic grammar and words influenced Persian and vice versa.[15] In the Safavid period, an estimated 1,200 Azerbai-

---

9.   Fizuli Muhammed Suleiman-Oglu (1498–1556) lived in Baghdad and died in Karbala, today part of Iraq.

10.   Roger Savory, *Iran Under the Safavids* (London: Cambridge University Press, 1980), p. 29.

11.   See A.H. Morton, *The Early Years of Shah Isma'il in the Afzal al-tavarikh and Elsewhere*, Pembroke Papers 4 (1996), pp. 27–51; and Savory, *Iran Under the Safavids*, p. 2.

12.   Shah Isma'il reportedly only learned Persian as a young adult. See E. Denison Ross, "The Early Years of Shah Isma'il," *Journal of the Royal Asiatic Society* (1896), p. 288.

13.   Vladimir Minorsky, "The Poetry of Shah Isma'il I," *Bulletin of the School of Oriental and African Studies*, Vol. 10, No. 4 (1942), p. 1007a. Not only was his poetry in the Azerbaijani language, but its form was also influenced by Azerbaijani folk poetry, and the traditional 'āšeq style. See H. Javadi and K. Burrill, "Azeri Literature in Iran," *Encyclopedia Iranica*, p. 251.

14.   A. Caferoğlu, "Adhari (Azeri)," in *Encyclopedia of Islam*, (New Edition) Vol. I, (Leiden: E.J. Brill, 1986), p. 193.

15.   John R. Perry, *Persian in the Safavid Period: Sketch for an Etat de Langue*, Pembroke Papers 4 (1996), pp. 272, 279.

jani words entered Persian, mainly those dealing with administration and military spheres, areas that were chiefly in the hands of the Turkic peoples in Iran at this time.[16] The dominant ideology of the regime was Shi'i Twelver Islam. Yet, despite this banner of unity, Turco-Persian tensions characterized the Safavid regime.[17] Nevertheless, Shi'i identity and identity with the Iranian Safavid state were strong enough that during the various periods of confrontation with the Ottoman Empire there were few incidents of desertion to the Ottoman side, with whom the Turks of Iran shared a Turkic language.[18] The advent of the Safavid regime was an important event in the development of Azerbaijani national identity. The Safavids, considered by many Azerbaijanis today as an "Azerbaijani" dynasty, and portrayed as such in Azerbaijani historiography, serve as an important symbol of Azerbaijani identity and power.[19] At the same time, the Safavid imposition of Shi'i on the peoples of Iran and the regime's antagonism and rivalry with the Ottomans and Uzbeks, and the major Turkic regimes competing with them during the period, divided the Azerbaijanis from the rest of the Turkic peoples and increased their ties to Persians. However, being the only major Turkic people of Shi'i domination, over time, bound the people north and south of the Araz River, and contributed to the formation of their distinctive and common Azerbaijani identity.

Between 1514 and 1603, and again from 1722 to 1728, Tabriz and other parts of Azerbaijan were frequently attacked and occupied by the Ottomans. Due to its vulnerability to Ottoman attack, the capital of Iran

---

16.   G. Doerfer, "Azeri (Adari) Turkish," *Encyclopedia Iranica*, p. 246.

17.   See Savory, *Iran Under the Safavids*, p. 31.

18.   In contrast, there were some incidents of desertion to the Uzbek dynasties (which are also of Turkic origin), especially during periods of heightened confrontations during the Safavid period.

19.   For official historiography in the Soviet period, see "Shah Ismayïl" in *Azärbayjan Sovet Ensiklopediyasï*, Vol. 10 (1987), p. 473–474, and "Iran," *Azärbayjan Sovet Ensiklopediyasï*, Vol. 4 (1980), p. 504. Other works from the Soviet period: I.A. Huseinov, *Ismail Sefevi* (Baku, 1943); and O.A. Efendiev, *Obrazovanie azerbaidzhanskogo gosurdarstva Sefevidov v nachale XVI v.* (Baku, 1961). Examples of the Safavids being termed an "Azerbaijani government" in the post-independence period: Oqtay Efendi, *Azerbayjan Sefeviler Dovleti* (Baku: Azerbaijan State Government Publishers, 1993), Mahmud Ismaïl, *Azärbayjan Tarikhi* (Baku: Azerbaijan State Government Publishers, 1993); p. 151; and *Azärbayjan Tarikhi: Än Gädim Dövrlärdän XX Äsrin Ävvällärinä Gädär* (Baku: Elm, 1993), p. 164. In 2001, the five-hundredth-year anniversary of the dynasty was celebrated in the Republic of Azerbaijan at official state functions. In addition, the Safavids are often venerated in Azerbaijani literature and art forms, especially carpets. One of the central pieces in the Baku State Carpet Museum is a carpet depicting the Safavids.

was moved from Tabriz to Qazvin, and later on to Isfahan. This last move strengthened Persian language in the Safavid court, although Turkish was still of great consequence.[20]

Following the demise of the Safavid regime in 1722 and the assassination of its first successor, Nadir Shah, in 1747, the Iranian empire fell into chaos. Lack of central rule in the eighteenth century led to a period in which various groups vied for power; in south Azerbaijan the chief contenders were Afghan groups, Qajar chiefs, and local Kurdish chiefs.[21] Principalities were formed in Tabriz, Urmiya, Ardebil, Khoi, Maku, Karadagh, and Maraga.[22] In the north, local leaders took advantage of the power vacuum to assert their independence, establishing local khanates in Baku, Kuba, Sheki, Shamakhi, Karabagh, and Nakhchivan. Regional identity was strengthened in this period. The khans who ruled these states in the north were of Turkic origin.[23]

Central rule was reinstated in Iran in 1779 with the establishment of the Qajar dynasty.[24] The Qajar drive to reimpose rule on the khanates in northern Azerbaijan led to conflict with Russia, which also aspired to incorporate them. Under Qajar rule, Azerbaijan became the residence of the heir apparent, and Tabriz, with its location on Iran's major trade routes with Russia and Europe, was the major commercial capital of Iran. Thus, the Azerbaijanis were exposed more than other peoples in Iran to foreign ways and ideas. Many foreign states had consulates in Tabriz, and Azerbaijanis formed a large percentage of Iran's representatives abroad.[25]

During the Qajar regime, Turkish was the predominant spoken language at the Iranian court, while Persian was the predominant literary language.[26] Linguistic diversity was characteristic of the Qajar re-

---

20.   E.G. Browne, *A Literary History of Persia*, Vol. 4: *Modern Times* (1500–1924) (London, 1924), p. 14.

21.   See Bosworth, "Azerbaijan," *Encyclopedia Iranica*, p. 230.

22.   Tadeusz Swietochowski, *Russia and Azerbaijan: A Borderland in Transition* (N.Y.: Columbia University Press, 1995), p.2.

23.   Audrey Alstadt, *The Azerbaijani Turks* (Stanford, Calif.: Hoover Institute, 1992), p. 8.

24.   The Qajar Turks had served in the Safavid administration as lords and local governors. See Ira M. Lapidus, *A History of Islamic Societies* (Cambridge: Cambridge University Press, 1988), p. 300.

25.   Hasan Taqizadeh, "The Background of the Constitutional Movement in Azerbaijan," *Middle East Journal*, Vol. 14 (1960), p. 457.

26.   Henry D.G. Law, "Modern Persian Prose (1920s–1940s), in Thomas M. Ricks, ed., *Critical Perspectives on Modern Persian Literature* (Washington, D.C.: Three Continents Press, 1984), p. 132.

gime.[27] The position of the Azerbaijani language and of the Azerbaijanis themselves was so significant that all of the students first sent abroad in the beginning of the nineteenth century from Iran to study in Europe were from Azerbaijan.[28] To the astonishment of their hosts abroad, most had not even mastered Persian.[29]

THE SPLIT OF AZERBAIJAN

In the early nineteenth century, Russia and Iran fought for control of the Caucasus and southern Azerbaijan. Iran was defeated in the first military campaign. The sides concluded the Treaty of Gulustan in 1813, and Iran ceded a large part of the Caucasus to Russia. Major confrontation erupted again in 1825, and once more Iran was defeated. In February 1828, the Treaty of Turkmenchay was signed, and Iran lost the rest of the Caucasus. The border was set at the Araz River, thus dividing the Azerbaijanis under two separate regimes. In the eyes of many Azerbaijanis, this treaty symbolizes the separation of the people, and how one felt about it became an indicator of national identity. This section focuses on the Azerbaijanis north of the Araz River, since they became incorporated into the Russian Empire while those in the south remained under the same rule.

As part of the Turkmenchay agreement, Russia gained special economic rights in southern Azerbaijan, and so exerted its influence over this territory as well. Despite the formal division of Azerbaijan, direct ties between the Azerbaijanis on both sides of the border continued, especially due to the active economic interaction between the two areas. Iran and northern Azerbaijan seemed to remain one intellectual and cultural sphere. Mutual influences were quite significant, and important thinkers and activists constantly moved between the territories of northern and southern Azerbaijan. Mutual cultural ties continued and common poetry, songs, and fables developed among the Azerbaijanis on both sides of the Araz.[30] Moreover, the split gave the Azerbaijanis a unique role as conduit

---

27.   Ervand Abrahamian, "Kasravi: The Integrative Nationalist of Iran," in Elie Kedourie and Sylvia G. Haim, eds., *Towards a Modern Iran: Studies in Thought, Politics and Society* (London: Frank Cass, 1980), p. 99. Toward the end of the Qajar dynasty, Persianization of the court and the elite occurred.

28.   Pierre Oberlang, "Iran," in Margaret Bainbridge, ed., *The Turkic Peoples of the World* (London: Kegan Paul, 1993), p. 151.

29.   Major Southerland, report from July 16, 1812: P.R.O., F.O., 60, in David Menashri, *Education and the Making of Modern Iran* (Ithaca: Cornell University Press, 1992), p. 49.

30.   Swietochowski, *Russia and Azerbaijan: A Borderland in Transition*, p. 21.

of ideas among the three empires around them, especially since they could read texts published in Turkish and Russian (among them works translated from European languages) and could pass on the ideas in them to their co-ethnics in Iran. They could also pass along ideas prominent among Iranian intellectuals, Muslims in the Russian Empire, and the Ottoman Empire.

Muslim groups in the Russian Empire were the first Muslims to fall under European colonial rule. As part of Russia's colonial policy, most of the powers of the Muslim clerical establishment were usurped. Freed from the constraints of the ulama (clerical establishment), the Azerbaijanis and other Muslims in Russia became a beachhead of secularism and strong proponents of modern education in the Muslim world.

Three major trends in the collective identity of the Azerbaijanis emerged in the second half of the nineteenth century. First, the majority of the political activists seemed to possess a Muslim identity that was chiefly supra-ethnic and was especially identified with a greater Muslim sphere that included Iran, the Russian-occupied Caucasus, and parts of the Ottoman Empire. Their careers often spanned different parts of this zone, and their ideological works seemed to be concerned with the situation in all these areas. Azerbaijanis could consider themselves as both Turks and Iranians, or Russian subjects, with little conflict. Some were active in political movements in all three of the regions, concurrently or at different times of their careers.

Second, regardless of the nature of the political movement to which they belonged, many prominent Azerbaijani intellectuals advocated liberal values. Many rejected authoritative rule, including that led by Muslims, and supported freedom of thought and the establishment of modern education, free from the limitations of the traditional Muslim religious establishment. Many Azerbaijanis attempted to merge liberal values with ideologies such as Pan-Islam, which was particularly attractive to Azerbaijanis as a way to bridge the gap between their unique combination of identity as Shi'i and Turks.

Third, some Azerbaijanis were beginning to write about local Azerbaijani nationalism. Most of them viewed Turkic cultural identity as an important component of Azerbaijani identity and most advocates of Azerbaijani national identity in this period referred to themselves as Azerbaijani Turks. The most important expression of the emerging Azerbaijani nationalism was the appearance of the Azerbaijani language press toward the end of the nineteenth century. In this period, Azerbaijani nationalism was significantly more prominent in north Azerbaijan, probably because of Russian authorities' discrimination against them, especially in the economic field.[31]

THE IMPACT OF RUSSIAN COLONIAL RULE ON AZERBAIJANI NATIONAL IDENTITY IN THE NORTH

Within fifteen years of its conquest, Russia abolished the khanate (local principality rule) system and the tül land allocation system in the parts of Azerbaijan under its rule.[32] These reforms, while upsetting the traditional administrative and legal systems, contributed to the internal cohesion of the Azerbaijanis of the Caucasus; they removed a level of division that had promoted local particularism and they facilitated the economic integration of northern Azerbaijan.[33]

In contrast to British and French colonial rule in the Arab East, the Russian Empire struck at the power of the Muslim clerics in the areas it ruled, denying them control over education and personal status. Much of the Muslim clerical assets and properties were confiscated and the functions of the Shari'a courts were limited. Many mosques and madrasas (Muslim schools) were closed, and the remaining clerics were expected to show loyalty to Russia.[34] Although this policy generated animosity among many of the Azerbaijanis, it also released them, at an earlier stage than most of the Muslim world, from the constraints of the traditional clerical establishment and enabled the introduction of secular education.[35]

As subjects of the Russian Empire, Azerbaijanis in the north were allowed to study in the institutions of the Russian civil service, and in the 1840s a group of professionally trained Azerbaijani bureaucrats emerged who had been exposed to European-style education. In addition, the Azerbaijanis learned about and participated in limited local government.

---

31. The Russian authorities extended more rights to the Christian Armenians than to the Muslim subjects in the Caucasus. The Armenians often served as facilitators of Moscow's policies in the area. See Alexandre Bennigsen, "Azerbaijan" (paper prepared for conference of the Kennan Institute for Advanced Russian Studies, The Wilson Center, May 1979), p. 4.

32. The tül is the traditional system of land allocation between the local nobility (*beys* and *aghas*).

33. Swietochowski, *Russia and Azerbaijan: A Borderland in Transition*, p. 16. Strong regional identity still persists among the Azerbaijanis, in both north and south Azerbaijan.

34. Muriel Atkin, *Russia and Iran 1780–1828* (Minneapolis: University of Minneapolis, 1980), p. 150.

35. Alstadt, *The Azerbaijani Turks*, p. 18.

The Russian Empire Municipal law of 1870 provided for the formation of local assemblies (Duma); the election of mayors and municipal councils, and in 1878, in Baku, a local government council was formed. This exposure to small-scale self-rule may have influenced the co-ethnics in Iran; Azerbaijanis in Tabriz were later the driving force of the Constitutional Revolution and the subsequent movements to preserve its accomplishments.

Russian education also led to the emergence of an Azerbaijani "intelligentsia"[36] who had received a Russian version of European-style education. The emergence of this secular, educated class was exceptional at this time in the Muslim world, especially in neighboring Iran, where very few had been exposed to this type of education. Thus, the Azerbaijanis began to emerge as the spearhead of many important movements for change in their part of the Muslim world. In fact, two of the main political thinkers influencing Iran at the time, Mirza Fath 'Ali Akhundzade and 'Abdul al-Rahim Talebzade, were Azerbaijanis who lived most of their lives and published primarily outside of Iran, in the Caucasus.[37] There, Muslims were free from the threats of the ulama cleric establishment and could produce more radical writings, as well as read Western writings.

As Muslims, Azerbaijanis were denied the right to become full citizens of the Russian Empire, making cultural and political assimilation within the Russian Empire unattainable. Therefore, most continued to see themselves as part of the Muslim world; their writings reflected this and tended to concentrate on the situation in the greater Muslim world, not just in Russia. This combination of anti-clericalism and radicalism, plus their concern for the plight of Muslims elsewhere, made their political writings unique and significant.

Mirza Fath 'Ali Akhundzade is an important national figure in both Iran and Azerbaijan. In Azerbaijan, he is venerated as the founder of the modern literary Azerbaijani language, while in Iran he is considered one of the chief Iranian enlightenment ideologists. His writings and those of thinkers influenced by him, such as Malkum Khan and Mirza Aqa Khan Kermani, had an important impact on the Constitutional Revolution in

---

36.   Until the Soviet takeover of north Azerbaijan, migration between the north and south was very frequent and many Iranian Azerbaijanis as well as northern were educated in the Russian-held Caucasus.

37.   Mirza Fath 'Ali Akhundzade (Akhundov), 1812–1878. He was born in Sheki. At the time of his birth, it was part of Iran. After the Turkmenchay Treaty, Sheki came under Russian rule. 'Abdul-Rahim Talebzade (Talebov) (1834–1909). Talebzade was born in Tabriz and emigrated with his family to the Russian-held Caucasus at age sixteen, where he resided mainly in Tbilisi, Georgia, which at the time had a large Azerbaijani population.

Iran.[38] Akhundzade was one of the most prominent Muslim advocates of secular education. He felt that it was necessary to break the hold of the Muslim clerics on the population and expressed his atheism in very strong terms for the time. Akhundzade campaigned for a major reform in the Arabic alphabet. Akhundzade wrote many of his works in Azerbaijani, which he referred to as *Türki*, in order to best communicate his liberal ideas to the masses.[39] His decision to write in Azerbaijani was an important precedent that broke the prevailing custom among the Azerbaijani elite of using Persian for publications.

In 1850–55, Akhundzade published in the Azerbaijani language the first European style plays in the Muslim world. These plays satirized the problems in Azerbaijani society, which he claimed were rooted in religious superstition and ignorance. Akhundzade's plays were written predominantly in simple colloquial Azerbaijani, and have been depicted as "full-scale portraits of the customs and mores of the people of Azerbaijan."[40] They were first performed by pupils in state schools in Azerbaijan toward the end of the 1870s.[41] The production of his plays in Baku was an important indication of the emerging Azerbaijani native cultural revival.

Akhundzade's career and activities epitomized the fluidity and often multi-layered collective identity among the Azerbaijanis at the time. He served as a Tsarist official, yet had a great interest in Persian culture, and emphasized the greatness of pre-Islamic Iran in his writings, which became a basis for the development of modern Iranian nationalism. He also used the term "vatan," a word of Arabic origin meaning homeland, to relate to both Iran and Azerbaijan, yet his writings in Azerbaijani played a major role in sparking the modern literary revival of the language and the consequent cultural and national assertion of Azerbaijani identity.

---

38. Further evidence of the magnitude of Akhundzade's impact on Iran was the discovery that some of Akhundzade's works were incorrectly attributed to Mirza Aqa Khan Kermani. For instance, Akhundzade's first volume of "Three Letters" of the strongly anti-Islamic "Kamal od Dowleh and Jalal od Dowleh" was erroneously credited by E.G. Browne to Kermani. See the note by Nikki Keddie and 'Abdul Hossein Zarrinkub in Taqizadeh, "The Background of the Constitutional Movement in Azerbaijan," p. 459.

39. Tadeusz Swietochowski, *Russian Azerbaijan, 1905-1920: The Shaping of National Identity in a Muslim Community* (Cambridge: Cambridge University Press, 1985), p. 26.

40. Hasan Javadi, *Satire in Persian Literature* (London: Associated University Press, 1988), p. 258.

41. "Akhund-Zada," in *Encyclopedia of Islam*, p. 332.

'Abdul-Rahim Talebzade, also of Azerbaijani origin, lived and worked in the Caucasus, and had a substantial impact on the liberal political awakening that took place in Iran. Like Akhundzade, he was exposed to Western thought through Russian translations and evidently Turkish publications as well. While Talebzade advocated constitutional restraints, he supported strong central government and large integrated state structures.[42] Writing in the Russian Empire, away from the threats of the ulama, Talebzade was, like Akhundzade, strikingly explicit in his support for the rule of secular law and anti-clericalism. He presented the ulama as a reactionary force whose unscientific approach "delayed human development," and he called the high-ranking clerics hypocrites.[43]

In contrast to Akhundzade, Talebzade published exclusively in Persian. His writings were read throughout Iran and the Caucasus. While Akhundzade seemed to possess a multi-sided identity, Talebzade apparently identified chiefly with Iran, which he stated should be united as one country, one nation, under one religion.[44] Yet, many of his ideas were influenced by his particular perspective as an Azerbaijani—he had the opportunity to work outside of Iran, where he could write strongly critical and anti-clerical treatises.

Talebzade played an important role in conveying ideas from Azerbaijan to Iran; he established, in Baku, the first Muslim school based on a modern secular curriculum, which later served as a model for the *Jadidist* schools in Iran that included Western, technological, and secular subjects in their curricula.

The rapid growth of the oil industries brought a major influx of foreigners to the area, and affected the formation of the identity of the Azerbaijanis in both the Russian Empire and Iran.[45] By the 1870s, Baku became a multi-ethnic commercial center. Contact with large numbers of non-Muslims strengthened the distinctive identity of the Azerbaijanis: the social discrimination they endured from the non-Muslims and their second-rate legal status in the Russian Empire helped cement the ties between the Azerbaijani elites and masses and fostered philanthropical

---

42.   This idea was later advocated in a more extreme form by Ahmad Kasravi.

43.   Quoted in Mongol Bayat, *Mysticism and Dissent: Socioreligious Thought in Qajar Iran* (Syracuse: Syracuse University Press, 1982), p. 157.

44.   Talebzade is quoted in M. Reza Ghods, *A Comparative Historical Study of the Causes, Development, and Effects of the Revolutionary Movements in Northern Iran in 1920–21 and 1945–46,* (Ann Arbor, Mich.: University Microfilms, 1991), p. 109.

45.   By 1891, Baku supplied half of the world oil consumption.

work by wealthy Azerbaijanis. In addition, the discrimination made left-wing political ideologies attractive to some Azerbaijanis.

A separate Azerbaijani identity was further strengthened by the economic differentiation of the oil industries. Toward the end of the nineteenth century, Russians and other non-Muslim foreigners owned the majority of the wells, Armenians filled most of the white-collar positions, and Azerbaijanis performed most of the menial, blue-collar jobs and were over all the poorest segment of the population.[46]

The oil boom in Baku also intensified contacts among the Azerbaijanis because a huge influx of Azerbaijani laborers from Iran came in search of jobs. While this strengthened the connections between the north and south, it also led to some animosity between the local population and the immigrants, who resented the superior financial position of the indigenous Azerbaijani population.[47]

This migration significantly strengthened the transmitting role of the Azerbaijanis. The migrant population was exposed to political ideas being developed among the Azerbaijanis in the Russian Empire, especially constitutionalism and socialism. Azerbaijani activists in the north subsequently mobilized this migrant Azerbaijani population and formed cells of many of their political movements within Iran.

A second generation of Azerbaijani intelligentsia emerged in Baku in the 1870s. Like the first generation, they generally advocated liberal and enlightened political thought, and stressed education, secularism, and constitutionalism. However, this group was highly influenced by the *Tanzimat* (constitutional reform, 1856–76) in the Ottoman Empire. This attraction to the *Tanzimat* seemed to augment their interest in their Turkic roots and strengthened their Turkic identity.

In the second half of the nineteenth century, ethnic tension between the Turkic and Persian speakers was evident, even among the religious Shi'i. Najaf, in Iraq, is the major center of Shi'a holy places and educational institutions. Muslim students came from around the Islamic world to study there. Islam recognizes no ethnic differences among believers, but evidence shows that even at this Islamic center ethnic differences af-

---

46. Ronald Grigor Suny, "Nationalism and Social Class in the Russian Revolution: the Cases of Baku and Tiflis," in R.G. Suny, ed., *Transcaucasia: Nationalism and Social Change* (Ann Arbor: University of Michigan Press, 1983), p. 244.

47. While the local Azerbaijans held predominantly unskilled jobs, their lot was better than that of the transient Azerbaijani population from the south. A small group of Azerbaijans owned oil wells and industrial plants and were among Baku's wealthy residents.

fected behavior. The sojourn to Najaf, instead of binding the Azerbaijanis to other Shi'i, often accentuated their differences and strengthened separate ethnic consciousness.[48] In Najaf, Azerbaijanis overwhelmingly tended to emulate Azerbaijani ayatollahs, such as Sheikh Husayn Najaf, while the Persian students there usually followed ayatollahs of their ethnic origin. Donors to the institutions in Najaf tended to earmark funds for students from their regions or ethnic group, a practice that reinforced separation on the basis of ethnic groups. In addition, interethnic marriages were very rare among the ulama families. The Azerbaijani ("Turk") students in Najaf experienced ethnic discrimination. They complained to the Azerbaijani ayatollahs that they suffered at the hands of Arab and Persian ayatollahs, and suggested that the Persian and Arab students should not be treated equally by the Azerbaijani clerics.[49] In Najaf, students were generally housed only with members of their own ethnic group and a madrasa was built for Azerbaijani students after they had protested that they suffered discrimination by Persians. Even the *ashura* precessions, the supreme unifying symbol of Shi'i Islam, were often conducted separately on an ethnic basis in Najaf.[50]

POLEMICS ON NATIONAL IDENTITY

In the last quarter of the nineteenth century, the internal debate over the national identity of the Azerbaijanis accelerated. Polemics were waged between differing ideologies that often espoused clashing identities. The Azerbaijani-language press, which emerged in Baku at this time, became a major arena for polemics.

In 1875, proponents of particularistic Azerbaijani identity began publishing the newspaper *Akinchi* (The Cultivator). Written in the style of the spoken Azerbaijani language, it caused much controversy on both sides of the Araz. *Akinchi* was circulated among the Azerbaijanis in Iran. Many local proponents of Pan-Islam protested against publishing a journal in any language but Persian. *Akinchi*'s editor, Hasan bay Zarbadi, often coined new words in Azerbaijani to avoid using Persian and Arabic terms. In 1877, *Akinchi* was forced to close down by the Russian authorities, on the premise that a Turkic-language newspaper should not be published in Russia during the Russian-Ottoman War.

---

48.   Meir Litvak, *Shi'i Scholars of Nineteenth-Century Iraq: The 'Ulama' of Najaf and Karbala* (Cambridge: Cambridge University Press, 1998), p. 31.

49.   Ibid., pp. 33–34.

50.   Ibid., p. 34.

One of the other newspapers founded in this period was *Kashkul* (Dervish's ritual dish). *Kashkul* introduced in writing the term "Azerbaijani Turk," and dealt directly with the question of Azerbaijani peoplehood and the ties between the Azerbaijanis on both sides of the Araz, while drawing a distinction between the nation and the religious community. In *Kashkul*, authors criticized the use of the term *millet* to denote both nation and community.[51] An imaginary dialogue published in *Kashkul* reflects the exploration of identity in Azerbaijan:

Question: What is your nationality (*millet*)?
Answer: I am a Muslim and a Turk.
Question: Are you an Ottoman?
Answer: No, I am *bijanli* (a play on words in Azerbaijani meaning "soulless").
Question: Where is the land of the *bijanlis*?
Answer: As far as I can tell, on the other side of the Araz live the Azeris—on this side the *bijanlis*. Together, it makes Azerbaijani. But separately we are *bijanlis*.
Question: Your language is Turkic so you are a Turk?
Answer: There is no word to describe my position. I am a Turk, but *bijanli*.
Question: Instead of being a bijanli Turk, why don't you solve your dilemma by calling yourself an Azerbaijani Turk?[52]

The post-*Akinchi* press in Azerbaijan was written predominantly in Ottoman Turkish and turned away from the colloquial Azerbaijani language.[53] The written use of colloquial Azerbaijani received a decisive blow in 1891, when the Russian government ordered the closing of *Kashkul*.

Until 1904, no other Turkic-language journal received permission to publish in the north, but Azerbaijanis continued to air many social questions in the Russian-language *Kaspii*. The majority of its contributors advocated self-government for the Muslims of the Caucasus, within the framework of a liberalized and reformed Russia. Yet, in its liberal spirit, *Kaspii* printed articles reflecting a variety of orientations, including those espousing Pan-Turkism. *Kaspii* was edited by 'Ali Mardan-bay Topchibashi,[54] and was published under the sponsorship of the Baku oil baron Zeynal 'Abdin Taghiyev.

---

51. *Käshkül*, No. 22 (1891), quoted in Swietochowski, *Russian Azerbaijan 1905-1920*, p. 32.

52. Swietochowski, *Russian Azerbaijan 1905–1920*, p. 32.

53. Ibid., p. 29.

54. 'Ali Mardan bay Topchibashi (1868–1934).

The Azerbaijani-language press was renewed with the publication of *Sharq-i Rus*. Its editor, Mehmed Agha Shakhtakhtinskii, was a proponent of secular nationalism as the means for progress for Muslims.[55]

In Iran as well, some Azerbaijanis took an interest in the literary revival of the Azerbaijani language. Toward the end of the nineteenth century, Mirza Shadiq Asadulla-ogli published a book advocating the use of Azerbaijani as the language of instruction in elementary schools, and he wrote textbooks in the language.[56]

In the second half of the nineteenth century, some Azerbaijanis espoused Pan-Islamic ideology,[57] and many of the supporters of Pan-Islam identified with Iran at this time. In addition, many Azerbaijanis were interested in their Turkic identity in a cultural sense, but few supported political unity with other Turkic peoples.[58] However, some Azerbaijanis played an important role in the development of Pan-Turkism in Istanbul. The most significant was 'Ali bay Huseynzade (1864–1941). In Istanbul, Huseynzade became one of the founders of *Ittihad-i Osmaniyye*, which was a forerunner of the Young Turk movement. Huseynzade's poem, *Turan*, was the first poetic call for unity among all ethnic Turks.[59] The chief ideologist of the Pan-Turkist movement, Ziya Gökalp, cited Huseynzade as one of his most important teachers, from whom he adopted the slogan "Turklashtirmak, Islamlashtirmak, Avrupalashtirmak" (Turkify, Islamicize, Europeanize).[60] Ziya Gökalp's use of this slogan was embraced as one of the main mottoes of the Pan-Turkist movement.

---

55. See Edward J. Lazzerini, "Sayyid Jamal al-Din al-Afghani from the Perspective of a Russian Muslim," in Kedourie and Haim, *Towards a Modern Iran: Studies in Thought, Politics and Society*, p. 57.

56. Mirza Shadiq Asadulla-oghli, quoted in Sakina Berengian, *Azeri and Persian Literary Works in Twentieth-Century Iranian Azerbaijan* (Berlin: Klaus Schwarz Verlag, 1988), p. 47.

57. Many Azerbaijanis claim that Sayyid Jamal al-Din Afghani, the first modern proponent of Pan-Islam, was actually of Azerbaijani origin. Afghani was born in the late 1830s in an Azerbaijani-speaking village outside Hamadan, which indicates that he grew up in an Azerbaijani-speaking area. See Ervand Abrahamian, *Iran Between Two Revolutions* (Princeton: Princeton University Press, 1982), p. 62.

58. Swietochowski, *Russia and Azerbaijan: A Borderland in Transition*, p. 33.

59. Alstadt, *The Azerbaijani Turks*, p. 69.

60. Ziya Gökalp, *The Principles of Turkism* (Leiden, 1968), pp. 5–6; and U. Heyd, *Foundations of Turkish Nationalism: The Life and Teachings of Ziya Gökalp* (London: 1950), pp. 107–108, quoted in Swietochowski, *Russia and Azerbaijan: A Borderland in Transition*, p. 34.

Azerbaijani political attitudes were influenced by the confrontations with the Armenians during the Armenian-Tatar War (1903–05) that waged in the Caucasus.[61] It also affected the Azerbaijanis in Iran, for many of the Muslim victims of the violence were migrant Azerbaijani workers from the south.[62] In response to these events, a clandestine Azerbaijan self-defense organization, *Difai* (defense) was formed in Ganja, which represented an important shift away from dependence on Russian protection. This was one of the first developments in a series of events that gave Ganja a more pronounced Azerbaijani nationalism than Baku, among the cities in the north.[63]

THE REVOLUTIONARY ERA, 1905–20

In 1905–08, three major political revolutions occurred in the areas surrounding the Azerbaijanis: the 1905 Russian Revolution, the Constitutional Revolution of Iran in 1906, and the Young Turk Revolution in 1908. Many Azerbaijanis played a role in these events, which also catalyzed developments in their own national identity and orientation. These three revolutions were followed by further revolutions and counterrevolutions in these three countries, a world war, and periods of brief foreign occupation of parts of Azerbaijan by Ottoman and later British forces.

This period is marked by a number of substantial political developments. First, an Azerbaijani left-wing movement emerged. Second, an all-out Azerbaijani nationalism developed, which is best illustrated by the foundation of the Azerbaijan Democratic Republic in the north. Prior to the establishment of the republic, it seems that few Azerbaijanis felt complete independence was attainable, and had coupled their nationalism with an orientation toward a foreign power which they would join in a federation or confederation that could provide protection. Third, and in contrast to the north, many Azerbaijanis in Iran identified with and participated in the general Iranian revolutionary movements, and many advocated embracing Persian culture and language. Fourth, the role of the Azerbaijanis as conveyors of ideas and activists was especially pronounced in this period in Russia, Turkey, and Iran; activists in each of these countries passed the lessons they had learned to an adjoining arena. Finally, in almost all the movements they joined, the Azerbaijanis contin-

---

61.   This was a series of intensive violent clashes between the Muslims and Armenians in the Caucasus. In the Russian Empire, non-Muslims referred to Azerbaijanis and many other Muslim groups by the misnomer "Tatar."

62.   Swietochowski, *Russia and Azerbaijan: A Borderland in Transition*, p. 40.

63.   By 1897, the local population in Ganja had began to call themselves "Azerbaijani Turk." See Alstadt, *The Azerbaijani Turks*, p. 79.

ued to be at the forefront of Muslims advocating the adoption of liberal values and enlightenment. One example of this is the insistence on the emancipation of women advocated by political parties in both north and south Azerbaijan.

Revolutionary reforms in Russia, Iran, and Turkey ushered in a period of relative freedom that allowed the airing of views that had previously been censored. Indeed, the revolutionary events not only helped to shape the ideas of the Azerbaijanis, but also allowed their publication.

Following the 1905 limited constitutional Russian Revolution and the end to the ban on Turkic-language newspapers, a plethora of Azerbaijani newspapers, both in the local Azerbaijani vernacular and in modified Ottoman Turkish, began to appear in north Azerbaijan. The press reflected the Azerbaijani engagement with the question of self-identity, and the related polemics, such as the debate over what should be the preferred language and the appropriate remedies for improving their social situation. Among the terms that began to appear at this time in the Azerbaijani press are *milliyatchilik* (nationalism), and the foreign loan word, *nasyonalizm*.[64]

The choice of language generally reflected the political and often the national identity orientation of the newspaper. The newspapers *Sharq-i Rus*, *Taza Hayat*, and *Hayat* were written in Azerbaijani, and espoused a liberal, secular, ethnic-nationalist position. *Fuzuyat*, which was written in modified Ottoman Turkish, reflected the authors' secular-liberal orientation and support for strong ties with Turkey and Pan-Turkism. It was edited by 'Ali bay Huseynzade, who returned to Baku from Istanbul following the Young Turk Revolution. Huseynzade wrote that the Azerbaijanis, as Oghuz Turks, were basically the same people as the Ottoman Turks, and thus there was no need for separate identification.

Many of the Azerbaijani journals had an extensive following and much influence in Iran and the Muslim world. The most important and well-known journal was *Molla Nasreddin*, which rejected writing in foreign languages, such as Persian and Russian, and Ottoman Turkic grammar. It supported Azerbaijani in the style spoken by most of the people. One of the famous caricatures from the journal depicts an Azerbaijani man and three foreigners (representing Russian, Persian, and Arabic) trying to stuff tongues into his mouth; he responds, "Hey, brothers, I was not born tongue-less that you have to stuff my mouth with these tongues."[65]

---

64. Swietochowski, *Russian Azerbaijan, 1905-1920*, p. 57.

65. *Molla Nasreddin*, December 22, 1906.

After restrictions were relaxed in north Azerbaijan and after the 1905 revolution in Russia, the local intelligentsia led a cultural revival that included the founding of additional Azerbaijani-language schools. One of the highlights of this cultural revival was the staging in 1908 of the Azerbaijani opera, *Leyli and Majnun*, based on the poem of the famed Turkic poet, Fizuli, set to the music of the native composer Uzeir Hajibayli. This was the first Western-style opera performed in a language of a Muslim people. At this time, many Azerbaijanis expressed a desire to educate their children in the Azerbaijani language. In 1906, the Conference of Muslim Teachers convened in Baku and addressed the issue of the "nationalization of primary schools."[66] The teachers stressed the need to use Azerbaijani as the language of instruction in the schools and the importance of developing Azerbaijani-language textbooks, and pointed out that Muslim parents opposed sending their children to Russian-language schools. In addition, in July 1913 workers held a strike; one of their main demands was the establishment of Azerbaijani-language school.

In the Russian Empire, Azerbaijani national identity was affected by the discrimination of the Russian authorities against Muslims, and the competition and tension with the Armenians, who were granted preferential treatment by the imperial authorities. In addition, separate Azerbaijani identity was fostered by both the Muslim and Russian political parties, which tended to emphasize the Azerbaijanis' disadvantageous position in an effort to recruit them into their various movements.[67] Violence between Armenians and Azerbaijanis erupted a number of times in the first quarter of the twentieth century, and this affected the identity and political development of each of the sides.

Following the first Russian Revolution in 1905, leftist political forces became prominent among Azerbaijanis, especially in Baku. Among the most important of them was the *Himmet*, which drew its members chiefly from Azerbaijanis in Baku and the migrant workers from Iran. It was the predecessor of the communist parties of both Azerbaijan and Iran. Within the *Himmet*, a separate section, *Adalat*, was formed for the migrant workers from Iran, which later served as the basis for the socialist movement within Iran. *Adalat* published the bilingual Azerbaijani-Persian newspaper, *Hurriyet*. The *Himmet* was associated with the Russian Social-Democrat Workers' Party (RSDWP). The Azerbaijanis attained a unique status for the *Himmet* among the socialist organizations operating in the Russian

---

66. Quoted by Alstadt, *The Azerbaijani Turks*, p. 201.

67. Mangol Bayat, *Iran's First Revolution: Shi'ism and the Constitutional Revolution of 1905-1909* (N.Y.: Oxford University Press, 1991), p. 79.

empire: At the time of its founding in 1904, Lenin sanctioned their request that the *Himmet* retain its ethnic character and remain an all-Muslim group. In contrast, the Jewish Bund's request to retain exclusively Jewish membership was denied.[68]

The unique nationalistic character of the Azerbaijani left is also illustrated by the activities of some of its activists, such as Nariman Narimanov, one of the founders of the *Himmet*, who later became the Chairman of the Government of the Soviet Republic of Azerbaijan. Narimanov worked for the language rights for the Azerbaijanis, and in 1906 served as the co-chairman of a committee set up in Baku to address language rights in education.[69] At the time of the Soviet takeover of Baku, Narimanov asked the Russian Bolsheviks that Azerbaijan be granted independence.[70] Another *Himmet* leader, Azizbeykov, was also active in trying to set up educational institutions in the Azerbaijani language.

An additional sign of the national cohesion of the Azerbaijani left is that Azerbaijani workers showed little signs of class solidarity or cooperation with Russian or Armenian workers; clashes between them were frequent. During the period of the independent Azerbaijani Republic (1918–20), *Himmet* restricted its membership to Muslims. Even after the Soviet takeover of Azerbaijan, many Himmetist supporters sought to sustain Azerbaijani autonomy within a Soviet framework.[71]

At this time, no important figures in Azerbaijan called for the adoption of Russian cultural identity. In any event, the extreme Russian discrimination against Muslims effectively blocked assimilation. Some liberal bourgeois figures, such as Topchibashi, advocated close cooperation with Russia after the 1905 Revolution, although he did not express any form of self-identity with it. Even Topchibashi, after his expectations of achieving Muslim equality under Russian rule were not met, turned to Azerbaijani nationalistic activity. Most activists in north Azerbaijan had an ambivalent relation toward Russia, an important trend throughout the twentieth century. While they resented the Russian discrimination and condescension, they appreciated Russia's role as a conduit of secular and

---

68. Bennigsen, "Azerbaijan," p. 7; and Alexandre Bennigsen and S. Enders Wimbush, *Muslim National Communism in the Soviet Union: A Revolutionary Strategy for the Colonial World* (Chicago: The University of Chicago Press, 1979), p. 12.

69. Alstadt, *The Azerbaijani Turks*, p. 55.

70. Bennigsen and Wimbush, *Muslim National Communism in the Soviet Union*, p. 56. Narimanov claimed that as an independent country, Azerbaijan would be a role model for communist revolution in other Muslim-populated states.

71. Swietochowski, *Russian Azerbaijan 1905-1920*, p. 194.

scientific education. Since most groups in north Azerbaijan then believed that full Azerbaijani political independence was infeasible, many felt that some sort of federative relationship between Azerbaijan and Russia was inevitable.

Between 1905 and the collapse of the Russian Empire in 1917, some Azerbaijanis supported the establishment of a political federation with other peoples of the Caucasus. When the Russian Empire collapsed, Azerbaijan joined the Transcaucasian Federation, which fell five weeks after its founding. No major proponents of Caucasian identity emerged at this time.

After the 1908 Young Turk Revolution in Turkey, the language debate and the question of the identity of the Azerbaijanis as Turks intensified in north Azerbaijan. In Baku, Pan-Turkists advocated that all the Turkic peoples adopt the newly modified Ottoman Turkish, now devoid of many of its Arabic and Persian words. In 1912, Azerbaijanis who supported the adoption of Ottoman Turkish as the literary language of the Azerbaijanis began publishing *Shalala* in the new Ottoman Turkish. The declared goal of the newspaper was to "serve the cause of the unification of Turkic peoples on the basis of the Ottoman dialect used by the most advanced of all literatures in the Turkic-speaking world."[72]

The Azerbaijanis were singled out for special attention by the Ottoman Turks, due to their special affinity with them; their languages stem from the same Turkic group, the Oghuz. During this revolutionary period, a new ideological movement, *oghuzism*, emerged in Istanbul, stressing the special ties within this Turkic group. Some of the Azerbaijanis living in Istanbul were active in this group, while others there joined the Pan-Turkish movement that emerged after the Young Turk Revolution. A prominent Pan-Turkish proponent was Ahmad bay Agaoglu.[73] He became the leading writer of one of the most important Pan-Turkist journals, *Türk Yurdu*. Agaoglu's articles on Pan-Turkism and the Turkic nation in *Türk Yurdu* reflected the special Azerbaijani desire to bridge the Shi'a-Sunni split, which was especially important to the Azerbaijanis since they were both Shi'i and Turks, and were strongly anticlerical, as were many Azerbaijani intellectuals.

A few Azerbaijanis were active at this time in the Pan-Islamic movement in the Russian Empire, and especially in the formation of the *Ittifaq al-Muslim*. The Azerbaijanis' activities within this movement reflected

---

72. *Shälälä*, No. 21 (1913), quoted in Swietochowski, *Russian Azerbaijan 1905–1920*, p. 62.

73. Earlier in his career, Agaoglu had advocated Pan-Islamist ideology. Agaoglu is often referred to with a Russian name ending as Aghayev.

their unique perspective; they called for the need to put aside sectarian Sunni-Shi'i divisions, and for the Muslims of Russia to unite in the struggle to attain their rights within the empire. The members of this movement opposed Turkic nationalism and any form of particularistic Azerbaijani nationalism.

GROWING AZERBAIJANI IDENTITY: THE ESTABLISHMENT OF THE
AZERBAIJAN DEMOCRATIC REPUBLIC

The Young Turk Revolution in Turkey in 1908 gave impetus to Turkic cultural identity and to local nationalist trends that were emerging among the Azerbaijanis in the Russian Empire. These trends were accelerated by the return of absolute rule in Iran, which made Iran less attractive. The disillusionment with the Revolution of 1905 in Russia, which failed to end the extreme discrimination against the Muslims in the Russian Empire, also strengthened this process. Nevertheless, few Azerbaijanis called for full political independence; most saw this goal as unrealistic until the collapse of the Russian Empire during the 1917 Russian Revolution.

The rising Azerbaijani identity was embodied in the *Musavat* (Equality) Party, which was founded in 1911. Its first published platform included a commitment to secular Turkic nationalism and the establishment of an autonomous Azerbaijan in association with Russia, within a federation of free and equal states.[74] *Musavat* strove to encompass Muslims of different political orientations and create unity among them. The use of both phrases, "autonomous" and "free and independent," in the different platforms suggests that the authors were not clear on the actual degree of independence they desired for Azerbaijan, or at least they feared to call forthrightly for independence. *Musavat* formed cells within Iran, especially in Tabriz, Rasht, Ardebil, Khoi, and Maku, and also in the border area.[75] The collapse of the Russian army in the Caucasus during the Revolution gave the *Musavats* the opportunity to establish an independent state, initially as part of a Transcaucasian federation. When the federation dissolved, Azerbaijan became an independent state. During the period surrounding the declaration of the new state, Nasib bay Ussubekov, one of the chief activists of *Musavat*, expressed reservations about proclaiming a state in north Azerbaijan without the south, at a time when he estimated that Azerbaijani nationalist sentiments were high there as well.[76]

---

74. Swietochowski, *Russia and Azerbaijan: A Borderland in Transition*, p. 62.

75. Ibid., p. 129.

76. Ibid., p. 65.

On May 28, 1918, the Azerbaijan Provincial Council proclaimed the establishment of the new state, the Azerbaijan Democratic Republic (Azerbayjan Khalq Jumhuriyet). The declaration stated that:

1. Azerbaijan is a fully sovereign state; it consists of the southern and eastern parts of Transcaucasia under the authority of the Azerbaijani people.
2. It is resolved that the form of government of the independent Azerbaijani state will be a democratic republic.
3. The Azerbaijan Democratic Republic is determined to establish friendly relations with all, especially with the neighboring nations and states.
4. The Azerbaijan Democratic Republic guarantees to all its citizens within its borders full civil and political rights, regardless of ethnic origin, religion, class, profession, or gender.
5. The Azerbaijan Democratic Republic encourages the free development of all nationalities inhabiting its territory.
6. Until the Azerbaijani Constituent Assembly is convened, the supreme authority over Azerbaijan is vested in a universally elected National Council and the provisional government responsible to this Council.[77]

The retention of the name Azerbaijan fostered fears in Iran that the new republic intended, with Ottoman support, to detach south Azerbaijan from Iran. In an attempt to allay Iranian apprehension, the government referred to the new republic as the *Caucasian Republic of Azerbaijan* in much of its correspondence abroad.

The constitution of the new republic declared equal rights for all citizens regardless of religion, ethnic origin, or gender, making Azerbaijan the first Muslim state to grant women the vote.

Polemics continued to be waged over the national identity of the new state. Azerbaijan's external orientation shifted rapidly, mostly on the basis of which foreign state seemed willing to support the fledgling state's independence, and less on the basis of ideological factors or as a result of national identity.[78] The republican government declared Turkish the

77. Näsib Näsibzadä, *Azärbayjan Demokratik Respublikasï* (Baku: Elm, 1990), pp. 43–44.

78. Some Azerbaijanis unsuccessfully attempted to create an alliance with Great Britain, while others initiated negotiations with Iran toward confederation, mainly out of a desire to achieve ties with south Azerbaijan. See Swietochowski, *Russian Azerbaijan, 1905–1920*, pp. 157–158.

official language of the state. State employees were to conduct all business in that language within two years, in an attempt to end the predominance of Russian. A debate was conducted over whether to adopt Azerbaijani Turkish versus Ottoman Turkish. The *Musavat* Party Program, issued at the Second Party Congress in December 1919, stated that the Ottoman dialect would be mandatory in Azerbaijan's high schools. Turkic language instruction was introduced at all levels in all the schools in Azerbaijan, and the study of Russian history was replaced by the history of the Turkic peoples. One of *Musavat's* early goals was the opening of a university in Baku with instruction in Azerbaijani. In September 1919, this goal was realized. After the Soviet takeover of the republic, Russian was imposed as the primary language at the university.

The Red Army of the newly established Soviet state attempted to reconquer the territories of the former Russian empire that had declared independence. On April 27, 1920, Soviet forces, with the assistance of Azerbaijani communist supporters, conquered the Azerbaijani Democratic Republic, bringing its independent statehood to an end after only twenty-three months and incorporating it in the territory of the Soviet Union.[79]

Identity in Iran

In the beginning of the twentieth century, Iranian Azerbaijanis spearheaded the Iranian Constitutional movement, and most of the Azerbaijani intelligentsia identified as Iranians. Two main trends of identity emerged among the Azerbaijani activists in Iran at this time: Some supported the Persianization of the Azerbaijanis and other minorities in Iran, to increase unity and ease the development of a modern state. Others advocated the establishment in Iran of a reformed constitutionally-based and supra-ethnic regime that would allow for cultural autonomy. Some members of this group supported autonomy for the Azerbaijanis and the other ethnic groups in Iran as a means to form liberal political structures in Iran, at least on a local scale.

Generally, activists who had been educated in the Caucasus and had extended contacts with their co-ethnics in the north, including the leftists,

79. Swietochowski cites a Soviet source that claims that in April 1920 there were approximately 4,000 members of the Communist Party in Azerbaijan. In Swietochowski's opinion, the local communists were a less critical factor leading to the fall of the ADR than public fear of the overwhelming Soviet military might and infighting among the Azerbaijani nationalist groups. See Swietochowski, *Russia and Azerbaijan: A Borderland in Transition*, p. 91.

tended to support the preservation of Azerbaijani cultural and linguistic rights within Iran. In contrast, those who had not had extended contact with their co-ethnics in the north, and were most often educated in Tehran, usually supported the Persianization of the Azerbaijanis in Iran.

Tabriz, the major Azerbaijani-populated city, was the center of revolutionary activity in Iran in the first quarter of the twentieth century. The demonstrations that triggered the Iranian Constitutional Revolution of 1906 began in Tabriz. The majority of the Azerbaijani activists in the Iranian Constitutional Revolution wished to pursue goals that would affect the regime in all of Iran. However, in their efforts to preserve the constitutional regime, Azerbaijanis, on a number of occasions, threatened to separate from Iran in their confrontation with the Shah's regime.[80] This indicates at least an awareness of their distinctive identity within the Iranian framework, and a perception of its potential political power.

A few writers in Iran were working to strengthen particularistic Azerbaijani identity in this period. Among them was the Azerbaijani educator Mirza Hasan Roshdiyeh, who in 1905 published a textbook, *Vatan Dili*, in Tabriz. Written in Azerbaijani, it was based on Azerbaijani literature and folklore.[81] Some writers contributed to the bilingual Azerbaijani-Persian newspaper, *Azerbayjan*, which began to appear in 1907. It published varying views on the question of national identity, and emulated the satirical journal, *Molla Nasreddin*.[82]

After the 1906 Constitutional Revolution in Iran, local councils, or *anjumans*, were established to supervise local parliamentary elections. The Tabriz Anjuman extended its authority far beyond this role and even remained in permanent session after the elections, a move that illustrates Azerbaijani desire for local rule.[83]

In 1908, the Qajar Shah, Mohammad 'Ali, attempted to reverse the successes of the Constitutional Revolution and reimpose autocratic rule in Iran. Under the leadership of Sattar Khan, an Azerbaijani, the residents of Tabriz were the first to stand up against the Shah. Sattar Khan's troops captured Tabriz in the name of the Tabriz Anjuman, and replaced the Ira-

---

80. Abrahamian, *Iran Between Two Revolutions*, p. 91.

81. Mirza Hasan Roshdiyeh (1850–1943), *Vatan Dili* (Tabriz, 1905).

82. *Azärbayjan* often published caricatures in which the lines spoken by the sympathetic peasant are in Azerbaijani, while the lines spoken by the landowner, the tax collector, etc., are in Persian, reflecting an intertwining of ethnic and social grievances.

83. Janet Afary, "Peasant Rebellion of the Caspian Region during the Iranian Constitutional Revolution 1906-1909," *International Journal of Middle East Studies*, Vol. 23 (May 1991), p. 142.

nian flag with the flag of the Tabriz Anjuman. Sattar Khan declared that the "nation of Azerbaijan" refused to recognize the sovereignty of Mohammad 'Ali Shah, and declared Tabriz the temporary capital of Iran.

While the Azerbaijani activists in the Constitutional Revolution in Iran had mostly advocated the Persianization of the Azerbaijanis and the centralization of government in Iran, literature appeared during the period of Sattar Khan's revolt that glorified Azerbaijan's role in Iranian history, called Azerbaijan the homeland, and extolled the virtues of the Azerbaijanis. In addition, the publication of an Azerbaijani-language newspaper in Tabriz, *Ana Dili* (Mother Tongue), began at this time; it stressed indigenous Azerbaijani language and culture and often published literary works from north Azerbaijan.[84] Sattar Khan had close ties with the left-wing *Firqeh-i Ijtima'iyyun 'Ammiyyun* party, which was based in the Caucasus.[85]

The end of the Qajar monarchy was preceded by three revolts in north Iran: in Gilan, Khorasan, and Azerbaijan. Azerbaijani activists from both the north and south, as well as other groups from the Caucasus, were active in the uprisings. These revolts were led by reform-minded individuals who believed that the establishment of democratic reforms in their own regions would lead to the basis for liberalization of the rest of Iran.[86] Of the three revolts, the revolt led by Khiyabani in Azerbaijan was the most threatening to the Iranian regime. Khiyabani, a well-educated cleric, had embraced radical ideas while studying in the Caucasus.[87] He was exiled by the Turkish forces that had occupied Iranian Azerbaijan in 1915, because he rejected the Pan-Islamist ideology that the Turks were trying to promote at the time and had warned against what he viewed as their attempts to annex the province.[88] Early in the revolt he convened a conference of representatives from most of the towns in Iranian Azerbaijan. After the conference, a bilingual Azerbaijani-Persian newspaper, *Tajaddod*, was established and the name of the Azerbaijani branch of the Democratic Party was changed to the Democratic Party of Azerbaijan, emphasizing its separateness. The Tabriz Democrats established a chap-

---

84. Ghods, *A Comparative Historical Study*, pp. 135–136; and Berengian, *Azeri and Persian Literary Works in Twentieth-Century Iranian Azerbaijan*, pp. 47–48.

85. Afary, "Peasant Rebellion of the Caspian Region during the Iranian Constitutional Revolution 1906–1909," p. 151.

86. Atabaki, *Azerbaijan: Ethnicity and Autonomy in Twentieth-Century Iran*, p. 3.

87. Abrahamian, *Iran Between Two Revolutions*, p. 112.

88. Ghods, *A Comparative Historical Study*, p. 171.

ter in Baku, which in 1918 began to publish its own newspaper, *Azerbayjan*.[89] Among the demands the conference in Azerbaijan sent to Iran's central government were the appointment of a governor of Azerbaijan who would be trusted by the people of the province; the immediate reconvening of the National Assembly in Tehran; and the reconvening of the *anjumans*, as provided by the constitution.[90] In his closing speech at the conference, Khiyabani charged that Azerbaijan, despite the sacrifices that it had made in the Constitutional Revolution, received neither fair parliamentary representation nor equitable budgetary allocations from the central government.[91] When the Shah rejected their demands, Khiyabani proceeded to take over and govern the whole province of Azerbaijan, establishing the autonomous government of *Azadistan* (Land of Freedom) in April 1920.

Khiyabani decreed the right to use the Azerbaijani language in the province. His insistence on protecting journalists who wrote in Azerbaijani led to an open split with Ahmad Kasravi, who was deported from Iranian Azerbaijan because he criticized the use of the Azerbaijani language in the province.[92] Like many of his northern Azerbaijani counterparts, Khiyabani differentiated between identifying culturally as Turks and forging political links to Turkey; he supported the right of the residents of the province to use their native Turkic language, and also struggled against the Ottoman presence and its influence in Azerbaijan. Khiyabani also promoted a local literary revival under the direction of Mirza Taqi Khan.

Khiyabani's demands reflected both Azerbaijani and Iranian identity. Khiyabani did not aspire to separate the Azerbaijan provinces from Iran, but advocated a change between center and periphery relations and the retention of language rights for Azerbaijanis. He strove, as well, for the formation of a reformed democratic Iran that would allow for cultural pluralism. Khiyabani used the term *vatan* to refer to both Iran and Azerbaijan.[93] As part of the reforms he instituted during the short-lived autonomy, Khiyabani worked to establish Azerbaijani-language schools

---

89. Swietochowski, *Russia and Azerbaijan: A Borderland in Transition*, p. 65.

90. Abrahamian, *Iran Between Two Revolutions*, p. 112.

91. Similar claims were be made sixty years later by Azerbaijani activists, referring to their sacrifices in the Islamic Revolution.

92. Ervand Abrahamian, "Communism and Communalism in Iran: The Tudah and the Firqah-i Dimukrat," *International Journal of Middle East Studies*, Vol. 1, No. 4 (1970), p. 294.

93. Swietochowski, *Russia and Azerbaijan: A Borderland in Transition*, p. 99.

in Iranian Azerbaijan, often employing teachers from north Azerbaijan or Turkey.[94]

Khiyabani's reforms and cultural programs were cut short after his rebellion was quelled in September 1920 by Reza Khan's forces, which dispersed the Democrats and later executed Khiyabani. Reza Khan's success in subduing the autonomy movements was an important rallying point in his rise to power as Shah of Iran.

TIES AND MUTUAL INFLUENCES ACROSS THE ARAZ

Despite the division of the Azerbaijanis under separate and very different empires, they continued to interact as one intellectual and cultural sphere, and the commercial and family ties between the two populations remained vibrant. For most of the period, there was constant migration between the two sides, and each side was a refuge when turmoil occurred on the opposite side. The Azerbaijanis continued to play an important role as a conduit of ideas and as activists in Russia, Iran, and Turkey.

Azerbaijanis from Iran who had significant contact with co-ethnics from the north tended to be more attached to their Azerbaijani identity than those who did not have this contact. They usually strove to promote this ethnic culture even within the framework of other ideological movements, such as communism or Iranian nationalism. Many of the major liberal Azerbaijani political activists in Iran had spent time in the Caucasus, and had connections with and received aid from Azerbaijanis there. For instance, a group of Tabriz intellectuals who had spent time in Baku founded a literary circle in 1895 that later served as a basis for liberal oriented political and education activity and for secret and semi-secret activity devoted to constitutionalism.

Zeynal 'Abdin Taghiyev's philanthropical activities illustrate the social and cultural cohesion of Azerbaijanis from both sides of the Araz in the nineteenth century, and how identity with co-ethnics often extended beyond the border. Taghiyev's activities touched Azerbaijanis beyond his home in the north. In Tabriz, he underwrote the first *Jadidist* high school which served as a model throughout Iran and a modern library, and he funded the distribution of liberal newspapers to clerical students in Najaf.[95]

Free from the threats and limitations of the ulama, an educated and secular Azerbaijani intelligentsia emerged in the Russian Empire before anything similar in most places in the Muslim world. Many members of

---

94. Ibid., p. 97.

95. Ibid., *Russia and Azerbaijan: A Borderland in Transition*, p. 23.

this group were exposed to and adopted liberal political thinking. These ideas were easily transmitted to their co-ethnics in Iran. Through their frequent contacts with each other and common language, Azerbaijanis channeled ideas and influence to both sides of the Araz. In addition, many publications from Baku were distributed among Azerbaijanis in Iran and had significant impact there. The most prominent are the works of Miza Alekber Sabir Tahirzade, published mostly in the Azerbaijani journal *Molla Nasreddin*.[96] Sabir's works influenced not only the Azerbaijanis of Iran, but also intellectuals throughout the country. Many Iranian political movements, such as most of the Iranian socialist parties, were organized and run from Baku. The Azerbaijani migrant workers who formed the bulk of the membership worked in Azerbaijan for only part of the year, and brought back with them radical ideas and forms of protest when they returned to Iran.[97] Another illustration of Azerbaijanis' role as conveyors of activity was that volunteers from the Caucasus, many of Azerbaijani origin, joined in the struggle to retain the constitutional regime in Iran. For example, fighters from the Caucasus were among the forces that set out from Gilan and overthrew Muhammad 'Ali in Tehran on July 16, 1909, and arms were sent from Baku to the fighters in Tabriz.

On both sides of the border, many Azerbaijani intellectuals active during the late nineteenth and early twentieth centuries were often affected by the same revolutionary events. The intellectuals' careers also illustrate how both Azerbaijans functioned as one intellectual and political sphere with much movement between the two regions. The career of Mehmet Emin Rasulzade best reflects this mobility and the interconnections of events in north and Iranian Azerbaijan. One of the founders of the *Himmet* socialist party in Baku, Rasulzade also had been active during the Constitutional Revolution in Iran, and worked as the editor of the Persian newspaper, *Iran-i Nou*. When Iran returned to despotic rule, Rasulzade spent a period in Istanbul, and then became one of the leading activists of the Azerbaijani nationalist Musavat Party in Baku. There, he edited the Azerbaijani journal *Achiq Soz* from 1913. In his contributions to this paper, he referred to the Azerbaijanis by the term *Turk*. In 1918, Rasulzade was elected to serve as the first head of the National Council of the Azerbaijan Democratic Republic.

---

96.   Miza Alekber Sabir Tahirzade was born in 1862 in Shamakhi.

97.   Afary, "Peasant Rebellion of the Caspian Region during the Iranian Constitutional Revolution 1906–1909," p. 141.

Conclusions /

Prior to the mid-nineteenth century, it is difficult to speak of a separate "Azerbaijani" identity among the residents of this area; but rather, there was a separate Turkic, or Muslim, and regional identity. Even in the Safavid period, when the Azerbaijanis formed the ruling elite of Iran, and strongly identified with the Iranian state and the Shi'i people of Iran, a distinct Turkic identity existed and Turco-Persian tensions remained high. Later, balancing between those groups became a mark of the Qajar regime. Thus, even in this period, there were distinctions of identity between Turks and Persians in the area. Nevertheless, during the Safavid and Qajar periods, Azerbaijanis could identify with Iran in supra-ethnic terms, especially since the political leadership of these regimes shared a common ethnic and linguistic background with them, and in this period ethnic identity was less pronounced in general. There was no inherent conflict between identifying with the Iranian state and Turkic culture. In later years, the Safavids came to symbolize for many Azerbaijanis their own sovereignty and leadership over Iran. Today, when some Azerbaijanis say that they identify themselves as Iranians, they are not necessarily implying that they identify with Persian culture and leadership, but rather with an Iran that accommodates both Turkic and Persian culture and language, along the lines of the Safavid model.

The imposition of Shi'a on the population of Iran led to important developments in terms of collective identity. Adherence to Shi'a expanded the ties between Azerbaijanis and Persians and linked them together in the Shi'i state of Iran. Yet, as the only major Turkic-speaking Shi'i group, Azerbaijanis in Iran forged a separate Azerbaijani identity that cemented the ties between the Turkic speakers on both sides of the Araz River. Thus, the Shi'i factor that unites the Azerbaijanis with Iran also links them with Azerbaijanis beyond the borders of Iran.

In later periods the cultural orientation chosen by certain Azerbaijanis was not always directly translated into a political orientation. For instance, interest in and identification with Turkic culture did not always lead to a desire for political alliance with or orientation toward Turkey.

During the late nineteenth and early twentieth centuries, forces from different ends of the political spectrum promoted Azerbaijani cultural rights in the Russian Empire, especially the use of their language. In Baku, many groups, including Marxist ones such as the *Himmet* and the *Firqeh*, as well as individuals such as Nariman Narimanov and Mehmet Emin Rasulzade, supported Azerbaijani cultural rights. Even more orthodox Marxist groups were often willing to use rhetoric in support of

Azerbaijani cultural and language rights, which illustrates their assessment that these goals were popular among many Azerbaijanis and that such a stance would help mobilize support. In contrast, many prominent Azerbaijanis in Iran advocated assimilation into Persian language and culture. One of the reasons for the difference may be that in the Russian Empire, Muslims could not assimilate into the majority group. In Iran, in contrast, Azerbaijanis and members of other minority groups could choose to identify themselves as Iranians. Furthermore, Russian discrimination against Azerbaijanis and other minorities and Azerbaijani contact with non-Muslims in the Russian Empire seem to have reinforced the minorities' distinctive identities. In contrast to their co-ethnics in the north, during the nineteenth century, Azerbaijanis in Iran had much less frequent contact with non-Azerbaijanis in Iran. In this period in Iran, provincial power was predominant, and the Qajar Shahs had limited control and influence outside of the capital.[98] Moreover, official cultural discrimination emerged later in Iran, as part of Reza Shah's centralization policies; as will be shown in the next chapter, this had a significant impact on the collective identity of the Azerbaijanis in Iran.

---

98. See Nikki R. Keddie, "The Iranian Power Structure and Social Change 1800–1969: An Overview," *International Journal of Middle East Studies* Vol. 2 (1971), p. 3; and Shaul Bakhash, "Center-Periphery Relations in Nineteenth-Century Iran," *Iranian Studies* Vol. 14 (Winter–Spring 1981), p. 35.

Chapter 2

The Azerbaijanis under the Soviet and Pahlavi Regimes

A new period for the Azerbaijanis was ushered in with the fall of the short-lived independent Azerbaijan Democratic Republic and its subsequent Sovietization, and the crushing of Khiyabani's autonomous Azerbaijani movement in Iran and the rise of the Pahlavi regime (1921–79). This chapter covers the period from the Soviet conquest of the Azerbaijani Democratic Republic in 1920 through the late 1970s; and the rise of the Pahlavi regime in Iran in 1921, the brief Provincial Azerbaijani Government, and the second Pahlavi reign until 1979.

Ties between the Azerbaijanis across the border were severely limited by the new regimes. Until this period, interchange and contacts between the two sides of Azerbaijan, especially in the spheres of commerce, family, and culture, were quite free despite its political division since 1828. These ties were significantly restricted (except for a brief respite in 1941–46) from the beginning of Stalin's purges in the Soviet Union until the end of the 1970s, when new opportunities for limited contact were created after the Islamic Revolution in Iran.

Under Iran's Pahlavi regime, the Azerbaijanis in Iran and other ethnic minorities began to experience extreme cultural suppression and discrimination. As in the Russian Empire a century earlier, where a policy of discrimination toward non-Christians had catalyzed an exploration of collective identity among the Azerbaijanis and forced the prioritization of identities, the policies of the new regime in Iran greatly affected the development of national identity among the Azerbaijanis there. Reza Shah set out to increase the centralization of his regime in Iran and to extend the regime's power in the periphery, and he allocated more resources to the center. In addition, Reza Shah forced most of the nomads in Iran—many of whom were Turks—to settle.

The new regime's extension of government functions into various outlying regions of Iran made contact between members of the minority groups and the Persian-dominated center more intense. Toward the end of the Qajar period, state control outside the capital was weak and most areas of the periphery enjoyed de facto autonomy. Some Azerbaijanis made their first contact with non-Azerbaijanis in Iran in this period. The interaction with the center propelled many Azerbaijanis in Iran to begin to explore their relationship with the center and their relationship with their co-ethnics.

Reza Shah also implemented a policy of fostering Iranian nationalism by merging the identity of the Iranian state and nation with those of the Persian people and the Persian language. In this manner, Reza Shah merged state identity with the identity of the largest ethnic group in Iran. As part of this policy, the regime aggressively attempted to assimilate the various ethnic groups in Iran. This policy included closing minority-language schools and publications. This policy hit the Azerbaijanis hardest of all the ethnic minorities in Iran, since they were more urbanized than the other minority ethnic groups and had developed their own institutions and publications in their own language, unlike many of the other ethnic groups.[1] By the 1930s, many places in Azerbaijan were given Persian names, and the authorities put obstacles in the way of those who wished to give their children non-Persian names. Many of those interviewed for this book recounted the almost comical manner in which Azerbaijani teachers, who usually had very distinctive accents in Persian, were forced to conduct their lessons with Azerbaijani students who themselves struggled to answer in Persian. Yet private exchanges with the teachers, such as questions during recess, or greetings when meeting the teacher in the street or at a wedding were always in Azerbaijani. Some interviewees described how they were beaten or fined for speaking Azerbaijani in the classroom.[2]

Reza Shah singled out the Azerbaijanis for special discrimination, economic disadvantages, and cultural repression, possibly to punish them for their part in the Khiyabani-led rebellion in 1920.[3] In 1937, most

---

1. Abrahamian, *Iran Between Two Revolutions*, p. 163.

2. See also "Letter from Nosarat Khavani," *Varliq* (April–June, 1991), p. 93.

3. Homayoun Katouzian, *The Political Economy of Modern Iran* (London: Macmillan, 1981), pp. 133, 150.

of Azerbaijan, which had been administered as one Iranian state *(iyalat)*, was divided into two provinces *(ostan)*.[4] Some of Azerbaijan's traditional territories were annexed to other Iranian provinces.[5] The poor economic situation of the province in this period—caused largely by Tehran's policies favoring development of the center, specific discrimination against the Azerbaijani provinces, and the severing of direct economic ties with Soviet Azerbaijan and Russia—led to emigration within East Azerbaijan province to Tabriz, and from the Azerbaijani provinces to the center of Iran, mainly to Tehran. A significant portion of Azerbaijan's merchant class moved to Tehran under Reza Shah's reign. A large number of middle-class Azerbaijanis moved to Tehran during World War II, and the largest exodus took place in the 1970s as people went in search of the jobs created by the increased oil revenues. The economy of the Azerbaijani provinces was also damaged because Azerbaijanis could no longer travel to Baku for seasonal work, which had been a major source of income in Iranian Azerbaijan.

The migration to central Iran increased contacts between Azerbaijanis and Persians. For some Azerbaijanis this led to assimilation; for many others this interaction accentuated the differences between themselves and the Persian citizens of Iran and hastened the development of their particular Azerbaijani identity. Despite the extreme limitations of the Pahlavi period, some Azerbaijanis still expressed desire for ties with their co-ethnics in Soviet Azerbaijan, which can be an articulation of Azerbaijani identity.

One of the most momentous events during this period was the establishment of the autonomous Provincial Government in Iranian Azerbaijan during 1945–46. This local government and its subsequent demise had a major effect on the development of the identity of Azerbaijanis in Iran.

---

4.   Iran was previously divided into four large *iyalat* (Azerbaijan, Khorasan, Fars and Kerman), which each had their own governor, and numerous smaller *velayat*. Under the new division of the country, inaugurated between 1937–38, Azerbaijan was divided into two *ostans*: the Third Province (today known as East Azerbaijan) with Tabriz its capital, and the Fourth Province (today known as West Azerbaijan), its capital Reza'iyeh (formerly Urmiyeh, an important historical name in Azerbaijan, renamed in honor of Reza Shah). Parts of Kurdistan province, including the cities of Mahabad and Sardast, became part of East Azerbaijan. See Atabaki, *Azerbaijan: Ethnicity and Autonomy in Twentieth-Century Iran*, p. 59.

5.   Shokat Tagieva in interview in "Istoriia odnoi granitsy," *Bakinskii rabochii*, March 24, 1990, p. 3.

Identity in Iranian Azerbaijan

During the Pahlavi period, three major trends of identity emerged among the Azerbaijanis in Iran. One group advocated assimilation into Persian culture and language. They associated diversity with inefficiency and unity with progress. While they advocated Persianization of the Azerbaijanis in Iran and the elimination of a separate Azerbaijani identity, it would be difficult to call them Persian nationalists. They tended to see Persian culture and language in a utilitarian way, as a tool to unite all the citizens of Iran and promote the implementation of their social and political programs. For most there was no emotional identification as Persians; rather, they identified as Iranians and felt that they were among the inheritors of ancient Iranian culture and history. This stance was prominent among Azerbaijani intellectuals from the 1920s through the beginning of the 1940s. During World War II and after this position became less popular.

A second position advocated an Iranian state identity and Azerbaijani ethnic identity. It aimed for Azerbaijani cultural autonomy within the Iranian state. Proponents saw Iranian identity as predominantly supra-ethnic, and did not equate it with Persian identity. The formation of the Provincial Government of Azerbaijan (1945–46) by the leaders of the *Firqeh-i Dimukrat* during the Allied occupation of Iran in World War II was a manifestation of this conception of identity. However, some of the activists of the Provincial Government identified more as Azerbaijanis than as Iranians.

A third trend was the emergence of class identity, held by proponents of socialist and communist ideologies. Days after the abdication of Reza Shah in September 1941, the *Tudeh* Communist Party was founded. Under the Pahlavi regime, many Azerbaijanis pursued universalistic ideologies, which espoused eliminating ethnic differences, partially in the hope that this would end discrimination against members of the minority groups. Orthodox Marxists, such as the majority of the Azerbaijani *Tudeh* members in the 1940s, advocated Persianization as a means to achieve their political goals. In contrast, a second group of communists advocated retaining Azerbaijani cultural autonomy within Iran.

ASSIMILATION INTO PERSIAN-BASED IRANIAN IDENTITY

The most outspoken Azerbaijani advocate of Persianization was Ahmad Kasravi. Kasravi published chiefly in the 1920s to the 1940s. He fanatically opposed any form of autonomy for different sectors in Iran, whether based on class, ethnicity, or religion. He defined a nation as the inhabitants of a territorial unit, and he rejected diversity within those units.

Kasravi's treatment of the origins of the Azerbaijanis in Iran reveals many contradictions. In 1922, for instance, he wrote in the journal *al-'Irfan*:

The Turkish speakers among the Iranian population who were spread through every region of Iran were not Persians who were forced to abandon their original language and forgot it and learned Turkish. No one spoke Turkish as a result of being vanquished by the Turkish conquerors over their lands, as was the opinion spread throughout Iran.[6]

In his later writings, he adopted the opposite view of the ethnic origins of the Azerbaijanis, claiming that they and the other Turkic speakers in Iran were actually Iranians who had been forced to speak Turkish beginning in the tenth century.

Kasravi is often referred to as the "father of Iranian nationalism"; his ideology is instrumental. He viewed unity and the formation of large units within a state as a fundamental key to achieving modernization.[7] By advocating a utilitarian approach to the linguistic and cultural assimilation of the Azerbaijanis, he echoed the statements of other Azerbaijanis that preceded him, such as Talebzade. Kasravi's preference for Persian over Azerbaijani or other minority languages in Iran was not motivated by an emotional attachment to Persian: "These languages are all good, but their existence within one state causes dissension. It is always best to have one common language in a nation."[8] Kasravi wrote that Azerbaijani, in its own right, "has all that a language needs in order to be a refined language, despite the fact that it is not a literary language; indeed, it meets within it all the criteria and has qualities that distinguish it over many refined languages."[9]

Kasravi wrote many works dealing with the ancient and modern history of Azerbaijan. Yet, his ideologically laden view of history and his vehement opposition to expressions of Azerbaijani nationalism suggest that he did not objectively reflect events and forces in Azerbaijan. According to Abrahamian, for example, Kasravi's opposition to the use of minority languages was so intense that he even distorted facts in his own autobiography: in describing how, as a cleric in Azerbaijan, he refused to preach

---

6. Kasravi, *al-'Irfan*, pp. 121–123.

7. Abrahamian refers to Kasravi as the "integrative nationalist of Iran." See Abrahamian, "Kasravi: The Integrative Nationalist of Iran," pp. 97–131.

8. Ahmad Kasravi, "Concerning Languages," *Parcham-i Haftagi* (April 22, 1944), quoted in Ibid., p. 115.

9. Kasravi, *al-'Irfan*.

to his followers in Arabic which he opposed as a foreign influence on Iran, he does not mention that he preached in Azerbaijani, not Persian.[10]

In Kasravi's works *Tarikh-i Mashrutah-i Iran* and *Tarikh-i Hijdah Salah-i Azarbayjan*, he focuses on his view that the destiny of Azerbaijan is with the rest of Iran and that the autonomy movements hurt Iran's reform efforts. His attacks on the autonomy movements and discussion of the issue of Azerbaijan's relations with the center show that Azerbaijanis' connection with the rest of Iran was an important question at the time.

Among the prominent Azerbaijanis who advocated Persian assimilation was Dr. Taqi Arani, a prominent figure in "the Fifty-three" Movement in Iran.[11] Arani's views seem to have been based on orthodox Marxism and his view that centralization was a key to state efficiency. Arani also saw events in Azerbaijan as an integral part of the history of Iran. *Tudeh* activist Khalil Maleki shared Arani's support for the Persianization of Azerbaijanis and often angered his fellow Azerbaijanis by refusing to talk with them in his native language.[12]

Most of the Azerbaijanis who advocated cultural assimilation in Iran, such as Arani and Maleki, had been educated in Iran and had not spent much time in north Azerbaijan. Conversely, most of those who had spent significant time in north Azerbaijan, such as Jafar Pishaveri, generally emphasized Azerbaijani identity, often together with socialist or liberal goals.

In the 1940s, the *Tudeh* leadership, which was composed mainly of Persians and assimilated Azerbaijanis who lived in the center of Iran, were often confronted with grassroots demands from Azerbaijanis for ethnic autonomy and a solution to the ethnic-based conflicts that broke out among workers, evidence of the tensions between different ethnic groups in Iran.[13] Conflict within the *Tudeh* leadership emerged in 1944 over the refusal of Azerbaijani delegates to the First Congress of the *Tudeh* to address the delegates in Persian; instead, they chose to speak in their native Azerbaijani. In its political activities, the *Tudeh* succeeded in reach-

---

10. W. Stele, "The Intellectual Development of Ahmad Kasravi" (unpublished Ph.D. dissertation, Princeton, 1966), quoted by Abrahamian, "Kasravi: The Integrative Nationalist of Iran," p. 129. A recently unearthed document reveals that Kasravi admitted that Persian was not his native language. See Kasravi, *al-'Irfan*.

11. "The Fifty-three" refers to a group of 53 men who were arrested in 1937 and accused of Marxist activities. Most of them were Persians and this was not an ethnic-based group. This group became the nucleus of the *Tudeh* Party.

12. Abrahamian, "Communism and Communalism in Iran," p. 305. His insistence was almost comical; Maleki spoke Persian with a strong Azerbaijani accent.

13. Ibid., p. 302.

ing people beyond the elite level and it discovered that many Iranian citizens could not even speak Persian.[14] Azerbaijanis who espoused Azerbaijani nationalism, such as 'Ali Shabistari, the editor of the party newspaper in the province, who had spent most of his life in north Azerbaijan, were ousted from the *Tudeh* in this period.[15]

WORLD WAR II—AZERBAIJANI AUTONOMY IN IRAN AND THE RENEWAL OF TIES BETWEEN NORTH AND SOUTH

The Allied invasion and consequent abdication of Reza Shah in 1941 ushered in a period of political liberalization in Iran that tolerated open political activity and made it possible to publish many ideological and cultural works that had been written earlier. Some of the publications and activities revealed that Reza Shah's centralization policies had generated much resentment in Iran; many of these resentments were voiced by the Azerbaijanis in Iran.

Under the Allied occupation of Iran during World War II, Azerbaijan was in the Soviet sector, and there was a renewal of contacts between Azerbaijanis on both sides of the Araz River. Many border installations and customs posts were removed, facilitating direct contact.[16] The Soviets placed predominately Azerbaijani-speaking troops in northern Iran and sent Azerbaijanis from Soviet Azerbaijan to operate Soviet propaganda organs in Iran. The Soviet Azerbaijanis led the production of many Azerbaijani-language publications, such as the newspaper *Vatan Yolunda* (published in Arabic characters). A common theme of these publications was the shared heritage of the Azerbaijanis on both sides of the Araz and the importance of renewing ties between them. Moscow clearly had an interest in this policy; it wished to promote admiration for the Soviet Union among the ethnic minorities in Iran, and to encourage ethnic-based sentiments as a possible lever for pressure on Tehran. However, it seems that the main proponents of this policy were from Baku, and many of them used it to advance their own ethnic-based agenda.

In September 1945, the *Firqeh Dimukrat Azarbayjan* movement was formally established in Iran under the leadership of Jafar Pishaveri. The Azerbaijani branch of the *Tudeh* Party almost immediately defected to the *Firqeh*. The *Firqeh*, like the *Tudeh*, was communist and Soviet-oriented.

---

14. Ibid., p. 303.

15. Afterwards, Shabistari continued to publish *Azärbayjan* as the organ of the *Firqeh*. Shabistari also founded the Society for Azerbaijan, which was dedicated to the preservation of Azerbaijani culture and language.

16. Ivar Spector, *The Soviet Union and the Muslim World 1917–1958* (Seattle: University of Washington Press, 1959), p. 197.

However, it advocated language rights for the ethnic minorities in Iran, and differed from the *Tudeh* on the degree of centralization that Iran should have in relation to the provinces, and on the question of priority of ethnic identity over class identity. The *Firqeh* advocated Azerbaijani unity more than class conflict. The founding nucleus of the *Firqeh* consisted of Azerbaijanis who had spent significant time in Soviet Azerbaijan. In contrast, most of the *Tudeh* activists lived in the Persian-dominated center of Iran. The new organization adopted the same name as Khiyabani's political movement to illustrate continuity; indeed, many of its founding members had been part of the Khiyabani revolt. In its first declaration, the *Firqeh* defended Iranian Azerbaijan's right to have its own provincial councils and to use the Azerbaijani language in its schools, among other points.

In October 1945, protected from Tehran's wrath by the Soviet troops that occupied northern Iran, the *Firqeh* led an almost bloodless revolt for control of southern Azerbaijan, and established the Provincial Government of Azerbaijan. In January, a similar revolt was led by Kurdish activists, who established a provincial government in Mahabad, the capital of the Kurdish province. Most Western accounts of the revolt in Azerbaijan and the short-lived provincial government in 1945–1946 tend to present it as a Soviet puppet-state, not a local phenomenon.[17] While Soviet support was clearly essential in providing opportunity and tools, many of the goals and demands of the provincial government were primarily local. Initially, local support for the provincial government was quite extensive, and at first, most of the population supported the measures taken in the spheres of economy, infrastructure, and status of the Azerbaijani language.[18] In contrast to most external references to the Provincial Government, its leaders never referred to it as the Azerbaijan Democratic Republic (ADR). This name creates the impression that the Provincial Government was simply a Soviet fiction instead of the fruit of independent autonomous aspirations.

In its first statement as a provincial government, the *Firqeh* leaders declared that the Azerbaijanis were a distinct nation *(millet)*. They also stated that they did not aspire to secede from Iran. They voiced three ma-

---

17. See for instance, Robert Rossow, "The Battle of Azerbaijan, 1946," *The Middle East Journal*, Vol. 10 (Winter 1956), pp. 17–32, and Richard W. Cottam, *Nationalism in Iran: Updated Through 1978* (Pittsburgh: University of Pittsburgh Press, 1979), p. 118.

18. Many middle-class merchants, however, moved to Tehran in this period, evidently due to the severance of economic ties with the center, where their major business were.

jor demands: the use of the Azerbaijani language in local schools and government offices; the retention of tax revenues for the development of the region; and the establishment of the provincial assemblies promised in constitution.[19] The *Firqeh's* leadership denounced Tehran for disregarding their provincial grievances and proclaimed that their language, history, and culture had endowed the people of Azerbaijan with a "distinct national identity."[20]

In its proposed program, presented in November and reaffirmed by the National Majlis in Tabriz in December 1945, Azerbaijan is clearly referred to as a nation *(millet)*. At the same time, the program states a commitment to the preservation of the integrity of Iran. This declaration reflects the *Firqeh* leaders' national identity as Azerbaijanis, within a political framework of Iran. The program states:

1. The people of Azerbaijan have been endowed by history with distinct national, linguistic, cultural and traditional characteristics. These characteristics entitle Azerbaijan to freedom and autonomy, as promised to all nations by the Atlantic Charter. 2. The Nation *(millet)* of Azerbaijan has no desire to separate itself from Iran or to harm the territorial integrity of Iran, for it is aware of the close cultural, education, and political ties that exist between itself and other provinces and is proud of the great sacrifices it has made for the creation of modern Iran. 3. The Nation of Azerbaijan officially and openly declares that it has the right to form its own government, like other living nations, and to administer its internal and national affairs, observing the integrity of Iran. 4. The Nation of Azerbaijan has a special attachment to its national and mother language. It realizes that the imposition of another language on the people of Azerbaijan has hindered their historical progress. This Congress therefore instructs its ministers to use the Azerbaijani language in schools and government offices as soon as possible.[21]

Linking themselves to Azerbaijani history, the new regime called their military forces *Babak*, after the infamous leader of the revolt against Arab rule in Azerbaijan, and *Qizilbash*, the name of the Turkic military forces of the Safavid regime.

Under the Provincial Government, the Azerbaijani language was used in the schools and the Azerbaijan University, the first provincial uni-

19.   Abrahamian, *Iran Between Two Revolutions*, p. 399.

20.   Ibid., p. 217.

21.   National Congress of Azerbaijan, "The Declaration of National Autonomy," *Azerbaijan*, Vol. 26 (November 1945), quoted in Abrahamian, *Iran Between Two Revolutions*, pp. 400–401.

versity established in Iran, was established in Tabriz; it conducted lessons on Azerbaijani language and literature.[22] A radio station broadcasting in Azerbaijani was also opened in Tabriz.[23] In the summer of 1946, the authorities published a series of textbooks that dealt intensively with Azerbaijan's history and culture. In this series, only one reference is made to Iran.[24] During this period, Azerbaijani literature flourished and Azerbaijani-language plays resumed in 1941, becoming quite popular. Among the staged performances were: *Shah Ismail*, *Arshin Mal Alan*, *Koroghlu*, *Mashdi Ebvad*, and *Anamin Kitabi*.[25]

Like Khiyabani before him, Pishaveri did threaten to secede from Iran if Tehran did not meet the provinces' demands, though he had seemed initially committed to the preservation of the territorial integrity of Iran.[26] The local population was enthusiastic about the Provincial Government's policy toward the Azerbaijani language and culture, but many Azerbaijanis—especially those who had commercial ties to Tehran and other cities in the center—became increasingly apprehensive about rumors that the Provincial Government intended to secede.[27]

In September 1946, the Pishaveri government unveiled a new flag for the province and the Iranian national anthem was abolished in the territory.[28] In the second half of 1946, local support for the Pishaveri regime began to wane as the province's economy deteriorated due to its isolation from the Iranian economy.

After the withdrawal of Soviet troops from north Iran in May, Tehran could now attack the provincial government in Tabriz. On December 12, 1946, the local government in Azerbaijan surrendered to troops from Tehran. The terms of submission reflect the importance the Azerbaijanis attached to retaining language rights and the economic autonomy of the province: the demands included the right to educate their children in

---

22.   Shahrzad Mojab and Amir Hassanpour, "The Politics of Nationality and Ethnic Diversity," in Saeed Rahnema and Sorab Behdad, *Iran after the Revolution: Crises of an Islamic State* (London: I.B. Tauris, 1996), p. 232.

23.   Javad Heyat, "Regression of Azeri Language and Literature under the Oppressive Period of Pahlavi and its Renaissance after the Islamic Revolution," *First International Conference of Turkic Studies* (Bloomington, Ind.: May 19–22, 1983), p. 11.

24.   Atabaki, *Azerbaijan: Ethnicity and Autonomy in Twentieth Century Iran*, p. 167.

25.   Heyat, "Regression of Azeri Language and Literature," p. 12.

26.   *Azärbayjan*, Vol. 5, No. 9 (1945), quoted in Swietochowski, *Russia and Azerbaijan: A Borderland in Transition*, p. 143.

27.   Ghods, *A Comparative Historical Study*, p. 563.

28.   Jody Ememi-Yeganeh, "Iran vs. Azerbaijan (1945–46: Divorce, Separation or Reconciliation?)" *Central Asian Survey*, Vol. 3, No. 2 (1984), p. 15.

their native language; the retention of 75 percent of tax revenues collected in the province; and the allocation of 25 percent of the customs revenue from the province to the Azerbaijan University.[29]

Tehran did not honor this agreement. Cultural repression against the Azerbaijanis became even harsher. In addition, Tehran's troops executed thousands of Azerbaijanis, and many others were forced to flee.[30] Many members of the Pishaveri regime and cultural figures fled to Soviet Azerbaijan, where they later fostered ties with Iranian Azerbaijan and continued the development of their common culture, symbols, and literature. Many of the prominent poets of Soviet Azerbaijan in the post–World War II period were from Iranian Azerbaijan.

The loss of family members in the purges that followed the demise of the Provincial Government and the forced exile and escape of many Azerbaijani activists became an important factor in shaping the identity of the Azerbaijanis in Iran. It instilled in many a sense of hatred toward the Pahlavi regime; according to activists, this hatred propelled some Iranian Azerbaijanis to take leading roles in the 1979 revolution against the Shah.

Even after Moscow withdrew its forces from north Iran as part of a deal with Tehran, Baku continued to produce many literary and other works that expressed a strong desire to renew ties with Iranian Azerbaijanis and condemned the cultural repression of the Azerbaijanis in Iran. In 1947, for example, Baku released a film in the Azerbaijani language about Iranian Azerbaijan, dramatically showing the repression of the Azerbaijanis in Iran and the restrictions on the use their native tongue. Throughout the film, the Araz River is portrayed as a strong symbol of the separation of the Azerbaijanis. The continued production of cultural materials expressing a desire for ties between the Azerbaijanis after the Soviet withdrawal and Moscow's change in policy toward Iranian Azerbaijan shows that this activity had roots in Baku, and was not just ordered by Moscow.

---

29. "The Agreement Between the Iranian Central Government and the Representative of Azerbaijan (June 13, 1946), F.O. 371/52740, Tabriz Diary, June 1946, as it appears in Atabaki, *Azerbaijan: Ethnicity and Autonomy in Twentieth-Century Iran*, Appendix.

30. Amirali Lakhrudi, chairman of the Democratic Party of Azerbaijan (the successor of Pishaveri's party, which moved its headquarters to Baku in 1946), and a witness to the December 12, 1945, takeover in Tabriz, stated that when Tehran retook the city, 30,000 people were killed and 300,000 deported, and 10,000 emigrated to Soviet Azerbaijan. *Zerkalo*, December 2, 1995, p. 8. Other Azerbaijani participants in the Provincial Government have estimated that more than 10,000 Azerbaijanis were killed in the takeover. Iranian government reports estimate that 800 were killed. See, Atabaki, *Azerbaijan: Ethnicity and Autonomy in Twentieth-century Iran*, p. 220.

In the post–World War II period, during the premiership of Muhammad Mossadiq, some political restrictions were relaxed in Iran, allowing limited Azerbaijani literary activity, mainly within the framework of Azerbaijani cultural societies centered in Tehran.[31] Examples of these are the *Azerbaijan Dostlari Jam'iyati* (the Society of Friends of Azerbaijan), and the *Azerbaijan Yazichilar Hey'ati* (The Association of Writers of Azerbaijan). The publication of a bimonthly literary periodical in Azerbaijani, *Edebi Eserler*, was begun in 1951 by Sayyed Hasan Qorashiyan.[32] This and other Azerbaijani-language papers were forced to cease publication with the end of Mossadiq's premiership.

The most important Azerbaijani literary piece written in the post–World War II period in Iran is the poem by Muhammad Huseyn Shahriyar, *Heydar Babaya Salam* (Greetings to Heydar Baba).[33] This poem, published in Tabriz in 1954 and written in colloquial Azerbaijani, became quite popular among the Azerbaijanis in Iran and in Soviet Azerbaijan and in many places in the Turkic-speaking world. In *Heydar Babaya Salam*, Shahriyar expressed his identity as an Azerbaijani attachment to his homeland, language, and culture. Heydar Baba is a hill near Khoshknab, the native village of the poet.

ON THE EVE OF REVOLUTION IN IRAN

Despite the extreme limitations imposed on ethnic minorities under Muhammed Reza Pahlavi's regime throughout the 1960s and 1970s, Azerbaijanis in Iran continued to explore their collective identity often through literature, folklore, and children's stories, with which it was easier to circumvent the censor. This subject was also examined in political manuscripts that were distributed unofficially and formally published after the fall of the Shah's regime.

In the 1960s, many Azerbaijanis were active in left-wing movements and promoted both Azerbaijani culture and leftist political ideas. Among them were Samad Behrengi and Gholam Husein Sa'edi. Both were concerned with the situation of Iran's poor and opposed the Pahlavi regime. Behrengi's stories reflect his abhorrence of the income gaps in Iranian so-

---

31.   Mossadiq was of Qajar origin. He had served as Governor of Azerbaijan Province and he spoke Azerbaijani.

32.   Sayyed Hasan Qorashiyan had served in a senior position in the Pishaveri regime. See Berengian, *Azeri and Persian Literary Works in Twentieth-Century Iranian Azerbaijan*, p. 189.

33.   Mähämmäd Hüseyn Shähriyar, "Heydar Babaya Salam," (1954), in *Yalan Dünya* (Baku: Azärbayjan Ensiklopediyasï, 1993). Shahriyar was born in Tabriz in 1906.

ciety and the need to change, if necessary by violent means.[34] Behrengi was outspoken in his drive to preserve Azerbaijani language, literature, and culture. In his works, he often mocked Azerbaijanis who tried to assimilate into Persian culture and who had given up their native language. Most notable in this respect is his poem *Agha-ye Cox Bakhtiar*.[35] In one of his most famous works, *Kand va Kav Dar Masa'el-e Tarbiati-ye Iran* (An Investigation into the Educational Problems of Iran), Behrengi criticizes how children in Tabriz are forced to call their fathers by the Persian word of endearment, baba, instead of the Azerbaijani ata or dada.[36] He insisted that his colleagues call his native language Azeri, and not Turki, as the regime referred to it.[37] Behrengi published collections of Azerbaijani folk-tales and primers for teaching reading to Azerbaijani school children, which he was forced to translate into Persian after his request to publish them in Azerbaijani was rejected.[38] He often wrote in the style and language of Azerbaijani folk tales. According to his colleagues, Behrengi felt an ethnic and linguistic connection to the Azerbaijanis in the north and was "aware of this separating sickle which is (the) Araz."[39] Upon his death by drowning in the Araz River, the writer Al-e Ahmad eulogized, "He has entered the Araz! This separating sickle, this bisector of one culture and one language. You see, I had known that these names were as sacred to Samad as Medina is to his older brothers."[40] Here, Al-e Ahmad referred allegorically to the change in national identities from one generation to the other, from Muslim to Azerbaijani.

---

34. See, for instance, "Twenty-Four Restless Hours" and "The Bald Pigeon-Keeper" in Samad Behrengi, *The Black Fish and Other Modern Persian Stories* (Washington, D.C.: Three Continents Press, 1987).

35. Samad Behrengi, "Agha-ye Cox Bakhtiar" (A Very Lucky Man), unpublished poem.

36. Quoted in Brad Hanson, "The 'Westoxication' of Iran: Depictions and Reactions of Behrengi, Al-e Ahmad, and Shari'ati," *International Journal of Middle East Studies*, Vol. 15, No. 1 (February, 1983), p. 5.

37. Jalal Al-e Ahmad, "Samad and the Folk Legend," in Michael C. Hillmann, ed., *Iranian Society: An Anthology of Writings by Jalal Al-e Ahmad* (Lexington, Ky.: Mazda Press, 1982), p. 138.

38. One of the folktale collections is *Afsanaha-ye Azarbayjan* (Tales of Azerbaijan), translated from Azerbaijani into Persian. Vol. 1 (Tabriz, 1965). Vol. 2 (Tehran, 1968) which was co-authored with fellow Azerbaijani writer, Behruz Dihqani, who was killed under torture in a Savak prison.

39. Al-e Ahmad, "Samad and the Folk Legend," p. 138.

40. Ibid., pp. 141–142.

Behrengi's friend and colleague, Gholam Husein Sa'edi, also dealt with the position of the poor of Iran in his works, which are strongly anti-clerical and anti-religious. Like Behrengi, Sa'edi wrote regularly in an Azerbaijani supplement to the Tabriz weekly, *Mahad Azadi*, a legal Azerbaijani publication. In contrast to many of Sa'edi's earlier works, which are set in Azerbaijan, the setting for most of his later writings is in the south of Iran, in the Persian Gulf coastal area.[41] Behrengi wrote that Sa'edi's works reflect his Azerbaijani spirit.[42] Close friends of Sa'edi spoke of the importance Sa'edi attached to his Azerbaijani identity, and his hope of producing a journal in the Azerbaijani language in Iran.[43]

In 1964–65, a group of Azerbaijani intellectuals in Tabriz, encouraged by a visit from Al-e Ahmad, organized an Azerbaijan cultural group. Among their activities was the compiling of an Azerbaijani dictionary and the composition of songs in Azerbaijani, with accompaniments for Azerbaijani instruments. Among the participants in this group was the author Reza Baraheni, who wrote in this period about his self-identity as an "Azerbaijani Turk" in Iran, and about the cultural suppression of ethnic minorities under the Pahlavi regime. These themes appeared in his works published in the late 1960s and early 1970s.[44] In *Crowned Cannibals*, Baraheni wrote how Azerbaijanis in Iran were not even allowed inscriptions on their tombstones in their native language, and described the punishments inflicted on teachers taught in Azerbaijani.[45] Baraheni explains why he struggled for the rights of the ethnic minorities in Iran in the Persian language and how Persianization had affected him, and his national self-identity:

I came to feel that I had been cheated out of the most valuable aspect of my identity. I came to recognize my enemy, the present establishment in Iran. I

41. For example, *Pani Namayishnamah; az ingilab-i mashrutit. (Tehran: Sazman-i Intisharat-i Ashrafi*, 1345 (1966).

42. See Samad Behrengi, "A Look at Today's Literature: A Study of (Gholam Hosayn Sa'edi's) the Mourners of Bayal," in Thomas M. Ricks, ed., *Critical Perspectives on Modern Persian Literature* (Washington, D.C.: Three Continents Press, 1984), p. 351.

43. Based on conversations with close friends of Gholam Sa'edi.

44. Among Baraheni's works that deal with the question of ethnic minorities in Iran published during the Pahlavi regime are *Masculine History*, written in 1969 and published in 1972; his poems, "The Forest and the City" (1963) and "The Culture of the Oppressor and the Culture of the Oppressed" (1973) and *Tala dar Mes* (Tehran: Zaman, 1968).

45. Reza Baraheni, *The Crowned Cannibals: Writings on Repression in Iran* (New York: Vintage Books, 1977), p. 88.

raised my voice, trying to strike back at the enemy who had done all he could to paralyze the language of my entire consciousness. I could not hit back in the language of which I had been deprived through an historical necessity devised by the enemy. I took the sword of the enemy in my hands.[46] The enemy, by imposing his conditions on me, had given me training useful in combat. The enemy's strongest weapon was his language, his culture, and these I had learned as much as any of the songs of the daughters of the enemy. I tried to be the tongue of my oppressed nationality in the language of the oppressor. Linguistically speaking, the deep structure of my revolt against the establishment was in the language of my own nationality, but under the given historical conditions the deep structure had transformed itself into the surface structure of the Persian language. I tried to sing in the words of the master against the dominion of that very master. Now the falcon could not hear the falconer, the center could hold no longer. I was free.[47]

In the 1960s, two prominent Azerbaijani thinkers, 'Ali Tabrizli and 'Ali Reza Nabdel, wrote treatises on the Azerbaijani national question in Iran. Neither were allowed to officially publish their works in Iran, but both spread their ideas in underground literature among opposition groups in Iran and among Azerbaijani youth.[48] Both Azerbaijani authors, though ultimately representing two very different points of view, agreed on the irrelevance of arguments about the ethnic origins of the Azerbaijanis to the contemporary national question in Iran. Official Iranian literature published at this time emphasized that the Azerbaijanis were of Persian ethnic stock in attempt to delegitimize separate identity. According to Nabdel, "Chauvinists try to make the most of the fact that the population of Azerbaijan had spoken Persian, let's say eight hundred years ago, and they imagine that having proved this fact . . . they have already solved the crucial problem of our time."[49] Nonetheless, Nabdel, who was a radical Marxist, condemned those, such as Pishaveri, who raised ethnic-based grievances, instead of only class issues. He wrote, "No nation is superior to others, and there must be unity of the masses for class struggle. Any other method of struggle is doomed to fail. Death to Persian chauvinism, death to provincial nationalism. Provincial nationalism in-

---

46. He refers here to the Persian language.

47. Baraheni, *The Crowned Cannibals*, p. 113.

48. Nasib Nasibzade, "A. R. Nabdel i A. Tabrizli: Dva uklona v ideologii natsional'no-osvoboditel'nogo dvizheniia azerbaidzhantsev v Irane," AVAz.SSR *Izvestiia*, Seriia istoriia filosofii, No. 2 (1988), p. 60.

49. A.R. Nabdel, *Azärbayjan va masala-yi melli*, p. 4, quoted in ibid., p. 61.

jures Marxism."[50] Thus, for Nabdel, primary identity was class identity, and he rejected both Persianization and Azerbaijani nationalism.

Tabrizli emphasized a more Azerbaijani and Turkic identity. He idealized the ancient "Turks" of Azerbaijan in many books glorifying the history of Azerbaijan, and saw the struggles between Turks and Persians as a major theme in Iranian history.[51] Tabrizli seemed to support the preservation of Azerbaijani ethnic identity within a reformed supra-ethnic Iranian framework. He maintained that "each ethnicity is distinguished from the other by its language, literature, history, and culture, but all of them together constitute the 'Iranian nation.'"[52] At the same time, Tabrizli used the term "Turkish nation of Iran" to refer to the Azerbaijanis, and claimed that of all the names used to describe his ethnic group—Turk, Azerbaijani Turk, Azeri, Azerbaijani, etc.—the name Turk was the most appropriate.[53]

In the 1960s, Tehran launched a literacy campaign throughout the country, partly as cover for a Persianization campaign aimed especially at Azerbaijan and Kurdistan. The campaign indicates that the Azerbaijani language continued to be widely spoken in Azerbaijan. Many Azerbaijanis commented in interviews that most residents of East Azerbaijan Province could not speak Persian on the eve of the Islamic Revolution in Iran.

In the 1970s, extensive development of infrastructure, such as roads and communications, was conducted in Iran. Abrahamian claims that technological advances helped consolidate separate ethnic identity in Iran:

These developments, together with the commercialization of agriculture and the settling of some tribes, produced two paradoxical results. In the central provinces, national identity took root in the countryside as the rural population lost its traditional insularity and forged links with both the towns and the central government. In the peripheral provinces, however, ethnicity grew as communal identity based on one's immediate village and tribe gave way to a broader identity based on one's language and culture. Villagers and tribesmen who had in the past viewed themselves as belonging to small local

---

50. A.R. Nabdel, *Azärbayjan va masala-yi melli*, quoted in Ghods, *A Comparative Historical Study*, p. 688.

51. His books include *Shah Isma'il, Vurgun Azerbayjan, Babak,* and *Atropat.* See Berengian, *Azeri and Persian Literary Works in Twentieth-Century Iranian Azerbaijan*, p. 195.

52. Tabrizli in Nasibzade, "A. R. Nabdel i A. Tabrizli: Dva uklona v ideologii natsional'no osvoboditel'nogo dvizheniia azerbaidzhantsev v Irane," p. 63.

53. Ibid.

communities now saw themselves as Kurds, Turkomans, Arabs, Lurs, Baluchis, or Azeris.[54]

The rise of oil prices in the international market brought higher revenues to Tehran and created many new jobs in the capital that led to a large migration of Azerbaijanis from West and East Azerbaijan to Tehran in the 1970s.[55] The rate of migration from rural settlements in the Azerbaijan provinces to Tehran and Tabriz was the highest in Iran.[56] Communal cohesiveness among many of the Azerbaijanis who went to Tehran remained. In the slum neighborhoods of south Tehran, Azerbaijanis and other Turkic-speakers continued to live together more than other communal groups.[57] Many of these Azerbaijanis worked in the construction industry, which further contributed to their cohesiveness.[58] Migration to the center strongly affected Azerbaijani collective identity in Iran. For the first time, many saw the gaps in income and opportunity between their provinces and the Persian-dominated center, and encountered prejudice and neglect by the regime. The Azerbaijanis were commonly the subject of ridicule and jokes by Persians. Far from their native province, many Azerbaijanis felt a longing for their native culture, and thus grew to appreciate it more.

At the same time, many Azerbaijanis in Tehran succeeded in assimilating into Persian culture. Many married into Persian families, and during the Pahlavi regime, Persianized Azerbaijanis formed a large segment of the Iranian elite. For instance, the Shah's wife, Farah, is of Azerbaijani origin and often spoke in the language with Azerbaijani guests at the palace.

In the 1960s and 1970s, the Shah's regime implemented social and economic programs that increased the gaps between the Persian-dominated center of the country and the Azerbaijanis (and the other eth-

---

54.   Abrahamian, *Iran Between Two Revolutions*, p. 428.

55.   From 1971 to 1976, 601,200 people over the age of five migrated from East Azerbaijan to Tehran. At the same time, 113,600 arrived from West Azerbaijan. Estimates of the Azerbaijani-speaking population in the Iranian capital reached 1.5 to 2 million. See Plan Organization, Statistical Center: *Census of Population of Housing*, Tehran Sharestan (Tehran Plan Organization, 1979), quoted in Akbar Aghajanian, "Ethnic Inequality in Iran: An Overview," *International Journal of Middle East Studies*, Vol. 5 (1983), p. 223; and Swietochowski, *Russia and Azerbaijan: A Borderland in Transition*, p. 178.

56.   Farhad Kazemi, *Poverty and Revolution in Iran: The Migrant Poor, Urban Marginality and Politics* (New York: New York University Press, 1980), p. 30.

57.   Ibid., p. 65.

58.   Sabri Tabrizi, *Iran: A Child's Story, A Man's Experience*, p. 243.

nic minorities). Moreover, the ethnic minorities in the provinces gained little from the overall improvement of the Iranian economy that came with the oil boom, which made the distribution of resources among the ethnic communities more unequal.[59] The state mainly invested oil profits in the industrial sector, which was Persian-dominated, further enlarging the income gap with the predominantly agricultural minorities.[60] By 1975, half of Iran's manufactured goods were produced in Tehran, where only 22 percent of the country's industrial labor force lived. Relative to the center, Azerbaijan was predominantly agricultural. In Tehran, for every worker employed in manufacturing, 0.7 were employed in agriculture. In East Azerbaijan, on the other hand, the ratio was 1:2.6 and in West Azerbaijan 1:13. In contrast to Persians, Azerbaijanis in the provinces were disadvantaged by almost every common standard of measurement, although less so than the Baluchis and Kurds. For instance, in the mid-1970s the literacy rate in Tehran was 62 percent, and 27 percent in East Azerbaijan. The percentage of children attending school was 74 percent in Tehran, but 44 percent in West Azerbaijan. In the mid-1970s, Tehran had one doctor for every 974 people, one dentist per 5,626, and one nurse per 1,820 people. In contrast, East Azerbaijan had one doctor per 5,589, one dentist per 66,156, and one nurse per 12,712.[61] In addition, an estimated 75 percent of the Persian households had electricity, compared with 25 percent of the Azerbaijani households.[62] However, government allocations strongly favored the Persian-dominated center of the country. For instance, in 1972–73, the central province, with 20.7 percent of the country's population, received 32.7 percent of the budget; East Azerbaijan, with 10 percent of the population, received only 4.8 percent of the budget.[63]

Abrahamian claims that the resentments created by these ethnic and class inequalities were hidden in the early 1970s, but once "cracks appeared in the Pahlavi regime, they rushed forth into a torrent to engulf the whole society."[64] An expression of this resentment is that Azerbaijanis

59. Aghajanian, "Ethnic Inequality in Iran," p. 222.

60. Ibid, p. 221.

61. Abrahamian, *Iran Between Two Revolutions*, p. 449.

62. Aghajanian, "Ethnic Inequality in Iran," pp. 216–217.

63. Ibid., p. 221. See also Nasib Nasibzade, "K ekonomicheskoi politike shakhskogo pravitel'stva v Iranskom Azerbaizhane v 60-70-kh godakh," *Problemy ekonomicheskogo razvitiia stran Azii i Severnoi Afriki* (Moscow: Nauka, 1983).

64. Abrahamian, *Iran Between Two Revolutions*, p. 449.

were the main founders of underground opposition groups to the Shah, such as the *Mujahedin*.[65] Other Azerbaijanis formed the opposition group *Nahzat-i Radikal* (the Radical Movement).[66]

On the eve of the revolutionary period of the 1970s, the regime made some concessions to the Azerbaijani provinces' demands for local language use. These concessions included the publication of a few books in Azerbaijani and permission for some lectures at Tabriz University to be conducted in the Azerbaijani language.

Soviet Azerbaijan: Institutionalization of Identity

After the establishment of the Soviet Union, Moscow attempted to mobilize the non-Russian peoples to support the new regime.[67] The Soviet Union encouraged the development of ethnic groups' literature, though with heavy censorship on the content of works. Thus, Moscow facilitated the development of Azerbaijani literature and culture. The Latin alphabet was officially adopted in Soviet Azerbaijan in 1924, predating its adoption by the Republic of Turkey in 1928.[68]

In the 1930s, though, Stalin's purges stifled independent cultural and political expression in almost any form throughout the Soviet Union. Between 1934 and 1937, almost all the members of the Central Committee of the Communist Party of Azerbaijan were executed. Among the first to be killed were the past members of the *Himmet*, who had founded the Azerbaijani Communist Party. Moscow's extreme secularization campaigns accelerated the weakening of Azerbaijanis' and other Soviet Muslims' ties to Islam, and especially to its clerical institutions. In addition, Stalin had severely limited direct contacts between Azerbaijanis across the border. During World War II and the Soviet occupation of north Iran,

---

65. Ibid., p. 489.

66. Ibid., p. 504.

67. For an excellent discussion of Soviet nationality policies, see Ronald Grigor Suny, *The Revenge of the Past: Nationalism, Revolution and the Collapse of the Soviet Union* (Stanford, Calif.: Stanford University Press, 1993).

68. In 1940 Moscow imposed the Cyrillic alphabet on Azerbaijan. Some authors claim that Ataturk's decision to adopt the Latin alphabet in the Republic of Turkey was influenced by the Azerbaijani precedent. See Hugh Seton-Watson, *Nations and States*, pp. 258–259. Azerbaijani activists who left Azerbaijan after the fall of the independent state in 1920 and found refuge in the Republic of Turkey evidently lobbied for the adoption of the Latin alphabet in Turkey. See Swietochowski, *Russian and Azerbaijan: A Borderland in Transition*, p. 114.

many of these restrictions were temporarily lifted. In addition, during the war Moscow encouraged the use of religious and ethnic symbols that were dear to the Soviet peoples to cultivate support for the war effort. For example, in this period Azerbaijani literature frequently featured Babak and his struggle for the motherland against foreign armies.

Soviet Azerbaijani collective identity was especially influenced by the stationing of many in Iranian Azerbaijan as part of the military and civilian occupation forces. While it seemed that Moscow wished to stimulate the attachment of the Iranian Azerbaijanis to the north, the influence flowed both ways, and among the northerners who served there, a sense of increased identity with their co-ethnics seemed to emerge.

The Azerbaijanis who worked to foster ties between the north and the south in Tabriz during World War II were not simply fulfilling Moscow's orders. After returning home, most of those who had been active in the propaganda organs in Tabriz continued to express a desire for a renewal of ties in Azerbaijani journals in Baku that were not intended for consumption in Iran. On the grassroots level, the desire to renew ties was fostered by the fact that most Soviet Azerbaijanis had relatives in Iran. Some authors suggest that the head of the Communist political leadership in Baku, A.A. Bagirov, proposed to Moscow the adoption of a policy aimed at uniting Soviet and Iranian Azerbaijan.[69]

By the postwar period, Azerbaijani identity had become the primary collective identity of most of the Azerbaijanis in the Soviet Union. They were among the least Russified of the Soviet peoples.[70] Many Azerbaijani cultural figures praised their ethnic cultural tradition, and continued to produce numerous works in their native language. Even members of the republic's communist leadership implemented policies that showed their commitment to the preservation of Azerbaijani language and culture. For instance, in the 1950s, First Communist Party Secretary Imam D. Mustafayev advanced a policy encouraging the migration of Azerbaijanis into Baku in order to tip the balance in favor of the indigenous population.[71] He also promoted the economic autonomy of the republic and resisted

---

69.   Ghods, A Comparative Historical Study, p. 479.

70.   Soviet Azerbaijanis, for instance, seldom intermarried with non-Azerbaijanis and had one of the lowest rates of emigration from their national republic in the Soviet Union. See S. Enders Wimbush, "Divided Azerbaijan: Nation Building, Assimilation, and Mobilization Between Three States," in William O. McCagg, Jr., and Brian D. Silver, eds., Soviet Asian Ethnic Frontiers, (New York: Pergamon Press, 1979), p. 71.

71.   Alstadt, The Azerbaijani Turks, p. 165.

Moscow when it sought to change the status of the local languages in the schools in the non-Russian republics. His stand on this issue may have been the reason for his dismissal by Moscow.[72] In addition, Azerbaijan Communist Party and later Politburo candidate member Heydar Aliyev at times tried to promote Azerbaijani interests within the limits of the Soviet system. He worked to create jobs inside the republic so that Azerbaijanis would not leave in search of work. He objected to Moscow's plans to move "surplus labor" from Azerbaijan to Siberia. Aliyev also brought the body of nationalist playwright Husein Javid to Azerbaijan for burial.[73]

Some Azerbaijanis interviewed stated that during the Soviet period, Azerbaijanis fiercely sustained their cultural traditions in their homes, which were seen as the only place Soviet and Russian culture could not permeate. For example, most Azerbaijanis devotedly prepared their traditional foods.

Throughout the 1960s and 1970s, the Azerbaijan SSR Writers' Union and intellectual groups continued to grapple with the issue of Azerbaijani cultural and national development. The Azerbaijani intelligentsia's writings of the 1960s and 1970s revealed a firm interest in Azerbaijani identity and culture and an effort to preserve that culture. For example, many works of traditional Azerbaijani *ashug* poetry were published.[74] Many Azerbaijani dictionaries and other philological works were produced throughout the 1960s and 1970s, and many literary works expressed identity with Azerbaijan. Azerbaijani literary journals published many works extolling the Azerbaijani homeland that had been written earlier by poets who were Communists who had been decorated by the regime. These works were not rejected by the censor due to the positions of the authors in the regime. Their poems included the obligatory praise of Communism, but also their love for Azerbaijan as their homeland. A posthumously published book on Samad Vurgun's poetry includes the following poem:

---

72.   Yaroslav Bilinsky, "The Soviet Education Laws of 1958–59 and Soviet Nationalities Policy," *Soviet Studies* Vol. 14, No. 2 (October 1962), pp. 138–157.

73.   Husein Javid was killed in 1937 in a Siberian labor camp during Stalin's purges. He was accused of being a "bourgeois nationalist" and "Pan-Turkist."

74.   See, for instance, Muzäffär Shukur, ed., *Ashïk Shämshir* (Baku: Azerbaijan State Publishers, 1973); "Ashïk Ädäbiyyatï," *Azärbayjan,* Vol. 12 (1964), pp. 72–74; and "Ashïk Äläsqärin Anadan Olmasïnïn 150 Illiyi," *Azärbayjan,* Vol. 5 (1972), pp. 16–34.

The nation knows that you are mine,
My homeland,[75] my nest, you are my home,
They say, you are my native land!
I have been separated, heart from soul?[76]
Azerbaijan, Azerbaijan!

In 1967, poet Bakhtiyar Vahabzade expressed his anger at the attempts to stifle the Azerbaijani language, evading the censor by referring to the Latin language, in his poem "Latin Dili":

If you cannot say in your mother tongue
"I am free, I am independent."
Who would believe that you are?
What kind of freedom is that, which cannot say its name
If your mother tongue is prisoner[77]

Many Azerbaijani nationalistic writers and academics later served as the hard core of political activists who led the opposition and national movement that were openly active in the end of the 1980s. Among the most important activists is Abulfez Elchibey, who was imprisoned in 1975 due to his nationalistic political activity in Azerbaijan.

The use of the Azerbaijani language remained prevalent in the republic. In April 1978, Azerbaijan, along with Armenia and Georgia, rebuffed Moscow's efforts to grant Russian the same status as the local languages in the republics' constitutions.[78]

Nationality Policies of Moscow and Tehran

The extremely different policies of the Soviet Union and the Pahlavi regime in Iran toward their ethnic minorities affected the development of the national identity of each Azerbaijani population in different ways.

---

75. Here he uses the Turkic word *yurd* and not the Arabic-origin word *vatan*. *Samed Vurgun 1906–1956: Bibliografiya* (Baku: Azerbaijan SSR Academy of Sciences Publishing, 1965), p. 11.

76. This is possibly a reference to the separation between north and south Azerbaijan.

77. Bakhtiyar Vahabzade, "Latin" (1967), as published in Hadi Sultan-Qurraie, ed., *Selected Works of Bakhtiyar Vahabzade* (Bloomington: Indiana University Turkish Studies Publications, 1998) pp. 52–53.

78. "O proekte Konstitutsii (Osnovnogo zakona) Azerbaidzhanskoi Sovetskoi Sotsialisticheskoi Respubliki i itogakh ego vsenarodnogo obsuzhdeniia," *Bakinskii rabochii*, April 21, 1978, pp. 2–4.

Moscow's policy toward ethnic minorities and the intensity of its drive for Russification fluctuated throughout the Soviet period, but overall, the Soviet regime was strikingly more tolerant in allowing collective expressions of Azerbaijani culture than was Tehran in this period.[79] Iran attempted to centralize its regime and the identity of all its citizens. The Soviet Union, except during part of the Stalinist era, more or less granted autonomy to local elites in the Muslim republics in exchange for their maintaining stability and the flow of resources to the center.

Moscow stressed both ethnic and territorial-based identity; this created inherent tensions. The Soviet Union termed many of the larger ethnic groups in the country as nations, and granted them territorial units. In addition, it institutionalized the ethnic identity of its citizens: in internal passports, most other identifying documents, and many official administrative forms, the ethnic identity of the citizens was always noted. This process strengthened the ethnic awareness of each citizen. Rogers Brubaker claims that this Soviet policy of incorporating ethnic identity into the state structures was an

unprecedented displacement of nationhood and nationality, as organizing principles of the social and political order, from the state-wide to the sub-state level. No other state has gone so far in sponsoring, codifying, institutionalizing, even (in some cases) inventing nationhood and nationality on the sub-state level, while at the same time doing nothing to institutionalize them on the level of the state as a whole.[80]

Children automatically received the ethnic identity of their parents. Those that were born to parents of two different ethnic groups could choose the ethnic identity of one of their parents at age sixteen, but they could not freely select their self-identification. Thus, paradoxically the Soviet system prevented the assimilation of ethnic groups into larger units, despite its Russification policy.

Every Soviet citizen was born into a certain nationality, took it to day care and through high school, had it officially confirmed at the age of sixteen and then carried it to the grave through thousands of application forms,

---

79.   This is illustrated by Javad Heyat's claim that the Akhundzade Library in Baku contains more than 50,000 books published in Azerbaijani from 1930s to the 1980s. In the same period, fewer than fifty books were published in Azerbaijani under the Pahlavi Regime in Iran. See Heyat, "Regression of Azeri Language and Literature," p. 10.

80.   Rogers Brubaker, *Nationalism Reframed: Nationhood and the National Question in the New Europe* (Cambridge: Cambridge University Press, 1996), p. 29.

certificates, questionnaires and reception desks. It made a difference in school admissions and it could be crucial in employment, promotions and draft assignments.[81]

Moscow's political interest in institutionalizing ethnic identity was to present itself, in contrast to capitalist states, as a country in which minority groups have cultural rights. However, since the Soviet Union imposed extreme limitations on expressions of identity, policies that increased individuals awareness of their own distinctive identity simultaneously created an inherently agitated situation.

Despite ideological rhetoric, Russian society rarely allowed full assimilation of many of the non-Russians, especially the Muslim minorities, though complete loyalty to the Soviet regime gave Azerbaijanis access to positions of power and resources and minimized the discrimination against them as non-Russians.

The political borders and the ethnic borders were rarely congruent. Thus, many Soviet citizens lived in republics belonging to ethnic groups other than their own. This also created tension, due to the problematic relationship between the republics and their co-ethnics beyond their borders in other Soviet republics, and between members of the ethnic minorities within the republics. This became evident in many of the conflicts that erupted in the glasnost and post-Soviet period, such as the Nagorno-Karabagh conflict between Azerbaijan and Armenia.

In contrast, the Pahlavi regime of Iran offered the option of assimilation and Persianization, and this served as a way to enter into the country's upper echelons. Tehran discriminated against non-Persian groups, but rarely against individual non-Persians who accepted the Persian language and culture. In contrast to the Soviet Union, the Pahlavi regime and the Islamic Republic did not note the ethnic status of citizens of Iran in any official form and did not recognize separate ethnic groups. For example, since the 1950s Tehran has not included in official censuses questions on ethnic identity. In Pahlavi Iran, Azerbaijani and Iranian identity could not coexist. The Pahlavi regime defined Iranian identity as Persian. Iranian identity was no longer supra-ethnic, encompassing all the national groups in Iran. No collective rights were recognized by the Pahlavi regime for non-Persian ethnic groups. While Moscow allowed Soviet and ethnic identity to coincide, the Pahlavi regime in Iran demanded that the

---

81.   Yuri Slezkine, "The USSR as a Communal Apartment, or How a Socialist State Promoted Ethnic Particularism," in Geoff Eley and Ronald G. Suny, eds., *Becoming National* (New York: Oxford University Press, 1996), p. 228.

members of the minority groups Persianize and assimilate in order to participate fully and advance.[82]

The regimes differed greatly in their handling of government appointments and language policy. Moscow generally appointed a member of the main indigenous ethnic group to head a republic's communist party. The leaders of the republics generally had local power bases and were versed in the culture and ways of the dominant ethnic group. They routinely appointed associates who were close to them, often from their own ethnic and even regional and clan grouping. In contrast, Tehran generally appointed people from outside the dominant ethnic group to serve as governors of the provinces, and most often non-natives of the region.

Tehran did not tolerate the use of languages other than Persian in any official public capacity. Children who mistakenly used Azerbaijani and other "tribal" languages in the classroom were fined and sometimes beaten. Permission to publish in the ethnic languages was rare. By the eve of the Islamic Revolution, most educated Azerbaijanis were well-versed in Persian and it was their primary language for reading and writing. However, the majority of the Azerbaijanis were still monolingual and illiterate at this time. Overall, Tehran succeeded in instilling its message that Persian is a "higher" and more developed language than the Turkic and other languages used by many of the peoples in Iran, and its use became a mark of prestige by many of the members of the non-Persian groups.

Moscow achieved similar results through very different methods. Most of the non-Russian languages were officially recognized and the development of their literatures encouraged within the limitations of official ideology. Cultural elites in the republics were allowed to write in their "national languages" and to publish classical "national" literary pieces as long as they included revolutionary and pro-proletarian messages. From the 1930s, Moscow implemented a policy of Russification among the Soviet peoples. Instead of formally limiting the official use of non-Russian languages, generally positive incentives for Russification were created: greater resources were given to the Russian language schools in the republics, lessons at the top universities across the Soviet Union were conducted in Russian, and access to positions of power in the center required a full command of Russian. Members of the non-Russian groups had to learn Russian to attain major positions of power in their own republics and in the center, whereas Russian residents of non-Rus-

---

82. Fred Halliday, *Iran: Dictatorship and Development*, 2d. ed. (London: Penguin Books, 1979), p. 216.

sian republics were not forced to learn the local languages, even when they filled important positions in those republics.

In Soviet Azerbaijan, the Azerbaijani language remained both the primary literary and spoken language in the republic. Mostly the educated elite adopted Russian as its primary language. In Iran, Azerbaijani was chiefly a spoken language. Due to the limitations on publications in languages other than Persian, few writings were produced in Azerbaijani. These were read mostly by highly educated Azerbaijanis, who also knew Persian and thus did not need these publications to be written in the Azerbaijani language.

Ties between Azerbaijanis

Despite the limitations imposed on both sides after World War II, interest in cross-border ties persisted among the Azerbaijanis. Soviet Azerbaijan intellectual publications indicate that the subject of the connection between Azerbaijanis in the north and south was of constant interest throughout the post–World War II period. These writings, produced primarily for readers in the republic of Soviet Azerbaijan, were published almost exclusively in Azerbaijani and rarely appeared in Russian. In certain periods, such as 1941–46, Moscow encouraged Soviet Azerbaijanis to inspire a heightened identity among their co-ethnics in Iran. The drive to encourage Azerbaijani identity continued after Moscow stopped promoting this policy, indicating that it was based on local desires of many Soviet Azerbaijanis.

After the Soviet Azerbaijanis returned from Iran at the end of World War II, many who had served in Tabriz, as well as many veterans of the Pishaveri regime who had fled to Soviet Azerbaijan after its fall, continued to publish literary works on their emotional attachment to the south, and on the ties between north and south Azerbaijan. One of the most important works of this period is Suleyman Rustem's *Iki Sahil* (Two Shores) published in 1950. The title refers to the two banks of the Araz River.

Mirza Ibrahimov was for a long time the most outspoken champion in Baku of the cause of "South Azerbaijan." Ibrahimov served for many years as the head of the republic's Writers' Union. He and many other writers in Soviet Azerbaijan set many of their literary works in Iranian Azerbaijan and used the Araz and Tabriz as important motifs.[83] While he was head of Azerbaijan's Writers' Union, Ibrahimov received many

---

83. See, for example, Mirza Ibrahimov, *Qüläbätin* in *Azärbayjan*, Vol. 10 (1965). Famil Mehdi, "Täbriz Khalïsï," and "Män Kichik Deyiläm," *Azärbayjan*, Vol. 5 (1978), pp. 128–129, 134–136.

awards from the republic's political leadership, exemplifying their support or at least their tacit acceptance of his drive to increase contact between the Azerbaijanis.[84]

In 1958 one of Azerbaijan's most important poets, Bakhtiyar Vahabzade, wrote "Gulustan," about the 1813 Gulustan Treaty, which divided Azerbaijan between the Russian and Persian Empires. "Gulustan" was published in 1960 in a local newspaper in Sheki. The poem describes the tragedy of two brothers who became separated as a result of this treaty, allegorically referring to the separation of the two Azerbaijans. The author asserts that Iran and Russia had no right to divide up a land that they do not own—"After all, this land has its owners!"[85] Vahabzade and the editor of the newspaper were reprimanded by the authorities.[86] Despite the official ban on the poem, it became well known among the Azerbaijanis, many learning it by heart.[87]

Balash Azeroglu, a Soviet Azerbaijan poet, expressed solidarity with co-ethnics in Iran and distress over their lack of cultural rights in his poem, "The Motherland Demands Just Such a Son." Among its lines: "No schools to teach the language of Azerbaijan/ No Alphabet to learn the ABC/ This is the vengeance of great Tehran/ 'We are a mighty nation,' says Iran. Encouraging, they pat our shoulder blade, yet use of our own language, they forbade . . . Who will pay for this atrocious crime!"[88]

Official cultural institutions of the Azerbaijan Republic consistently portrayed Iranian Azerbaijan as an integral part of Azerbaijan. For instance, in the Carpet Museum in Baku, carpets from different regions of Azerbaijan, such as Karabagh, Kuba, and Tabriz, were displayed without

---

84. In *Azerbaijanian Poetry: Classic, Modern and Traditional* (Moscow: Progress Publishers, 1969), Mirza Ibrahimov discusses cities of north and south Azerbaijan as part of one entity. For example, he states, that "Ganja, Tabriz, Ardebil, Baku, Shamakhi, Nakhchivan, Urmiya, Shusha, and other ancient towns mentioned in medieval historical literature are situated on Azerbaijanian soil and it is these towns which gave Azerbaijanian culture its splendid poets, musicians, artists, architects, and sculptors." (p. 24).

85. Bakhtiyar Vahabzade, "Gülüstan," quoted in Hadi Sultan-Qurraie, "Introduction," in *Selected Works of Bakhtiyar Vahabzade* (Bloomington, Ind.: Indiana University Turkish Studies Publications, 1998), p. 16.

86. In September 1988, "Gülüstan" was republished in the Azerbaijani journal *Genjlik*.

87. Mirza Michaeli, "Azerbaijan Notebook," *Report on the USSR* (RFE/RL) 155/1989 (March 15, 1989), p. 29.

88. Quoted in Ibrahimov, ed., *Azerbaijanian Poetry: Classic, Modern and Traditional,* p. 411.

any note that Tabriz is in Iran. In the historical museums, the maps of Azerbaijan included south Azerbaijan, and exhibits presented historical and cultural figures from Iranian Azerbaijan as part of Azerbaijani history, without pointing out that they are in a separate country.

The press in Soviet Azerbaijan often published articles about Azerbaijani authors and poets from Iran, such as Behrengi, and published their works both in Azerbaijani and translated from the Persian in which they were usually forced to publish.[89] Throughout the post–World War II period, many academic works published in Soviet Azerbaijan dealt with Iranian Azerbaijan.[90]

Radio Baku broadcasts targeted to Azerbaijanis in Iran were another means used for forging ties between Soviet and Iranian Azerbaijan. In interviews, some people stated that these broadcasts had a wide following in Iran, especially in the Ardebil region, where the broadcasts were picked up very clearly. Some of the interviewees mentioned that they listened to the broadcasts to hear music in their native language. Others said that they tuned in to Baku in order to hear classical music.

Music continued to be a bond between the Azerbaijanis on both sides of the Araz River. In the 1960s, 'Ali Salim's "Ayriliq" (Separation) was immensely popular among Azerbaijanis in Soviet Azerbaijan and Iran.[91] The singer Rashid Behbudon, of Baku, and the singer "Gugush,"of Tehran, a popular singer of Azerbaijani descent, popularized the song, which later played a symbolic role in Baku's quest for independence in the 1980s. Tapes of Azerbaijani music from Soviet Azerbaijan were quite popular and frequently purchased, clandestinely, by Azerbaijanis in Iran. In addition, Azerbaijani intellectuals in Iran often succeeded in obtaining Azerbaijani books in Arabic script published in Baku.[92] Many interviewees from Iran stated that despite the formal restrictions, many Azerbaijanis maintained ties with relatives on the other side of the border. Some Azerbaijanis illegally crossed the border into Soviet Azerbaijan, while others traveled through Moscow to Baku.

---

89. See for instance, Sämäd Bähränqi, "Mähäbbät Naghïlï," in *Azärbayjan*, Vol. 6 (1976), pp. 190–202; Ilqar Gasïmov, "Äbädi Mubarizädä," *Ädäbiyyat vä Injäsänät*, December 9, 1978, p. 6.

90. For examples, see *Vostokovednyetsentry v SSSR*, Vol. I (Azerbaijan, Armenia, Georgia, Ukraine) (Moscow: Glavnoe izdatel'stvo vostochnoi literatury, 1988), pp. 40–41.

91. 'Ali Salim, a musician of Azerbaijani origin, lived in Iran. Born in Baku, his family emigrated to Iran in 1938.

92. Based on a conversation with an Azerbaijani from Urmiya.

Conclusions

Azerbaijani identity was often strengthened by the discrimination, cultural repression, and economic disadvantages propagated by the regimes that ruled the Azerbaijanis, both in Russia and Iran. Since 1828, Russian colonial rule exposed the north to discrimination and foreign rule. In the south, the Pahlavi regime's centralization policy achieved some results opposite of those intended: while the policy aimed to create national unity, the more the center pressed for Persianization, the faster it seemed to alienate some Azerbaijanis from the regime and motivate them to explore alternative identities. By equating the Iranian state and nation with the Persian people and language, the Pahlavi regime gave rise to the question of the identity of the Turkic-speakers in Iran.

During the Pahlavi period, the regime propagated the theme of the greatness of the Iranian nation as a Persian people, the magnificence of Persian literature and language, and the exalted level of Persian culture. Non-Persian cultures in Iran were generally treated by the regime as primitive, uncivilized, and underdeveloped. Many non-Persians internalized these messages and viewed their own ethnic culture through the prism of the regime. Samad Behrengi's poem "Agha-ye Cox Bakhtiar" mocks the assimilated Azerbaijani who has given up his native culture and language while attempting to assimilate into Persian culture. The embracing of Persian culture and the attempt to assimilate into it was common among Azerbaijanis, especially in Tehran in the late Pahlavi period, and so Behrengi's poem reflects a substantive trend. By the eve of the Islamic Revolution in Iran, a significant percentage of the Azerbaijanis living in the center of Iran had adopted Persian culture.

Most scholarship on Iran describes the Azerbaijanis in the Pahlavi period as well absorbed into Iranian society and cites few illustrations of Azerbaijani nationalism or lack of affinity with the regime.[93] Azerbaijani national activity, when mentioned at all, is described as a phenomenon belonging to the period following the Islamic revolution, or more frequently, following the breakup of the Soviet Union. In fact, this chapter shows that a separate Azerbaijani or Turkic identity was expressed by some of the Azerbaijanis during the Pahlavi period.

Extreme limitations and sanctions were imposed on any expressions of Azerbaijani national identity in the Pahlavi period, and individuals who engaged in nationalistic activity were subject to torture and impris-

---

93.   See, for instance, Cottam, *Nationalism in Iran: Updated Through 1978*, pp. 118–133.

onment, and some were even killed.[94] Thus, most expressions were subtle and limited to the cultural field.

In almost all the instances when central authority was weakened during the Pahlavi period, temporarily removing the threat of repercussions, Azerbaijanis and other ethnic minorities voiced cultural demands and tried to acquire autonomy. These episodes indicate that ethnic aspirations probably existed when central authority was strong, but fear and the regime's oppression prevented their open declaration.

Leading political scientists have claimed that advances in infrastructure and communications should augment citizens' identity with their state.[95] In contrast, the Azerbaijani example shows that advances such as mass communications and modern infrastructures can work to reinforce alternative identities. Some felt that modern advances would significantly boost identity with the state by increasing exposure to the center, creating attractive institutions, generating and facilitating contacts with citizens outside one's community, and through the state's use of the means of mass communications to cultivate state identity. The Azerbaijani example, particularly in the case of those living in Iran, showed that increased interaction with the center, which was facilitated by technological advances, often led to increased ethnic-based identity. These infrastructures brought the state to the village, and as such disrupted traditional aspects of life, often producing indignation. As the center extended infrastructures to all corners of the state, questions and competition arose regarding such issues as distribution of resources and the language that would be used in these newly established institutions. The interaction between Azerbaijanis and Persians, while often fostering common Iranian identity, also contributed to emphasizing the contrasts between the two peoples and the elements shared with co-ethnics.

Throughout the Soviet period, Azerbaijani national identity was retained in Soviet Azerbaijan by most of the ethnic Azerbaijanis in the republic. Literary works were the major venue reflecting nationalist Azerbaijani identity.

---

94. Many Iranian Azerbaijanis believe that Samad Behrengi, for instance, did not die in an accident, but rather was killed by the regime.

95. Karl Deutsch, *Nationalism and Social Communication* (Cambridge, Mass.: MIT Press, 1953); Ernest Gellner, *Nations and Nationalism* (Oxford: Basil Blackwell, 1983).

Chapter 3

The Islamic Revolution and the Azerbaijanis

The "Islamic Revolution"—the 1979 overthrow of the Shah—was carried out by a wide coalition of forces with varying ideological orientations and goals, united by their shared opposition to the monarchy in Iran. Only some wished to establish an Islamic Republic, and few of the Islamists envisioned that this element would prevail and eventually eliminate all other political forces. During the revolutionary period, when the Shah was overthrown, members of ethnic minorities played an especially prominent role. Many of them expected that democratization of Iran would bring greater freedom for the ethnic minorities. Tabriz, with the highest Azerbaijani population in Iran, was a center of the revolutionary activity that precipitated the fall of the Pahlavi regime. Members of the ethnic groups took advantage of the regime's weakened hold over their activities to express ethnic identity and make ethnic-based demands, and many publications appeared in the minority languages such as Azerbaijani, Kurdish, and Armenian.[1] The day after the Shah fled Iran, Azerbaijani activists began publishing the first Azerbaijani-language newspaper of the period, *Ulduz*.[2] Its authors called for ethnic rights, starting with the right to use the Azerbaijani language.[3] In its first year, the Islamic Republic's publication policy was relatively lenient, but after the

---

1. See Hasan Javadi, "Research Note: Azeri Publications in Iran," *Critique*, No. 8 (Spring 1996), p. 85.

2. *Ulduz* began publication on January 17, 1979, and included articles in Azerbaijani and in Persian.

3. E. Ch. Babaev, "Iuzhnyi Azerbaidzhan v iranskoi revoliutsii 1978-1979 gg," *Jänubi Azärbayjan Tarikhi Mäsälläri* (Baku: Elm, 1989), p. 128.

consolidation of the regime many non-Persian publications were forced to halt production and it became more difficult to publish books in the ethnic languages.

Ayatollah Khomeini gained power in Iran in February 1979. By the spring of that year, the regime faced demands from all the major ethnic groups in Iran. Through most of 1979, the regime engaged in an all-out military confrontation with the Kurds to establish control in the Iranian Kurdish province, and conducted a second military offensive against the Kurds beginning in April 1980. Azerbaijani activists rebelled against Khomeini in December 1979 and effectively controlled Tabriz for over a month. Confrontation between Ayatollah Kazim Shariatmadari, the Azerbaijanis' most widely followed religious figure in this period, and Ayatollah Khomeini posed one of the most serious threats to the legitimacy of the Islamic regime in the initial period. Many of the provinces that were populated predominantly by ethnic minorities boycotted some of the new regime's first attempts to legitimize its rule, such as the referendum on the establishment of the Islamic Republic (April 1979), the referendum on the establishment of ultimate power in the hands of a supreme leader (December 1979), and the first presidential and parliamentary elections (1980).[4]

The events of the revolutionary period initially led to a significant weakening of the center. As in other periods of Iranian history, various ethnic groups took advantage of the regime's weakened hold over their ·activities, to express their ethnic identity and make demands. Yet few works have chronicled and analyzed the special role and goals of the ethnic minorities in the revolutionary period. Some studies examine the Kurds, the Arabs, or even the Turkmen, but very few mention the Azerbaijanis.[5]

Ethnic minorities played an especially important role in the Islamic Revolution for three reasons. First, ethnic minorities had developed networks of connections among themselves in different locations throughout Iran, making them a force that was relatively easily mobilized for the anti-regime activity of the revolution. Second, the ethnic groups had compounded grievances toward the Pahlavi regime, which had suppressed

---

4.   Mojab and Hassanpour, "The Politics of Nationality and Ethnic Diversity," p. 238–239; and Ervand Abrahamian, *Radical Islam: The Iranian Mojahedin* (London: I.B. Tauris, 1989), pp. 59–62.

5.   On the demands of the Kurds and other ethnic groups in Iran at the time of the Islamic Revolution, see Mojab and Hassanpour, "The Politics of Nationality and Ethnic Diversity," pp. 229–250; and Dilip Hiro, *Iran Under the Ayatollahs* (London: Routledge and Kegan Paul, 1985), pp. 111–115.

their ethnic culture and given preferential treatment in the economic sphere to the Persian-dominated center. Lastly, many Azerbaijani and Kurdish families had relatives who had been killed or exiled by the regime after the fall of the provincial governments in 1946.

In the initial period of the revolution, the primary goals of most of the Azerbaijanis were all-Iranian; by the end of the period, their disappointment with the results of the revolution strengthened some Azerbaijani ethnic identity and activity. For example, the revolution's failure to bring significant democratization attracted some Azerbaijanis, who had previously identified themselves chiefly as Iranian, to ethnic-based messages. Most Azerbaijanis in Iran had assumed that democratization would end the restrictions on their language and culture, so even those with nationalist Azerbaijani goals tended to be active in general Iranian political movements during the revolutionary period. Moreover, Ayatollah Shariatmadari's ostracism from the new regime, and his eventual defrocking and humiliation by it, contributed to a sense of alienation from the revolution and its messages by many Azerbaijanis who had previously supported and identified with the Islamic Revolution.

The Islamic revolutionary period provides an important opportunity to learn about the identity of the Azerbaijanis and other ethnic minorities in Iran. After the fall of the Pahlavi regime, most restrictions on publications were briefly lifted, including those on the use of the ethnic languages. Moreover, since the revolution led most Iranians to believe that individual and collective liberties would be respected, an unprecedented number of materials in the ethnic languages were published dealing with the role of the minorities in Iranian society. Thus, this brief period is a window into the ideas and beliefs of the Azerbaijanis in Iran.

This chapter concentrates on the collective identity of the Azerbaijanis in Iran that was expressed during the period of the Islamic Revolution. It begins with examining the events that precipitated the open revolutionary activity beginning in 1977 and continues through 1983, when the new regime had become consolidated and most opposition and ethnic political organizations and publications had been successfully suppressed. The impact of the Revolution on the identity of the Azerbaijanis in the Soviet Union is also briefly analyzed.

Revolutionary Tabriz

One factor that contributed to the wide early support for the revolution among the Azerbaijanis was their mass migration from the villages to the major cities in the Azerbaijani provinces and to Tehran in the 1960s and 1970s. At the time, the largest percentage of migrants to Iran's urban centers came from the Azerbaijani provinces, where high birth rates and a lack of new jobs produced surplus labor.[6] Many of these migrants lived in difficult conditions in shanty towns adjacent to Tehran and Tabriz that lacked the support and constraints of the traditional villages they had left. The children born in the shanty towns were further removed from the traditions of their parents' homes. Under these conditions the migrants were mobilized into revolutionary activity. In addition, in the Persian-dominated center of the country, many Azerbaijanis encountered for the first time treatment as second-class citizens and slurs from Persians, which contributed to their alienation from the regime. The Pahlavi state policy of economic discrimination toward the periphery,[7] and especially toward Azerbaijan, also fostered support for the revolution among the Azerbaijanis, as did the cultural suppression of ethnic minorities. However, although Azerbaijanis constituted a significantly large proportion of the revolutionary activists and Tabriz was a center of the anti-Shah demonstrations, Azerbaijanis could be found in the nucleus of the Pahlavi regime.

Toward the end of 1977, anti-Shah activity became assertive and openly oppositional. Tabriz, and especially its university, was a center of this activity. Although most of the activity was part of the general Iranian revolutionary movement, its particular intensity in the Azerbaijani provinces illustrates that their inhabitants were especially alienated from the regime. In addition, many Azerbaijanis involved in the revolution protested in their own language and called for collective ethnic rights. For instance, on November 28, 1977, participants, at a demonstration in the Tabriz bazaar, carried signs bearing anti-Shah slogans and cried out demands in Azerbaijani.[8] Many of the Tabriz *bazaaris* expressed their support for the demonstrators.[9] Following this, on December 3, 1977, a group of teachers and educational staff protested in front of the Supreme Administration of Education building in Tabriz. Among their demands was the release from prison of opposition writers and the establishment of professional unions which would defend their interests and rights.

Tabriz University was the focal point of some of the most aggressive anti-regime activity in this period. Beginning in December 1977, students

---

6. Kazemi, *Poverty and Revolution in Iran*, p. 30; and Babaev, "Iuzhnyi Azerbaidzhan v iranskoi revoliutsii 1978–1979 gg, pp. 99–100.

7. Aghajanian, "Ethnic Inequality in Iran," p. 221.

8. Babaev, "Iuzhnyi Azerbaidzhan v iranskoi revoliutsii 1978–1979 gg," p. 101.

9. Ibid.

conducted a wave of protests against the Pahlavi regime. On December 5, students gathered at the entrance of the university and shouted in Azerbaijani: "We demand democracy!" and "We demand freedom!"[10]

They staged one of their most important demonstrations on December 12 (21 of Azar according to the Iranian calendar). This date has important meaning for Azerbaijanis for it commemorates both the day of the establishment and the fall of the Provincial Government of Azerbaijan in Iran in 1945 and 1946.[11] Two hours into the peaceful demonstration military units began brutally attacking the students who had assembled there. The demonstration was only completely broken up the next day. Angry students leaving the university smashed cars near the guard booth of the campus and gathered in the main street of Tabriz, shouting anti-government slogans. Although most of their slogans supported common Iranian goals, the choice of the date illustrates their special awareness as Azerbaijanis and the importance they attached to the struggle of their predecessors.[12] Sensitive to any signs of ethnic political activity, the regime reported in the newspaper *Ettela'at* that the demonstration had taken place on December 19.

Anti-regime demonstrations in Iranian Azerbaijan were not confined to Tabriz. In February 1978, students conducted a number of demonstrations at the University of Reza'iyeh (Urmiya).[13] Throughout 1978–79, Azerbaijani *ashugs* frequently appeared in buses in Iran, promoting revolution through their poetry.

In Tabriz, the anti-Shah regime activity entered a new phase on February 18, 1978. In response to the killing of approximately 162 demonstrators in Qom on January 9, Ayatollah Shariatmadari called on the people of Iran to strike on the fortieth day of mourning for the victims.[14] Demonstrations were held throughout the country, but the protest in Tabriz was the most contentious and became violent. The incidents in Tabriz were followed by a series of disturbances throughout Iran that intensified, raising the level of confrontation with the Pahlavi regime.

---

10. Näsib Näsibzadä, "Täbriz Universiteti," *Ulduz*, Vol. 9 (1983), p. 46.

11. During the Shah period, the fall of the Provincial Government in Azerbaijan was celebrated on December 12 as a national holiday commemorating the regime's victory. These celebrations were not continued by the Islamic regime.

12. Babaev, "Iuzhnyi Azerbaidzhan v iranskoi revoliutsii 1978–1979 gg," p. 104.

13. Ibid., p. 106.

14. Muslims traditionally commemorate mourning on the fortieth day after death.

During the Tabriz incidents, the local police refused to fire on the demonstrators, so the Shah transferred military forces from outside the Azerbaijan provinces to quell the demonstrations.[15] This presumably reflects his lack of trust in the local forces, which were primarily composed of Azerbaijanis. After the disturbances, local police officers who had refused to give orders to open fire on the demonstrators were transferred from Azerbaijan. A purge was carried out in the local ranks of the SAVAK security forces because a number of its members had been unwilling to act against the demonstrators in Tabriz.[16] The demonstration soon became an uprising, and the city was paralyzed by the strikes of factories, bazaars, and schools. Demonstrators, incensed by the killing of one of the protesters, attacked property throughout the city.

Individuals from diverse sectors of the Azerbaijani population participated in the Tabriz incidents, where calls of "Death to the Shah!" were heard for the first time. The slogans at the demonstration reflect the different goals and forms of identity prevalent among the Azerbaijanis at the time. On the one hand, people had answered the call of the religious leadership to demonstrate, and many of their slogans were pro-Islamic. Yet, many other slogans called for democratization, and even left-wing organizations, such as the *Mujahedin Khalq*, played an especially active role. Most of the slogans were voiced in Azerbaijani, illustrating the goal of cultural expression and the centrality of the Azerbaijani language to the people.[17]

The regime responded to the uprising in Tabriz with massive repression and arrests. It took the security forces two full days to quell the clashes, and hundreds were left dead or injured. The Shah blamed ethnic separatism as a factor in the demonstrations. He added that, "in certain geographical regions, there is no alternative but chauvinism. Iran is one of these regions; otherwise, you would disappear and your name would no longer be Iran, but Iranistan."[18]

The Tabriz demonstration set off a forty-day cycle of similar events throughout Iran to commemorate the "Tabriz massacre." Following the

---

15.   Cottam, *Nationalism in Iran: Updated Through 1978*, p. 353.

16.   *Le Matin*, Vol. 16, No. 5 (1978), quoted in Babaev, "Iuzhnyi Azerbaidzhan v iranskoi revoliutsii 1978–1979 gg," p. 111; and Cottam, *Nationalism in Iran: Updated Through 1978*, p. 354.

17.   Babaev, "Iuzhnyi Azerbaidzhan v iranskoi revoliutsii 1978–1979 gg," p. 109; and "Report of the Patriotic Muslim Students of Tabriz on the Tabriz Uprising," *RIPEH/The Review of Iranian Political Economy and History*, Vol. 2, No. 2 (June 1978), p. 67.

18.   Interview with Muhammad Shah, Tehran Domestic Service in Persian, May 13, 1978 (FBIS-MEA-78–94).

Tabriz uprising, anti-Shah activity broke out all over Iran. This was one of the catalysts that shattered the control of the Pahlavi regime. In Tehran, the Azerbaijani *bazaaris* played an important role in mobilizing a strike of the bazaar in protest against the killings in Qom.[19] The Azerbaijanis published a statement supporting a strike, defying the instruction of Ayatollah Khonsari, the highest-ranking religious leader in Tehran at the time, who objected to such an action. However, the main ethnic Azerbaijani ayatollah, Shariatmadari, had called for protest.

On April 13, 1978, the main municipal bazaar in Tabriz closed as a sign of solidarity with the demonstrating students of Tabriz University, where a student had been killed. On May 8, another demonstration was held at the university, and in clashes with security forces another student was killed, and twenty-two seriously injured. Most of the teachers and staff at the university supported the student protests. Many Azerbaijanis were enraged during the mourning period; on May 10, 1978; government forces violated the traditionally respected right to take sanctuary in the homes of religious leaders. They chased a group of protesters and shot dead two theological students in Ayatollah Shariatmadari's home in Qom.

On May 22, a student demonstration in Urmiya spilled over to the city streets. On August 24, a large demonstration was held in Tabriz, simultaneous with protests in Tehran and Rasht. Mass rallies were held throughout Iran on October 1, including in Urmiya, Zenjan, and Hamadan, cities with large Azerbaijani populations. On October 21, demonstrations demanding the release of political prisoners were held in Tabriz and Ardebil. One of the biggest demonstrations of the revolution was held on December 10 in Tabriz; 700,000 people participated. On the same day, large demonstrations were also held in Ardebil and Zenjan. In a demonstration on December 18 in Tabriz, in which 15,000 protestors participated, soldiers of the Tabriz garrison whose job was to suppress the demonstrations instead joined them. Additional soldiers then joined the demonstrations.[20] Violent demonstrations broke out in Tabriz on January 8, 1979, and demonstrators set fire to many public buildings. The Shah left the country on January 16.

---

19. Misagh Parsa, *Social Origins of the Iranian Revolution* (New Brunswick, N.J.: Rutgers University Press, 1989) p. 111. The *bazaaris* in Tehran are organized by ethnic and regional groupings and generally maintain separate mosques and other religious institutions as well. The Azerbaijanis form the largest regional bloc within the Tehran *bazaaris* and the Azerbaijani mosques and institutions often have ties with the *bazaaris* and organizations in the Azerbaijani provinces.

20. Babaev, "Iuzhnyi Azerbaidzhan v iranskoi revoliutzii 1978–1979 gg," p. 126.

The next day, Azerbaijani activists immediately began publishing *Ulduz*, the first Azerbaijani-language newspaper of the period (the newspaper also included articles in Persian). The authors called in *Ulduz* for the granting of ethnic rights, especially, the right to use the Azerbaijani language, along with general Iranian goals.[21] The speedy publication of *Ulduz* proves that ethnic-based demands existed previously and that many Azerbaijanis assumed that the revolution would provide cultural freedom for them.

The Islamic Republic

The activities and expressions of the Azerbaijanis in the initial period after the return of Ayatollah Khomeini and the formal establishment of the Islamic Republic reveal the diversity of their identities. The Azerbaijani leaders of the Islamic Republic held a primary Iranian and Islamic identity, whereas leaders of the movement for liberal democracy in Iran and the left-wing movements expressed both Iranian identity and class identity, while many also held particularistic Azerbaijani identity. Those active in the Azerbaijani autonomy movements usually possessed both Azerbaijani and Iranian identity, and believed that democratization in Iran would provide for autonomy. They struggled for democracy throughout Iran, assuming that this would lead to autonomy for Azerbaijan.

The Islamic Revolution's slogans of equality between all the ethnic groups and its stress on the universalism of Islam led many members of the ethnic minorities to believe that they would be on equal footing with the Persians in the new regime. The Shah's regime was associated with Persian-centered policies and severe suppression of the various ethnic minorities; the new regime hated the Pahlavi policies, thus many of the members of the ethnic minorities were led to believe that it would eliminate those policies.

The initial vanguard of the Islamic Republic included a significant number of Azerbaijanis who seemed to share primarily Islamic and Iranian identity. This group included Ayatollahs Musavi-Ardebeli, Khoi, Khamane'i, and Khalkhali, and the first prime minister of the Islamic Republic, Mehdi Bazargan, who was appointed by Khomeini. The existence of this group and their predominant role in the revolution indicates that an important segment of the Azerbaijani population held chiefly Islamic and Iranian identity. Nevertheless, many members of this group played

---

21. Ibid., p. 128.

an important role in shaping Azerbaijani identity. Azerbaijani members of the clerical elite, such as Musavi-Ardebeli and Khalkhali, used Azerbaijani in public and in interviews in the Tabriz press. According to many Azerbaijanis who were in Iran in this period, this was an important factor in making it acceptable to use non-Persian languages in public, and instilled in them a sense of pride and the legitimacy of the use of their language; this was a stark contrast with the attitudes in the Pahlavi period. In addition, some clerics of Azerbaijani origin openly condemned the derogatory slurs commonly used against the Turkic population in Iran. It seems that the Azerbaijani clerics used their native tongue not because of rising Azerbaijani identity, but because many of them had difficulty in speaking Persian. The revolution propelled to power many second-rank clerics from the provinces. Moreover, representatives of the new regime wanted to communicate with the Azerbaijani masses, many of whom did not know Persian. Nonetheless, their decision to speak publicly in Azerbaijani was influential.

When problems arose in the Azerbaijani provinces during the initial revolutionary period, Azerbaijani clerics were generally sent to represent the regime or appeal to the residents in the name of the regime, due to their special link to their birthplace and their ability to speak Azerbaijani. Prime Minister Bazargan was of Azerbaijani origin, but was raised as a Persian-speaker and spent most of his career working for general Iranian issues. However, Bazargan illustrated his support for cultural rights for the ethnic minorities in Iran at a rally on March 25, 1979 in Tabriz, and apologized for making his address in Persian: "I would have wished— and it would have been more appropriate—to have spoken in the Turkish language."[22] Bazargan was fully committed to Iran's territorial integrity and held Iranian identity, yet he was not opposed to granting a limited form of autonomy to the provinces, including local government and control of schools. He stated that the local rights granted in the Islamic Republic would go far beyond those granted by the Pahlavi regime.[23]

As in the past, members of ethnic groups tended to emulate and accept the opinions of co-ethnic ayatollahs. During the revolutionary period, many traditional and secular Azerbaijanis highly respected Ayatollah Kazim Shariatmadari. Ayatollah Shariatmadari was not a part of the new regime, and did not seek to hold a political position in the Islamic Republic. He believed that clerics should not become professional politicians, but rather advise and assist them. The dispute over the desired role of

---

22. Tehran Domestic Service in Persian, March 25, 1979 (FBIS-MEA-79-059).

23. See Tehran Domestic Service in Persian, April 3, 1979 (FBIS-MEA-79-066).

clerics in politics and the degree of centralization of the regime was the major issue that divided between Ayatollah Shariatmadari and Ayatollah Khomeini.[24] Evidently, Shariatmadari's opposition to centralization of the regime in Iran was influenced by his background as an Azerbaijani who had spent most of his life in an Azerbaijani province.

THE ISLAMIC REVOLUTION'S "PRAGUE SPRING": LITERARY EXPRESSIONS OF AZERBAIJANI IDENTITY

Immediately after the Shah's departure, a plethora of new publications appeared in Iran, many of them in the minority languages. However, once the Islamic Republic was consolidated, its publication policy became far more severe; fewer non-Persian publications and books were published.

The only Azerbaijani-language publication that started in that period—and still exists—is *Varliq*. It was established in April 1978. It is published under the editorship of Professor Javad Heyat, and its original founders included Dr. Hamid Nothgi, and the poets Savalan and Sonmez. The founders chose the name of *Varliq*, which means "existence," to signify that the Azerbaijanis and their distinctive culture had continued to exist under the Pahlavi regime in Iran, and that the regime did not succeed in eradicating their separate identity. *Varliq* contains articles in Azerbaijani (in Arabic script) and Persian, along with poetry from Turkey and Soviet (and later the Republic of) Azerbaijan. In its first issue, which appeared in June 1979, it was stated that *Varliq* is the organ of the Committee in Charge of Cultural and Literary Affairs of the *Anjuman-i Azerbaijan* (The Council of Azerbaijan). *Varliq*'s opening editorial spelled out in Azerbaijani its goals:

Each and every people (*khalq*) of the world has the historical and legal right to preserve its national (*milli*) culture, identity and language, no matter how long those people have had historical and cultural affiliations with other peoples throughout history.

The people (*khalq*) of Azerbaijan, together with the other peoples living in Iran, have shared a common destiny and have contributed to the creation of a common culture, yet have retained a national identity, character, and mother tongue . . .

The people (*khalq*) of Azerbaijan, although they retained their national (*milli*) culture and language, nevertheless remained loyal to Iran, even more so than those who wave the flag of "national unity"; the Azerbaijan people did not fail to carry out their historical and revolutionary duty when their services were needed.

---

24. See David Menashri, "Shi'ite Leadership: In the Shadow of Conflicting Ideologies," *Iranian Studies*, Vol. 13 (1980), p. 126.

We believe that our journal, in the great and honorable path we wish to follow, will be well accepted and honored by everyone who respects the national and cultural freedom of all peoples.[25]

The founders of *Varliq* clearly express their national culture, identity, and language as being Azerbaijani, and their state identity as Iranian, stressing that they share with other Iranians a common culture. This declaration also illustrates the expectation that expressions of ethnic culture and freedom would be permitted. In its first issue, *Varliq* published a poem by the Soviet Azerbaijani poet Bakhtiyar Vahabzade, "Mother Tongue," demonstrating the editor's connections to co-ethnics in the north and their awareness of the cultural activity taking place there. In 1982, Javad Heyat commented that *Varliq* had accomplished two important tasks: "It has standardized written Azeri despite the various local spoken dialects and it has reformed and adapted the alphabet so as to phoneticise it."[26]

At this time, one of the most popular Azerbaijani publications in Tabriz was the left-wing journal *Yoldash*. The distribution of this journal was eventually stopped by Revolutionary Guards, who frequently confiscated it at check points. The government itself published a journal in Azerbaijani, *Islami Birliq*. It appeared in both Arabic and Cyrillic characters, evidently with the hope of influencing Azerbaijanis in the Soviet Union as well. This publication, which existed for three years due to its official sponsorship, had few readers; many of those who read Azerbaijani had left-wing or ethnic orientations, and did not enjoy the journal's religious approach. In addition, the articles were written mostly by clerics who had little experience with literary Azerbaijani, and it was unattractive to Azerbaijani intellectuals, who were the main consumers of writings in their native tongue.

In 1979, a limited number of editions of *Molla Nasreddin*, a journal with a leftist orientation, were published. It featured some articles on Azerbaijani historical cultural figures, such as Taherzade Sabir, who had written in the original version of *Molla Nasreddin*.[27] Other journals that appeared at this time in the Azerbaijani language include the literary journal *Dada Gorgud*, which often contained writing from Soviet

---

25. Editorial of *Varliq*, Vol. 1, p. 3. English translation found in Ilhan Bashgoz, "Varliq" (Book review), *Turkish Studies Association Bulletin*, Vol. 3, No. 2 (September 1979).

26. Heyat, "Regression of Azeri Language and Literature," p. 17.

27. *Molla Nasreddin*, Vol. 3 (May 16, 1979), quoted in Javadi, *Satire in Persian Literature*, p. 282.

Azerbaijan and by local Azerbaijani writers, and *Koroghlu, Ishiq* (published in Urmiya), *Chanlibel,* and *Azerbayjan Sesi.* Most of these Azerbaijani journals did not last beyond 1981.

Two professors of literature at Tabriz University have described the post-revolution period in Iran as "a renaissance in Azerbaijani litera-ture."[28] According to *Varliq*'s editor, Javad Heyat, more than 150 books were published in Azerbaijani in Iran in the years 1979–83, the majority of which dealt with literary and religious subjects, language instruction, linguistics and folklore.[29] A new edition of the *Quran* in Azerbaijani, prepared by Azerbaijani madrasa students in Qom, also appeared at this time.[30]

In the initial period following the Islamic Revolution, many works of Azerbaijani poetry were published. An important collection was *Qizil Qosh.*[31] The poetry of one of the main contributors, Abbas Barez, stands out in expressing the themes of devotion to the Azerbaijani people and love for the land of Azerbaijan.[32] Some Azerbaijani poets in Iran and in the Soviet Union wrote poetic responses to each other's works that dealt with Azerbaijani cultural themes.[33] The first year of the revolution saw the publication of *Seher Ishiklanir,* a collection of literary works by Azerbaijani writers, many of which had been written during the Pahlavi period and could not then be published.[34] Many of the poems included in this volume praised Azerbaijani as the "mother language" and criticized the policy that had banned its use. One of the poems was dedicated to the Soviet Azerbaijani poet, Suleyman Rustem, in whose work the subject of south Azerbaijan figured as a major theme:

---

28. Mohammad Hariri-Akbari and Behrooz Aazbdaftari, "A Brief Review of Contemporary Azerbaijani Poetry," *Critique,* No. 11 (Fall 1997), pp. 95–118.

29. Heyat, "Regression of Azeri Language and Literature," p. 17.

30. Ibid., p. 18.

31. Abbas Barez and Sayerin, *Qizil Qosh* (Tabriz: Nasr-e Khoususi, 1359 [1980–81]).

32. See Hariri-Akbari and Aazbdaftari, "A Brief Review of Contemporary Azerbaijani Poetry," p. 100.

33. A poem on the connection with south Azerbaijan by Hokuma Billuti was responded to by Savalan, an Azerbaijani poet from Iran. See Hokuma Billuti, *Ädäbiyyat vä Injäsänät,* May 23, 1980, p. 4. The response of Savalan appeared in *Ädäbiyyat vä Injäsänät,* July 25, 1980, p. 7. Bakhtiyar Vahabzade and Mohammed Shahriyar responded to each other's poetry in 1979–1981.

34. Häbib Sahir, *Sähär Ishiklanir* (Tehran, 1979), as reviewed by Väfa Äliyev, "Mübarize Illerinin Äks-Sädasi," *Azärbayjan,* No. 1 (1982), pp. 189–191.

Once from the north
A guest arrived to us
There was darkness between friends
But, in his hand a lamp arrived.[35]

In this period, academic scholarship on the Azerbaijani language reflected and increased interest in the status of the language in Iran. A number of Azerbaijani grammars, dictionaries, and self-teaching tapes and guides were published and distributed, among them Farzanah's 1979 Azerbaijani grammar *Dastur-e Zanban-e Azerbayjani*.[36] One of the most important dictionaries published in the post-revolutionary period was Payfun's *Farhang-i Azerbayjani*.[37] This Azerbaijani-Persian dictionary includes a section that shows the Azerbaijani words in both Arabic and Cyrillic alphabets, to help those wishing to read texts from Soviet Azerbaijan.

Some Azerbaijani intellectuals in Iran explored the question of which was the most appropriate alphabet for Azerbaijani and created revised versions of the Arabic script. In 1980, Habib Azarsina independently published a pamphlet suggesting a revised Latin alphabet for Azerbaijani in Iran. Upon its publication, Azarsina was arrested. One of the questions asked during his formal interrogation was whether or not he was a "Pan-Turkist."[38] In this period, many writers began adding vowel markers to the Arabic script when writing Azerbaijani, a highly vowel-based language.[39]

Despite the limitations, the Islamic Republic was significantly more tolerant than the Pahlavi regime had been of the culture and languages of the non-Persian groups in Iran. Nevertheless, according to Heyat, "the cultural inheritance of the previous regime has not vanished" and many limitations were "still in place on the propagation and extension of Azerbaijani culture in Iran."[40] In addition, he claimed, many Azerbaijani

---

35.   Ibid. p. 190.

36.   Muhamma 'Ali Farzannah, *Dastur-e Zaban-e Azarbayjani* (1979), in the Persian language. Also, Samineh Baghcheban, *Galin Turkja Danishaq* (Tehran: Offset Publishing House, 1981).

37.   Muhammad Payfun, *Farhang-i Azerbayjani* (Tehran: Danishneye Publishing, 1983).

38.   Author's interview with Habib Azarsina, February 1998, Washington, D.C.

39.   Described in Azäroghlu, "Fäkhr Etmäyä Haglïyïg," *Ädäbiyyat vä Injäsänät*, April 9, 1982, p. 6.

40.   Heyat, "Regression of Azeri Language and Literature," p. 18.

intellectuals had internalized the Pahlavi propaganda and became alienated from their own mother language. Heyat expressed hope that

Azeri Turkish, being the mother tongue of millions of Muslims, will become a language for education and writing on a wide scale and that Azeri literature will make parallel progress to Persian literature and regain the esteemed position it deserves.[41]

AZERBAIJANI POLITICAL ORGANIZATIONS

Many political organizations in Iran were informally organized on ethnic lines in this period. A week after Khomeini's supporters founded the Islamic Republic Party, associates of Ayatollah Shariatmadari established the Muslim People's Republican Party (MPRP, known as the *Khalq* or *Khalq-e Musulman*) on February 25, 1979. This party encouraged the membership of all ethnic groups, but was composed mainly of inhabitants of the Azerbaijani provinces and Azerbaijani *bazaaris* from Tehran. The MPRP's party program called for autonomous rights for the national minorities within the framework of a united Iran. It believed that the different *iyalats* (large provinces) in Iran should have their own parliaments. The MPRP's official newspaper, *Khalq-e Musulman*, was published in Persian, but dealt disproportionately with issues related to Azerbaijan. The aim of the party leadership was to fulfill goals for all of Iran, but the MPRP was most active in the Azerbaijani provinces and focused on issues connected with the decentralization of the regime in Iran.

This party was composed of people with different political orientations, including some liberal groups united predominately by their common Azerbaijani backgrounds who felt shielded from persecution under the organization's Islamic guise.[42] The MPRP established chapters in most of the towns and villages in the Azerbaijani provinces.[43]

The relations between Ayatollah Shariatmadari and the founders of the MPRP were very close, and in fact, Shariatmadari's son, Hasan, was one of its leaders. Both Ayatollah Shariatmadari and the movement were united in their struggle against *Velayat-e faqih*—the centralization of all state authority around one supreme leader.[44] The movement did not take

---

41.   Ibid.

42.   H.E. Chehabi, *Iranian Politics and Religious Modernism: The Liberation Movement of Iran under the Shah and Khomeini* (London: I.B. Tauris, 1990), p. 263.

43.   Based on interviews with former MPRP activists.

44.   *Velayat-e faqih* is the concept of the Supreme leader and jurist, advocated by Khomeini. According to Khomeini's vision of Islamic government, the Supreme Jurist is authorized to make all the major appointments, declare war and peace, and affirm

orders from Ayatollah Shariatmadari, nor did he attempt to run the party. It operated in a decentralized fashion, as illustrated by the elections to the Assembly of Experts. The Assembly of Experts was elected in August 1979 to draft the constitution of the Islamic Republic. Participation in the Assembly of Experts elections was a point of disagreement between Ayatollah Shariatmadari and the MPRP. Shariatmadari contended that the election should be boycotted, because he opposed the drafting of the constitution by a committee instead of a full elected assembly. The local branch in Azerbaijan of the MPRP felt that it was important to participate in the drafting of the constitution, especially to ensure that it would guarantee regional rights. As a decentralized party, the MPRP's branch in Azerbaijan was allowed to make its own decision and to field candidates. The MPRP representatives from Azerbaijan were the only delegates elected to the Assembly of Experts who were not from Khomeini's party list.[45] This illustrates that the prevailing views in the Azerbaijani provinces were very different from the rest of the country.[46]

When the Assembly of Experts was convened, the Azerbaijan branch of the MPRP was promoting the idea of establishing an Assembly of Provinces (*Majles-e Iyalat*), as part of the Majlis in Tehran. In September 1979, the MPRP organization in Azerbaijan, the United People's Party of Azerbaijan, called for the establishment of a parliamentary body to represent the provinces. A proposal was presented at the Assembly of Experts by Moqaddam Maraghe'i, the leading representative from Azerbaijan:

The establishment of the Assembly of the Provinces and the Assembly of Iran's Peoples (*khalq*) will help prevent the concentration of all the power in the hands of the central government and will weaken the decision-making power of the central provinces. The establishment of such an institution will help achieve real equality between the peoples (*khalq*) of Iran.[47]

This statement reflects the desire for expanded representation of the provinces and minorities in Iran and the Azerbaijani desire for extended decision-making power for the provinces.

---

that all laws comply with Islamic law. See Ervand Abrahamian, *Khomeinism: Essays on Islamic Law* (Berkeley: University of California Press, 1993) for further explanations.

45.   Three MPRP Azerbaijani representatives were elected to the Assembly of Experts, which was comprised of seventy-five members.

46.   The MPRP and Ayatollah Shariatmadari had also disagreed over the staging of a demonstration against the government's closing of the newspaper *Ayandegan* in May 1979. Shariatmadari called on the people not to participate in this demonstration, while the MPRP supported it.

47.   *Khalq-e Musulman*, September 1, 1979 (15 Mehr 1358), p. 8.

One of the most important organizations established after the advent of the new regime in 1979 was the *Anjuman-i Azerbayjan* (Council of Azerbaijan). In its official publications, it spoke about the rights and demands of "Azerbaijan" and "the people of Azerbaijan," instead of the "Azerbaijanis," thus emphasizing the territorial dimension of their ethnic identity. In its manifesto, the *Anjuman* demanded the recognition of the "national language and culture of Azerbaijan" and the rapid establishment of schools in the upcoming school year and mass media in the Turkish language, as well as the recognition of the right of the Azerbaijanis "to use their mother tongue" in the courts and other government offices.[48] The *Anjuman-i Azerbaijan* even demanded a confederate relationship with Tehran. While formally calling only for "regional autonomy," the *Anjuman-i Azerbaijan* demanded that all administrative, cultural, judicial, economic, and even security affairs be in the hands of local representatives and councils, who should be elected directly by the people of Azerbaijan.

Other politically oriented Azerbaijani organizations were the Society for Azerbaijanis Residing in Tehran and the Society of Azerbaijani Poets and Writers.[49] In discussing the importance of the Society of Azerbaijani Poets and Writers, Halil Naseri expressed in *Ülker* the ardent expectations of many Azerbaijanis that the Islamic Revolution would facilitate the restoration of Azerbaijani "national" (*milli*) culture:

The Islamic Revolution had a great impact on the liberation movement of Iran's Azerbaijan and gave them opportunity to restore their own culture and national identity. With this tremendous victory chains of slavery were destroyed and languages and local cultures became free. Under such conditions, Azerbaijani language and ancient culture, too, achieved real freedom. Bright prospects were opened for national culture.[50]

Typical of activists from many other national movements, the author expresses support for reviving a culture that had been lost, rather than preserving the present form of Azerbaijani culture in Iran:

Many words, proverbs, terms, folkloric works are forgotten. The majority of Azerbaijanis have forgotten their literary language and they cannot read and

---

48. *Varliq*, No. 1 (1979); and manifesto of Anjuman-i Azarbayjan, clause 7, as published in ibid.

49. Tabriz Domestic Service in Persian, December 8, 1979 (FBIS-MEA-79-238 supplement 036); and *Ayandegan*, June 11, 1979 (FBIS-MEA-79-118).

50. Halil Naseri, "Farhang-e Ma Huiyat-e Mast," *Ülker* Esfand, 1359 (February–March 1981), p. 6 (written February 7, 1980). *Ülker* was a journal published by left-wing Azerbaijani intellectuals in Tabriz from 1980-81.

write in their own native language. Now they are speaking in a dialect which differs from the real Azerbaijani language.

The Society of Azerbaijani Writers and Poets must take very effective steps towards reviving Azerbaijan's language and literature and ensuring their development and blossoming. Such steps may be an example for other Iranian peoples living in Iran. Such activities are very effective in the salvation of Azerbaijani national culture. The Society of Azerbaijan Writers and Poets will be supported not only by writers, poets, scientists, and philosophers, but also by the people and by all the persons who are not indifferent to the destiny of their language, literature, national roots, national and historical identity.[51]

Within many existing Iranian political movements, Azerbaijanis and representatives of other ethnic minorities strove to achieve cultural and language rights for their groups. Some of the movements had Azerbaijan sections, for example, the Democratic Party of Azerbaijan, which was the Azerbaijani party organization of the *Tudeh* movement.[52]

During this period, most of the communist movements in Iran advocated granting of collective rights to the ethnic minorities, especially since large numbers of the activists were members of minority groups, and the Soviet Union encouraged the pro-Soviet groups to work for recognition of ethnic rights as a way of gaining support. For instance, in April 1979, the *Tudeh's* Plenum declaration stated that:

The republic can grow stronger and experience an upswing only if all peoples in our homeland participate freely and actively in political and social life, if all religions, traditions and customs, national culture and language of all peoples are recognized and respected. The granting of administrative and cultural autonomy to all peoples of the country, within the framework of a united democratic republic, is a necessary condition for implementing national unity, and for protecting the country's independence and territorial integrity.[53]

Most of the clandestine broadcasts of the left-wing movements, such as the NVOI (National Voice of Iran), which was transmitted from the Soviet Union, devoted a significant proportion of their hours to Azerbaijani

---

51. Naseri, "Farhang-e Ma Huiyat-e Mast," pp. 6–7.

52. The Democratic Party of Azerbaijan was the successor to Pishaveri's movement, which fell after the Provincial Government in Tabriz in December 1946 and moved its headquarters to Baku; it renewed operation in Iran after the Islamic Revolution. See interview with Democratic Party of Azerbaijan chief, Amirali Lakhrudi, *Zerkalo* (December 2, 1995), p. 48.

53. Tudeh Central Committee Sixteenth Plenum Declaration, published in *Horizont* (East Berlin), No. 14 (1979), pp. 11–12 (FBIS-MEA-079-070).

programs that called for granting of rights to the ethnic minorities in Iran.[54]

Opposition movements operating outside of Iran in this period also broadcast some of their programs in Azerbaijani. The Free Voice of Iran announced that:

Ever since we started broadcasting the Free Voice of Iran, we have been trying to carry programs in the languages and dialects of Iran, and especially in the sweet Azerbaijani language. We are now glad to inform you that effective today and . . . each week at this hour we will broadcast a program in Azerbaijani. We hope to be able to broadcast this program in the future on a daily basis for you, the brave and dear Azerbaijanis and the dear Azeriphones of the homeland.[55]

Many Azerbaijani politicians and intellectuals were involved in insuring language rights for the ethnic minorities in the new constitution of the Islamic Republic and in public bodies. Article Fifteen of the constitution states that the Islamic Republic of Iran will officially permit the use of the "regional and tribal languages" in their press and mass media and allow the teaching "of their literature" in schools. Article Nineteen of the constitution states that "all people of Iran, whatever the ethnic group or tribe to which they belong, enjoy equal rights; and color, race, language, and the like, do not bestow any privilege."[56] Though the implementation of these clauses was prohibited, they later served as important bases of claims by Azerbaijani activists in Iran struggling for the right to use their language. The inclusion of these rights in the constitution illustrates that demands for language rights were voiced in the revolutionary period. For instance, during the 1979 Writers' Association Convention in Iran, Azerbaijani author Reza Baraheni worked for the inclusion in the association's charter of a clause supporting the right to use the minority languages.

The extent of political mobilization along ethnic lines in this period is illustrated by the overwhelming support that the Azerbaijanis gave to

---

54. See, for instance, NVOI (FBIS-MEA-079-083) which broadcast: "Our country's ethnic and national leaders, Iran's Democratic National Front, the Tudeh Party, the National Front of Iran, the Democratic Union of the Iranian People, Cerhikhav-ye Feda'i -ye Khalq and Mujahedin Khalq, and various other national and political organizations have announced that they support the rights of our country's peoples within the framework of Iran."

55. Free Voice of Iran (a clandestine station operating outside of Iran), September 13, 1980 (FBIS-SAS-80-181).

56. "Constitution of the Islamic Republic of Iran," *Keyhan*, November 17, 1979.

Ayatollah Shariatmadari throughout 1979 regarding the major issues of his confrontation with Khomeini. This confrontation came to a head over the issue of the draft constitution for the Islamic Republic. Shariatmadari felt that the centralization of power in the hands of the *Velayat-e faqih* would usurp the sovereignty from the people, and called for the granting of local rights. Aware of Shariatmadari's objection to the centralization of power in the new constitution, and presumably due to their own view that extreme centralization of power was contrary to the Azerbaijani provinces' interests, the majority of the Azerbaijanis, along with most of the other major non-Persian ethnic groups, boycotted the December 2, 1979, referendum on the constitution.

REBELLION IN TABRIZ

Despite Ayatollah Shariatmadari's opposition to the constitution, Radio Tabriz broadcast an announcement in his name stating that he had issued a *fatwah* to vote in its favor in the planned referendum. When the public became aware of the deception, it was infuriated. A large demonstration took place on December 2, 1979, in Tabriz, at which protesters complained of the unfair treatment of Azerbaijanis in the media and called the referendum "rigged."[57]

On December 5, Azerbaijanis from around the province and beyond streamed into Tabriz to participate in a demonstration organized by the MPRP for the following day.[58] On December 5, an attack was made on the home of Ayatollah Shariatmadari in Qom, and one of his guards was killed. This attack occurred after repeated requests by government officials to cancel the December 6 demonstration, suggesting that it may have been ordered by an arm of the government to frighten Shariatmadari and force the MPRP to acquiesce to its demands.

The large December 6 demonstration turned into a protest not only against the new constitution, but also against the assault on Shariatmadari's home. The demonstrators attacked and gained control of the communications tower in Tabriz, which broadcast Radio Tabriz, the source of the deceptive broadcast.

The demands of the demonstrators and the intensity of their actions reveals that the issue of the constitution and the attack on Shariatmadari merely triggered their anti-regime activity. Their demands reflected the two issues that had been the focus of contention between the government and the representatives of the Azerbaijanis throughout the summer of

---

57.   Tabriz Domestic Service in Azerbaijani, December 2, 1979 (FBIS-MEA-79-234).

58.   *Keyhan*, December 6, 1979.

1979: the local control over appointment of officials in the Azerbaijani province, and influence over the local media.[59] The protesters captured symbols of these two issues: the radio and television broadcasting center and the provincial governor's offices and residence. In addition, the protesters gained control of the civil airport, and the army forces stationed in Tabriz refused to confront them. The rebels received the support of the air force units in Tabriz, and soldiers in uniform participated in three demonstrations in support of Ayatollah Shariatmadari.[60]

The rebellion quickly spread beyond Tabriz, and Azerbaijani opposition forces gained control of many government installations around the Azerbaijani provinces such as those in Urmiya and Ardebil. MPRP branches in Urmiya and other cities expressed support for the uprising and for Shariatmadari in his confrontation with Khomeini.[61] Some of the citizens of Urmiya, seeking to emulate the action in Tabriz, attempted to takeover the communications there, but were averted at the last moment.[62] In the town of Germi, near Ardebil, local forces took over all the government installations, including the local prison; they released all the prisoners and incarcerated in their place all the local Revolutionary Guards.[63]

In a number of instances, the rebels stressed the people's desire to control the affairs of the province. For example, in a communique read on the radio, the MPRP called for the removal of the representatives of both the Ayatollah Khomeini and the general government in Azerbaijan. The document also asked that "the rights of the people of Azerbaijan, like those of the Kurds, be respected."[64]

During the demonstrations in Tabriz, some of the official MPRP banners displayed the slogan "self-determination for the peoples in Iran." According to an eyewitness who participated in the demonstrations, these banners were professionally produced, illustrating that it was one of the articulated goals of the MPRP. Interestingly, the banner was printed

---

59. In June 1979, a number of demonstrations were held in Tabriz, demanding the reinstatement of Moqaddam Maraghe'i as governor general of East Azerbaijan and freedom from censorship in the official media of the province. Maraghe'i was supported by the MPRP and was closely associated with Ayatollah Shariatmadari.

60. Based on an interview with an eyewitness. See also Sepehr Zabih, *The Iranian Military in Revolution and War* (London: Routledge, 1988), pp. 126, 237.

61. *Ettela'at*, December 10, 1979.

62. Tabriz Domestic Service in Azerbaijani, December 7, 1979 (FBIS-MEA-79-238, Supplement 036).

63. Based on a conversation with an eyewitness to the events.

64. AFP in Spanish, December 6, 1979 (FBIS-MEA-79-237).

in Persian. The eyewitness believes that this was to attract the support of other ethnic minorities in this struggle, mainly the Kurds. Participants in the demonstrations recounted that all the speeches were in Azerbaijani and anyone who attempted to speak in Persian, other than non-Azerbaijanis expressing support for the uprising, was heckled and booed.

During the time they controlled the communications tower, the rebels allowed a number of political groups to make announcements. One of them called for all-out control of the province on December 7 and announced the establishment of a provincial council that would be in charge of East Azerbaijan's affairs, calling on all officials to obey its orders.[65]

The rebellion received a serious blow on December 6, when Ayatollah Khomeini paid a visit to Shariatmadari's home, which was presented to the outside as a mission of conciliation. During this visit, however, Khomeini threatened Shariatmadari, stating that the Islamic Revolutionary Council had decided that if Shariatmadari's supporters did not vacate the communication tower within twenty-four hours, Tabriz would be bombed.[66] At the same time, Revolutionary Guards entered Tabriz by helicopter, setting up their base at Tabriz University, which was controlled at the time by Azerbaijani leftists who predominantly supported Ayatollah Khomeini during this confrontation. Ayatollah Shariatmadari feared Tabriz would become a "second Kurdistan"; the regime's attempt to quell the March rebellion there had resulted in a large massacre of Kurds. Thus, in his characteristic manner, Shariatmadari chose to avoid bloodshed and prevent confrontation between his supporters and the regime; he called on them to stop demonstrating, and to vacate the control tower and the government buildings. Shariatmadari's call to abandon the tower was presented to the public as part of a compromise that had been reached with Khomeini allowing more Azerbaijani control over local affairs and Shariatmadari's approval of all major appointments in the province. However, that the agreement seemingly granted Shariatmadari control over appointments in the province demonstrates that there was no agreement: Shariatmadari was adamantly opposed to the direct involvement of clerics in politics, and thus would not have requested such a role for himself.

---

65. AFP in Spanish, December 7, 1979 (FBIS-MEA-79-238, supplement 03).

66. Based on a conversation with Ayatollah Shariatmadari's son, Hasan Shariatmadari. The Islamic Revolutionary Council was part of the founding state power and was responsible for the shaping of overall policies, but in practice often dealt with day-to-day issues. In 1979, the Council seemed to have more actual power in Iran than the government. See Hiro, *Iran Under the Ayatollahs*, p. 107.

Shariatmadari's overriding concern was to avoid bloodshed. Nevertheless, he had contemplated confrontation with the regime, but decided in the end that Azerbaijan's chances of sustaining a rebellion were slight, especially since Azerbaijan lacked geographical features such as mountains that are conducive to the maintenance of underground movements.[67]

At Shariatmadari's request, on December 9 the demonstrators relinquished control of the communication tower and other government installations to Khomeini's supporters. Upon reoccupation of the buildings, government forces proceeded to attack the offices of the MPRP in Azerbaijan and to arrest many of its activists. Although they were unaware of the true nature of the conversation between Shariatmadari and Khomeini, the province's populace soon understood that Khomeini did not intend to honor a deal made with the rebels, and that they had vacated the government installations and communication tower in vain. A new cycle of violence between the rebels and government forces ensued, with the rebels regaining control of the communication tower; throughout December 1979 and the beginning of January 1980, control over the tower passed back and forth a number of times, but generally the Azerbaijani rebels had the upper hand.

During the first week of the conflict, a soldier stationed outside Tabriz who sympathized with the *Tudeh* Party (which supported Khomeini at the time of the rebellion), disabled the communications transmitter at Bonab, preventing the tower in Tabriz from transmitting and practically rendering the control of the tower there futile.[68] The MPRP lost its main means of communication with the people of Azerbaijan and thus its ability to mobilize and organize them easily. This was a significant blow to the rebellion's momentum.

Nonetheless, on December 13, a crowd of more than 700,000 demonstrated in Tabriz in support of Shariatmadari. The demonstrators rejected the new constitution, and demanded the release of Azerbaijani dissidents held by the government and the withdrawal of non-Azerbaijani military forces from the province.[69] On December 27, nine Revolutionary Guards

---

67. Conversation with Hasan Shariatmadari.

68. This evidently took place on December 9. See *Tehran Times*, December 10, 1979; also, interview with Hasan Shariatmadari.

69. Nicholas M. Nikazmerad, "A Chronological Survey of the Iranian Revolution," *Iranian Studies*, Vol. 13, Nos. 1–4 (1980), p. 366.

were taken hostage in Tabriz by supporters of Ayatollah Shariatmadari; they were subsequently released on January 2.

Khomeini was forced to send in soldiers from outside Azerbaijan to quell the uprising. The major installations in Tabriz changed hands for short periods a number of times, but effectively the rebels controlled them for more than five weeks. When the radio was under the control of the Khomeini guardsmen, messages from clerics of Azerbaijani origin, such as Ayatollah Musavi-Ardebeli, were broadcast. This shows that it understood that the ethnic issue was important to the protesters, and therefore it was worthwhile to broadcast in Azerbaijani. Fighting continued between the Azerbaijani protesters and the Revolutionary Guards and intensified in the second week of January. Shortly after eleven MPRP leaders were executed on January 12 in Tabriz and the party offices were occupied by Revolutionary Guards, confrontations increased sharply. On January 19, twenty-five air force officers and NCOs from the Tabriz Air Base were arrested, accused by the regime of supplying arms to the MPRP and of plotting to overthrow the regime.[70] The government continued to persecute those who it felt had been active in the rebellion and also eliminated other opponents. Additional executions of MPRP activists took place on May 22, 1980.

Ayatollah Shariatmadari did not concede to Khomeini's demands to formally disband the MPRP. Shariatmadari replied cynically, stating that there was no need to do so under the existing government policy, which could "itself declare all the political parties outlawed, gradually branding them as American, Zionist and anti-revolutionary"; he was referring to the government's attempts to slander the MPRP by using these labels.[71] According to a senior MPRP activist, the party did not try to renew its activities in Iran once its offices had been closed, for it did not believe in conducting an underground struggle against the regime, but only in open political activity. The MPRP has not been formally disbanded.

The events of December 1979 were a turning point for many of the Azerbaijanis in their relation to the Islamic Republic. Those who had expected that the revolution would bring an end to the ban on their language and culture realized that they had been overly optimistic. Azerbaijanis, especially older and conservative ones who had greatly respected Ayatollah Shariatmadari, saw him alienated and humiliated by the new regime, and many felt disaffection from the government. After

---

70.   *Tehran Times*, January 21, 1980.

71.   *Tehran Times*, December 12, 1979.

the rebellion was quelled, many Azerbaijanis declined to participate in the elections to Iran's national institutions, evidently having lost faith in their ability to influence them.[72]

After December 1979, Ayatollah Shariatmadari imposed public silence upon himself and stopped giving interviews and issuing public statements. He continued to receive hundreds of visitors everyday in Qom, most of them his followers from Azerbaijan. Shariatmadari supported the war effort against Iraq as long as it entailed defending the borders of Iran, but when Khomeini failed to end the war even after Iraqi forces had been expelled from Iranian territory, Shariatmadari began to speak to his followers against the war. Khomeini evidently perceived this as threatening, and in April 1982 fabricated Shariatmadari's involvement in a plot against the regime. Shariatmadari had heard of the plotters' intention, but had assumed that if he knew about it, then obviously the authorities also knew about it, so he did not report what he had heard. Furthermore, the idea that Shariatmadari would actively attempt to take power from Khomeini was completely inconsistent with his strong guiding belief that clerics should not fill political positions, but should guide politicians. A further indication that Shariatmadari had no involvement in the plot was the frequent complaints of many Azerbaijani activists of their disappointment in Shariatmadari's consistent unwillingness to confront Khomeini and take political action.

Khomeini used the plot incident as an excuse to defrock Shariatmadari from his position as Grand Ayatollah and publicly humiliated him, leaving him under house arrest and without proper medical care until his death in April 1986.[73] In reaction to the stripping of Shariatmadari's title and his arrest, supporters in Tabriz demonstrated and rioted on April 20, 1982.[74] At that time, many Azerbaijani devotees came from Tabriz to Qom to declare their willingness to defend him. Shariatmadari told them to return to Azerbaijan and not to act on his behalf. Most Azerbaijanis in Iran blame Khomeini for Shariatmadari's death, since he was often denied medical treatment. But even if Khomeini's actions did little to contribute to Shariatmadari's death, the fact that the Azerbaijanis

---

72. Abrahamian, *Radical Islam: The Iranian Mojahedin,* pp. 59–62. Abrahamian cites low Azerbaijani participation in the presidential elections and the elections to the parliament in 1980.

73. According to Amir Taheri, Shariatmadari was the first Grand Ayatollah ever to be defrocked. See Amir Taheri, *The Spirit of Allah: Khomeini and the Islamic Revolution* (London: Hutchinson, 1985), p. 287.

74. Nikola B. Schahgaldian, *The Iranian Military Under the Islamic Republic* (Santa Monica: RAND, 1987), p. 143.

blame Khomeini reflects how they feel about the regime. This perception influenced their identity as Iranians.

AYATOLLAH KAZIM SHARIATMADARI: SELF-IDENTITY AS A MUSLIM, IRANIAN, AND AZERBAIJANI

Ayatollah Shariatmadari exemplifies how individuals in Iran can simultaneously possess different collective identities that do not necessarily conflict.[75] Ayatollah Shariatmadari was one of the most senior religious authorities in Iran in the second half of the twentieth century. He recognized the Islamic concept of the *'umma* (people) of Muslim believers and identified as a Muslim. Yet, he also believed that Islam is experienced differently by each ethnic group and that ethnic identity is meaningful. In his words, "to be a Persian or to be an Azerbaijani was something." In the early stage of the revolution against the Pahlavi regime, Shariatmadari announced that: "We do not intend to create a society founded on religious rites . . . When we speak of a Muslim society and a Muslim government we are thinking of efforts of renewal to be undertaken by all the people, who will govern themselves according to their own history and their own culture."[76] He advocated the fulfillment of the commandments dictated by Islamic law, but through free choice by individual believers, not through force. Moreover, Shariatmadari was an ardent believer in democracy.

Shariatmadari also identified as an Iranian. He had supported Mossadiq's Iranian nationalist efforts in the early 1950s, and opposed Iran's dependence on foreign powers. At the beginning period of the Islamic Revolution, Shariatmadari often mentioned the "Iranian nation" and its sacrifices and struggles. It seems that he used this term much more than Ayatollah Khomeini, who often addressed the people as Muslims in this period. While Shariatmadari possessed strong identity as an Iranian, in the supra-ethnic sense he also strongly identified as an Azerbaijani and a Turk. At home, he spoke only Azerbaijani, which he referred to as *Türki*, and his wife was an Azerbaijani. It was important for him to preserve Azerbaijani identity; he referred to Azerbaijani culture as his "mother culture" and to the Azerbaijani language as his "mother tongue." Most of Ayatollah Shariatmadari's close friends were Azerbaijanis. He often told stories to his family of his childhood in Tabriz and described those days as good times, and he felt closely bound to the cul-

---

75. Ayatollah Shariatmadari's son, Hasan Shariatmadari, provided most of the information on the Ayatollah's experiences and attitudes.

76. Rome ANSA (in English), November 11, 1978 (FBIS-MEA-78-219).

ture of the province. Shariatmadari had in fact spent most of his life in Tabriz, even remaining there in the Pishaveri period (1945–46). He had mixed feelings toward the autonomous Provincial Government led by Pishaveri. He approved Pishaveri's accomplishments in the cultural arena, such as establishing Tabriz University, where instruction was conducted in Azerbaijani, and improving infrastructure in the province. However, since he rejected Iranian reliance on foreign powers, he sternly opposed the Provincial Government's dependence on the Soviet Union.

Shariatmadari was in his mid-forties when he left Azerbaijan for Qom, and this affected his ability to master Persian. Shariatmadari worked with many Azerbaijani clerics in Qom who had studied in Arabic and never fully learned Persian; and he himself had a strong Turkic accent in Persian. His difficulties in learning Persian influenced his opinion that pupils in Iran should learn to read in their native language, and only then learn Persian through the native language. In the Azerbaijani provinces, Shariatmadari always delivered his speeches in Azerbaijani. In Qom, he generally spoke in Persian, but he spoke with visitors from Iranian Azerbaijan in Azerbaijani.

Ayatollah Shariatmadari did not have any direct relatives in Soviet Azerbaijan, only "relatives of relatives"; nor had he visited there. Yet, he considered the people in north Azerbaijan as members of his same ethnic group. He used the term *shimali* (north) when referring to the Soviet Azerbaijan and *janubi* (south) when referring to Iranian Azerbaijan. Shariatmadari had followers in Soviet Azerbaijan, and the Sheikh el-Islam from Baku came to Qom several times to consult with him. Nevertheless, Ayatollah Shariatmadari did not possess an accurate picture of the state of Islam among the Muslims in Soviet Azerbaijan, tending to overrate both their piousness and that of the official Islamic establishment.

Shariatmadari believed in preserving the territorial integrity of Iran, yet he "was not angry" at those who voiced demands for secession. While supporting the aims of the protesters in the 1979 Tabriz rebellion, he chose not to acquiesce to the people's many requests to personally come to Tabriz, for in his mind this could lead to a drive for separatism of Azerbaijan from Iran.

He spoke out in favor of equality for all the ethnic groups in Iran, believing that all the rights granted to the Persian people—such as cultural freedom and a right to study in one's native language—should be given to all the peoples. In the early stage of the Islamic Revolution, Shariatmadari stated on a number of occasions that the question of the division of authority between the center and the different ethnic groups should be decided after a degree of stabilization was achieved by a permanent government. Yet, his statements on autonomy for the ethnic minorities in Iran were often contradictory. He frequently formally stated opposition to "autonomy" for the ethnic groups, but when explaining his ideas he seemed to endorse it. With respect to the Kurds he said: "Let the Kurds form their own assembly and speak their own language, but let money and revenues flow into a single treasury."[77] Thus, he advocated that they be granted the right to establish local government and cultural autonomy, but opposed economic separation of the provinces from the center. Later, Shariatmadari said, "As regards to autonomy, of course, if this is in the framework of remaining Iranian, it can be planned."[78] At another point, he was quoted as saying that he wanted to see the establishment of autonomous government for minority groups, except in the diplomatic and military spheres.[79] During the December 1979 crisis in Azerbaijan, Shariatmadari commented that "the constitution contains a provision to which the people of Tabriz are opposed; it creates obstacles to autonomy. What the people of Tabriz want is autonomy. It will have to be given to them; what the people desire must be respected."[80]

A main point of contention between Ayatollah Shariatmadari and Ayatollah Khomeini over the constitution was over the issue of *Velayat-e faqih*. Shariatmadari claimed that the people of Iran should be the sovereign, as embodied in Articles Five and Fifty-six of the Iranian Constitution. Shariatmadari's opposition to highly centralized power seems to emanate from his unwavering commitment to democracy, as well as his experiences as a member of a minority group and a resident of a peripheral province.

Ayatollah Shariatmadari's self-identity as a Muslim, an Iranian, and an Azerbaijani, and the importance he attached to all three of these identities, shows that for many in Iran, they were viewed as compatible.

Ties with Soviet Azerbaijan and Its Reaction to the Revolution

The Azerbaijani-language press in Soviet Azerbaijan differed somewhat from the general Soviet press in its coverage of the Islamic Revolution in

---

77. Interview with Ayatollah Shariatmadari in Istanbul *Jumhuriyet*, March 16, 1979, p. 6 (FBIS-MEA-79-056-21).

78. *Ettela'at*, August 14, 1979, p. 2 (FBIS-MEA-79-163).

79. NHK Television Network (Tokyo), December 14, 1979 (FBIS-MEA-79-243, supplement 041).

80. Shariatmadari interview to *Mundo Obrero* (Madrid), December 9, 1979 (FBIS-MEA-79-242, supplement 040).

Iran. In addition to the general Soviet themes on the revolution, during its initial period the press in Soviet Azerbaijan emphasized the factors that caused the revolution and the perspective of Iranian Azerbaijan, such as what "South Azerbaijan" gained and lost as a result of it, especially in terms of language rights.[81] Baku journals frequently carried articles on developments and culture in Iranian Azerbaijan, including information on new journals in Azerbaijani in Iran.[82] In April 1982, for instance, a regular column began to appear in the Azerbaijan teacher's newspaper, *Azerbayjan Muellimi*, called "Jenubdan Sesler" (Voices from the South). The goal of this column was to familiarize readers with articles appearing in the Iranian Azerbaijani media. *Ädäbiyyat vä Injäsänät* started a regular column featuring humor from Iranian Azerbaijan in October 1981.

When the revolutionary period of relative permissiveness in Iran ended and the majority of the national language publications were closed, the press in Soviet Azerbaijan criticized the Iranian government.[83] The Soviet Azerbaijani press also criticized the failure of the revolution to allow the opening of Azerbaijani-language schools, and the difficulties Azerbaijanis from Soviet Azerbaijan faced in getting permission to travel to Tabriz during visits in Iran.[84]

After the revolution, scholarly interest in Iranian Azerbaijan intensified in Baku, and in 1981 a new department for research on "South Azerbaijan" was established in the Oriental Institute of Soviet Azerbaijan in Baku.[85] At the Faculty of Journalism of the Kirov Azerbaijan State University, a course on "The Contemporary Press of Southern Azerbaijan" was added to the curriculum in 1981.[86]

---

81. *Azerbaijan-Iranian Relations* (Baku: FAR Centre for Economic and Political Research), May 1996, p. 6.

82. See, for example, *Azärbayjan*, No. 12 (1981), pp. 21–23, which discussed the journal *Ingilab Yolunda*; *Ädäbiyyat vä Injäsänät*, March 7, 1980, p. 7 (JPRS 76309); *Ädäbiyyat vä Injäsänät*, May 16, 1980, p. 7; *Ädäbiyyat vä Injäsänät*, September 5, 1980, p. 6; and *Azärbayjan*, No. 1 (1982).

83. For example, Arif Ibrahimov, "Täbrizdän Mäktub-Unvan: SSRI-Bakï," *Ädäbiyyat vä Injäsänät*, November 25, 1983, p. 8.

84. Näbi Khäzri, "Dokkuz Qün, Dokkuz Qeje-Iran Täässuratï," *Azärbayjan*, Vol. 9 (1983), pp. 104–158.

85. *Vostokovednye tsentry v SSSR*, Vol. I (Azerbaijan, Armenia, Georgia, Ukraine), p. 19.

86. *Kommunist* (Baku), January 24, 1982, p. 3.

Many new scholarly works on the history of Iranian Azerbaijan were published in this period.[87] An especially notable piece was written by Nasib Nasibzade on the history of Tabriz University.[88] Soviet Azerbaijani publications often discussed and published literature written by Azerbaijani authors in Iran; Samad Behrengi was featured more than any other southern Azerbaijani writer.[89] Behrengi's writings were suitable for publication in Soviet Azerbaijan: in addition to the nationalist Azerbaijani motifs, his works contain strong leftist messages and so were not problematic to the Soviet censors. One of the most important academic works published on Iranian Azerbaijan was *Jenubi Azerbayjan Edebiyyati Antoloqiyasi*. This was the first of four volumes of an anthology of south Azerbaijani literature, edited by Mirza Ibrahimov, and it covered the nineteenth century. A second volume, covering south Azerbaijani literature from 1900–41, was published in 1983.[90] In these volumes, the editor consistently refers to the "peoples of Iran," instead of the Iranian people, and to "South Azerbaijan and Iran" as if they were separate entities.[91]

After the Islamic Revolution, ties between the Azerbaijanis in the Soviet Union and Iran increased significantly. In 1979, for instance, direct telephone links between Iran and Baku were established.[92] In addition, many Azerbaijanis who had fled Iran, especially after the fall of the

---

87.   For example, Sh. Ä. Taghïyeva, "Azadlig vä Mäsläk Fädaisi," Azerbaijan SSR Academy of Sciences, *Khäbärläri* (History, philosophy and law series), Vol. 1 (1983) (Baku: Elm Publishers). This article was written to commemorate 100 years since the birth of Sheikh Mohammad Khiyabani.

88.   Näsib Näsibzadä, "Täbriz Universiteti." Other academic works by Nasibzade on Iranian Azerbaijan published in this period include, Nasib Nasibzade, "K ekonomicheskoi politike shakhskogo pravitel'stva v iranskom Azerbaidzhane v 60-70-kh godakh."

89.   See, for instance, "Sämäd Behränqi (Jänubi Azärbayjan)—Fäläyi Akhtaran Adam," *Ädäbiyyat vä Injäsänät*, August 14, 1981, p. 8; and Ilgar Gasïmov, "Ishïklï Ulduzlardan Biri," *Azärbayjan*, No. 10 (1983), pp. 148-153. A review of a book of Azerbaijani literature in Iran after the Islamic Revolution is found in Väfa Äliyev, "Mübarize Illerinin Äks-Sädasï," *Azärbayjan*, No. 1 (1982), pp. 189–191.

90.   Mirzä Ibrahimov, ed., *Jänubi Azärbayjan Ädäbiyyatï Antoloqiyasï* (Part I) (Baku: Elm Publishers, 1981); Mirzä Ibrahimov, ed., *Jänubi Azärbayjan Ädäbiyyatï Antoloqiyasï* (Part II) (Baku: Elm Publishers, 1983).

91.   The use of the phrasing "Iran and South Azerbaijan," was found in various works in the *Azärbayjan* journal as well. For example, Turan Häsänzadä, "'Molla Näsräddin' Zhurnalïnda Iran ve Jänubi Azärbayjan Mövzusu," *Azärbayjan*, Vol. 6 (1981), pp. 133–134.

92.   David Nissman, *The Soviet Union and Iranian Azerbaijan: The Uses of Nationalism for Political Penetration* (Boulder, Colo.: Westview, 1987), p. 67.

Pishaveri regime in 1946, returned in the wake of the revolution, with some taking an active part in political movements there. After the revolution, limited direct economic ties were reestablished. According to a press report, in this period, credit was provided to Azerbaijanis from Iran to purchase goods in the Soviet Union.[93] The wide-scale unemployment in Iran during the period of upheaval sent many Azerbaijanis to the Iranian border town of Astara, opening businesses that catered to the new traffic and trade flowing between the Soviet Union and Iran. In Astara, they made direct contact with many Azerbaijanis from the north and frequently watched television broadcasts from Baku, which could be picked up in Astara. As Tehran's television filled with religious programming that held little interest for most of the population, television from Baku became more popular in the Azerbaijani provinces.[94]

Some meetings took place between cultural figures from Soviet and Iranian Azerbaijan. For instance, during a visit to Iran in December 1982, the author Nebi Khezri met with the Iranian Azerbaijani poets Savalan and Sonmez. According to Khezri, they discussed the influence of television and radio broadcasts from Baku on Azerbaijani culture in Iran, and expressed a desire for their expansion.[95]

The poet Bakhtiyar Vahabzade wrote about Javat Heyat, the editor of *Varliq* (and a surgeon), and at the time one of the most important figures promoting Azerbaijani culture in Iran:

> Your divided motherland
> Expects from you this day a salve
> Brother, your weapons are two,
> By day—the knife, by night—the pen.[96]

Javad Heyat also expressed ties to the north. Referring to the division of Azerbaijan in 1828 as part of the Turkmenchay Treaty, he said:

This tragic incident, that may be considered the greatest catastrophe in the history of Iran, and especially in the history of Azerbaijan, was unable to cause a rupture in the heart of the Azeri people of this region who had a

---

93. AP, quoted by *Turkish Daily News*, May 30, 1980.

94. According to a number of interviewees in conversations with the author.

95. Näbi Khäzri, "Dokkuz Qün, Dokkuz Qeje-Iran Täässurati," p. 131.

96. Bäkhtiyar Vahabzadä, "Bïchak-Gäläm," *Azärbayjan*, No. 4 (1983), pp. 19-20, quoted by David Nissman, "The Origins and Development of the Literature of 'Longing,'" *Journal of Turkish Studies*, No. 8 (1984), p. 205.

unified language, religion, culture, history and nationality, or better yet, everything in common.[97]

Many Azerbaijani writers and cultural figures in the north expressed a desire for closer ties with the south, and after the Islamic Revolution they wrote extensively on the subject of their people's separation. One of the most active writers engaged in this area was Mirza Ibrahimov, the head of the Azerbaijan Soviet Socialist Republic Writers' Union, who was one of the main figures during the Soviet occupation of Tabriz during World War II. In 1980, Ibrahimov wrote an article entitled "Jenubda Dirchelish" (Revival in the South), in which he reviewed a number of the new Azerbaijani publications in Iran, and stressed the existence of a desire for cultural and political autonomy among the Azerbaijanis in Iran.[98] He set many of his works in Tabriz and other cities in Iranian Azerbaijan and published many scholarly works in this period on subjects connected to the south. A major collection of his works was published in this period, many of them dealing with Iranian Azerbaijan.[99]

A special section of *Azerbayjan* published in honor of Suleyman Rustem's seventy-fifth birthday carried a number of his poems, nearly all of them dealing with the desire for connections with south Azerbaijan. In "Tebrizden Gelen She're Javab" (An Answer to the Poem coming from Tabriz), Rustem wrote:

> The stars are counted
> A man has made it to the moon
> Why from this bank to that bank
> I can't cross you Araz?[100]

In many poems published in this period, the Araz river appeared as a symbol of the separation of the Azerbaijani people.[101] Also, the longing for Tabriz and Mount Savalan was stressed in many literary works, along with the idea that the Azerbaijanis from both sides of the border are the

---

97. Javad Heyat, "Regression of Azeri Language and Literature," p. 7.

98. Mirzä Ibrahimov, "Jänubda Dirchälish," *Azärbayjan*, No. 1 (1980), pp. 34–45.

99. Mirzä Ibrahimov, *Äsärläri On Jilddä* (Baku: Yazïchï, 1980, 1981).

100. Suleyman Rustäm, "Täbrizdän Gälän She'rä Javab," *Azärbayjan*, No. 4 (1981), p. 13.

101. Among the many examples, Fikrät Goja, "Aghrï," *Azärbayjan*, No. 9 (1981), p. 5; Aydïn Ibrahimov, "Araz Üstä Nar Baghï," *Azärbayjan*, No. 9 (1981), pp. 77-80; Novruz Qänjäli, "Rubailär," *Azärbayjan*, No. 12 (1981), pp. 96–97; and Oktay Shamil, "Araz Bayatilari," *Azärbayjan*, No. 9 (1983), p. 166.

same people.[102] Some Baku authors stressed the idea of a united Azerbaijan. Gasham Ilgar, referring to the Araz river, wrote "this side is the homeland, that side is the homeland," and Hasan Valeh wrote, "May Azerbaijan not be said twice!"[103]

The outpouring was rooted in the sentiments of the Soviet Azerbaijani intelligentsia; it was not simply a product of Moscow's policies to foster ties and spread Soviet influence. Most of these works appeared in Azerbaijani-language journals published for consumption in Baku and not abroad. None appeared in Russian-language publications.

At the same time, official policy organs in Soviet Azerbaijan invested significant resources in encouraging ties with the Azerbaijanis in Iran. Some journals in Soviet Azerbaijan began to publish editions in Azerbaijani in Arabic characters for readers in Iran.[104] In Baku, special publications in the Azerbaijani language in Arabic characters were produced for dissemination in Iran. One of the most significant was a collection of Bakhtiyar Vahabzade's poetry.[105] This volume contains many Azerbaijani nationalist works, such as his poem, "Azerbayjan." The book contains no indication in Azerbaijani that it was produced in the Soviet Union or in the Azerbaijan SSR; it simply says "Bakı" (Baku). Only the short summary of bibliographical information, which appears in Russian on the last page, indicates that this is a Soviet publication. The high quality of its print and its many color pictures indicate that large sums of money were invested in the production of this volume.

In its broadcasts to Iran, Radio Baku in Azerbaijani stressed the Azerbaijanis' ties to their culture, and especially their language. In 1979, for example, Bakhtiyar Vahabzade read his poem, "Mother Tongue" on the radio.[106] In Baku, some expressed interest in expanding the study of the Azerbaijani language to communities beyond the republic. In 1980,

---

102. On the themes of Tabriz and Mount Savalan see, for example, Adil Jemil, "Gozlerim Yol Chekir," *Azärbayjan*, No. 10 (1983); and a number of poems of Suleyman Rustäm, published in *Azärbayjan*, No 11 (1983). On the unity of Azerbaijani people, see Mämmäd Araz, "Hä Deyäk Bu Payïz Küklärinä," *Azärbayjan*, No. 12 (1981), pp. 15–19.

103. *Azärbayjan*, No. 7 (1981), p. 148, quoted in Nissman, *The Soviet Union and Iranian Azerbaijan*, p. 75; and Hasan Valeh, *Azärbayjan*, No. 9 (1981), pp.110-111, quoted in Nissman.

104. For example, in 1982 *Odlar Yurdu* began to publish in Azerbaijani in Arabic characters. *Odlar Yurdu* was published for Azerbaijanis abroad by the Azerbaijan Society for Friendship and Cultural Relations.

105. Bakhtiyar Vahabzade, *Mugham* (Baku: Azerbaijan SSR Government Publications, Yazïchï, 1982), in Azerbaijani in Arabic script.

106. Nissman, *The Soviet Union and Iranian Azerbaijan*, p. 52.

the Academy of Sciences in Baku published a Azerbaijani text book and announced its publication on the Azerbaijani-language radio broadcast geared to the Middle East.[107]

The leadership of Soviet Azerbaijan expressed support for strengthening relations with co-ethnics in Iran. At the Seventh Republic Writers' Congress held in Baku in 1981, Heydar Aliyev stressed the importance of cooperation with Azerbaijani writers from "South Azerbaijan" and the "propagandization of their works in the republic and abroad."[108] Aliyev also praised the works of the poet Suleyman Rustem, declaring that "the theme of South Azerbaijan and the struggle of his people for their social and national liberation occupies a prominent place in the poet's creativity."[109] In commenting on the works of Balash Azeroglu, Aliyev stated that through his "work we frequently encounter the theme of South Azerbaijan; it reflects the dreams and aspirations of his multimillion people."[110] In praising the works of Mirza Ibrahimov, Aliyev described his book *Gelejek Gun* as portraying the "movement for revolution in South Azerbaijan, and the struggle for the people's national and social independence."[111]

In this period, official Soviet Azerbaijani treatment of the status of the Azerbaijani provinces in Iran was unequivocal: in the *Azerbayjan Soviet Ensiklopediyasi* published in 1980, the entry "Iranian Azerbaijan," states, "*Bax Jenubi Azerbayjan*" ("See South Azerbaijan").[112]

Soviet Azerbaijan: In Light of the Revolution in Iran

In the late 1970s and early 1980s, a trend toward intensified expressions of Azerbaijani national identity appeared in Soviet Azerbaijan, and intellectuals explored the nature of Azerbaijani identity. This debate may have been influenced by the challenge to national identity presented by Iran's Islamic model, and also by the partial renewal of ties with the Azerbaijanis in the south.

---

107.   Radio Baku in Azerbaijani to the Near and Middle East, October 17, 1980 (FBIS-SOV-80-206).

108.   Speech of Geidar (Heydar) Aliyev to the Seventh Republic Writers Congress, *Bakinskii rabochii*, June 14, 1981, p. 2.

109.   Geidar (Heydar) Aliyev, *Bakinskii rabochii*, December 12, 1981 p. 1.

110.   Ibid.

111.   Heydar Aliyev, quoted in "H. E. Äliyev Yoldashïn Chïkhïshï," *Azärbayjan*, No. 10 (1981), p. 67.

112.   *Azärbayjan Sovet Ensiklopediyasï*, Vol. 4 (1980), p. 513.

In the period following the Islamic Revolution, an anti-Islam campaign was conducted by the regime in Soviet Azerbaijan.[113] The Soviet authorities may have wished to preempt any sympathetic response to the Islamic Revolution in Iran. In the Communist Party daily newspaper of Baku, party activists blamed Iran for causing a rise in Islamic activity in the republic. They stated that the Islamic activity can be "explained as a result of the religious-political movement led by Iran which shares a border to the south of our republic."[114] In one of the articles attacking the practice of Islamic rituals in Azerbaijan, the author pointed out that his intent was not to attack rituals which are part of the national (*milli*) culture of Azerbaijan, but only the explicitly religious ones.[115]

Many poems appeared that praised the Azerbaijan homeland, which was often referred to by the word *vatan* or the Turkic-origin word, *yurd*.[116] Previously, the identity of the homeland was often left ambiguous, so that the reader was not sure if it was the Soviet Union or Azerbaijan. In this period, explicit praise for Azerbaijan as the homeland was often pronounced. Some literary works focused on the Azerbaijanis' pre-Islamic past and their Zoroastrian roots, which may have been a way of expressing an aversion to the Islamic ideology disseminated by Iran. For example, Balaghlan Shafizade's poem "Vatan":

You are the flame of the great Zardusht's faith . . .
These cliffs, these mountains are my ancestors,
Their crystal waters flow in my veins . . .
In my body are grains from their every place,
It seems I am the sum total of those grains.[117]

In "Thank you, My Mother Tongue," Sabir Rustemkhanli writes:

---

113. See, for instance, F. Kocherli, *Kommunist* (Baku), February 12, 1982, p. 2; K. Mustafaev and E. Qurbanov, ibid., February 19, 1982; ibid., March 23, 1982, p. 1; and ibid., July 14, 1982, p. 3.

114. K. Mustafaev and E. Qurbanov, *Kommunist* (Baku), February 19, 1982, p. 2. Iran was blamed for contributing to a rise in Islamic activity in the republic, also in ibid., March 23, 1982, p. 1.

115. F. Kocherli, *Kommunist* (Baku), February 12, 1982, p. 2.

116. See, for example, Äliyar Yusifli, "Älinje Galasï," *Azärbayjan*, No. 12 (1981), p. 91; Kämalä, "Ana Yurdum-Azärbayjan," *Azärbayjan*, Vol. 12 (1979), p. 41; Näbi Khäzri, "Torpak Nejä Adlanïr?" *Azärbayjan*, Vol. 7 (1979), p. 6. This poem praises the land of Azerbaijan, and relates to it as the land of cultural figures from both north and south, such as Nizami and Babak, and writers, such as Sabir, Samed Behrengi and Behruz Dihqani.

117. *Azärbayjan*, No. 12 (1979), quoted in Alstadt, *The Azerbaijani Turks*, p. 188.

Along came the tongues of the Koran
The voices of the Prophet, the language of law.
They put you behind the door
You asked for justice, they robbed you.
But you were not destroyed, my mother, my dear language,
You made armies tremble, my hero Tongue![118]

Many historical novels allegorically addressed the question of Azerbaijani identity and its relations to the empires around them. A number of novels dealt with the reign of Shah Ismai'l, such as Azize Jafarazada's *Baku-1501* (1981), Alisa Nijat's *Qizilbashlar* (1983), and *Khudafarin Korpusi* (1983) by Farman Karimzade. The Safavid dynasty in Iran, which was founded by Shah Ismai'l, is viewed as an Azerbaijani dynasty in Azerbaijani historiography. The interest in publication of these works, which stress the Azerbaijani roots and political leadership of Iran may have been influenced by the question of the Soviet Azerbaijani's ties to Iran, which was aroused by the revolution and the partial renewal of ties with their co-ethnics in Iran.

Interest in the Azerbaijani language also grew in Soviet Azerbaijan in this period. A number of new grammars and dictionaries were published.[119] Many of them reflected a trend of the early 1980s toward the "purification" of the language, replacing Russian words with words based on Turkic roots.[120] One linguist, emphasizing the closeness of the Azerbaijanis to the Muslim peoples, pointed out that Arabic and Persian words have been generally completely absorbed into the language, while Russian and other words "of European origin" remained as "terms and technical vocabulary."[121] In these linguistic texts, the language spoken in the republic was usually referred to as the "Azerbaijani language," and not as Azerbaijani Turkish.[122] In an effort to bolster the language, linguists campaigned for direct translations of foreign literary and scientific works into Azerbaijani, and not from Russian translations, as was cus-

---

118. *Azärbayjan*, No. 6 (1982), quoted in ibid.

119. See, for instance, Färhad Zeyhalov, *Türkoloqiyanïn Äsaslarï* (Baku: Maarif Publishing, 1981). A grammar that discusses to a number of Turkic languages in addition to Azerbaijani; *Ruscha-Azärbayjancha Lüghät* (Baku: Azerbaijan ASSR Academy of Sciences, Nesimi Philological Institute, 1982).

120. See, for instance, *Ädäbiyyat vä Injäsänät*, November 4, 1983, p. 6 (JPRS-UP-S-84-028).

121. *Ädäbiyyat vä Injäsänät*, January 8, 1982 (JPRS 80867).

122. See, for instance, Zeyhalov, *Türkoloqiyanïn Äsaslarï*; and Ä.Ä. Orujovun, *Azärbayjan Dilinin Izahlï Lüghäti* (Baku: Elm Publishers, 1983).

tomary.[123] To attain this goal, a law was passed in May 1983, "The State of Translation in the Republic and Measures to Improve It."[124] In addition, many works examining Azerbaijani literature and culture were published in this period, and there was continued interest in traditional Azerbaijani literary works, such as *ashug* poetry.[125]

As part of a trend returning to eastern roots, many Azerbaijani intellectuals replaced western or Russian-style furniture with traditional pillows and carpets, especially in rooms where guests were received. A trend toward emphasizing traditional eastern and Azerbaijani motifs in architecture in new structures also emerged. In an article in Baku's *Kommunist*, Doctor of Art Kamil Memedzade criticized the fact that "there is no national form in the buildings we have constructed," and stressed "the study of the beautiful works of Azerbaijan architecture," which "is a great creative school for our modern architects."[126]

An important trend that reflected interest and concern for Azerbaijan was the drive to preserve historical and cultural monuments. Activity of this type is often associated with the glasnost period, but actually pre-dated it. A law was passed in 1992 in the Azerbaijan SSR, "On the Preservation of Historical and Cultural Monuments," and a public organization, the Azerbaijan Society for the Preservation of Historical and Cultural Monuments, was established.[127] In 1982, a new Main Administration for City Planning and the Preservation, Restoration and Utilization of Archaeological and Architectural Monuments was established under the Azerbaijan SSR Council of Ministers.[128] Intellectuals often wrote articles calling for the preservation of historical monuments and artifacts and praising efforts in this field.[129] At the Seventh Writers' Congress of the Azerbaijan SSR in 1981, one delegate pointed out the growing interest in ecology and also stressed the importance of preserving historical and

---

123. See, for instance, Zeydulla Aghayev in *Kommunist* (Baku), March 14, 1981, p. 4; March 6, 1981, p. 4; and November 19, 1983, p. 4.

124. *Kommunist* (Baku), July 6, 1984, p. 3 (JPRS-UPS-84-106).

125. Works on literature and culture include, *Azärbayjan Mahabbat Dastanlarï* (Baku: Elm, 1979); Ä. Akhundov, *Azärbayjan Khalg Dastanlarï* (Baku: Yazïchï, 1980); and Äli Saläddin, *Azärbayjan She'ri ve Folklor XIX-XX Äsrlär* (Baku: Elm Publishers, 1982). On ashug poetry see, for instance, "Ashïg Alïnïn Anadan Olmasïnïn 180 Illyi," *Azärbayjan* No. 11 (1981), pp. 151–153.

126. *Kommunist* (Baku), March 6, 1982, p. 3.

127. *Vyshka* (Baku), March 2, 1982, p. 2.

128. *Kommunist* (Baku), March 6, 1982, p. 3.

129. See, for instance, Sabir Äfändiyev, "Babalarïn Ämanäti," *Ädäbiyyat vä Injäsänät*, June 11, 1982, p. 5; and G. Abilova, *Ädäbiyyat vä Injäsänät*, May 23, 1980, p. 3.

cultural monuments.[130] In addition, many works published at this time explored different periods of Azerbaijani history and examined the ethnic origins of the Azerbaijanis.[131]

Few of the Soviet Azerbaijani publications, focusing on Azerbaijani identity, stressed its Turkish aspects. This is reflected in a piece, entitled "Dokkuz Gun, Dokkuz Geje-Iran Teessurati" (Nine days, Nine nights— Impressions of Iran), which chronicles the visit of Soviet Azerbaijani writer Nebi Khezri to Iran. The story relates the writer's encounters—by chance and as part of his business there—with Iranian Azerbaijanis. In a hotel, the author speaks to a bellboy who looked Azerbaijani to him:

> I said hello to him. He looked and inquired:
> Are you a Turk?
> I am an Azerbaijani. I am a Soviet Azerbaijani.
> You speak Turkish well.
> I speak Azerbaijani.
> He carried our things to the elevator.[132]

Another Azerbaijani encountered by chance asks Khezri, "Are you a Turk?" and he replied, "No, I am an Azerbaijani."[133] Some Soviet Azerbaijani intellectuals also criticized their co-ethnics in Iran for calling their common language Türki or Azeri, instead of Azerbaijani.[134]

Conclusions

The Azerbaijanis were one of the most active groups that worked for the overthrow of the Pahlavi regime in Iran, and Tabriz was one of the centers of revolutionary activity. Most Azerbaijanis who supported the revolution in Iran expected that it would bring democratization, and except for those who advocated Khomeini's version of Islamic government, most believed that democratization would bring an end to the ban on the

---

130. Araz Dadashzade, *Bakinskii rabochii*, June 16, 1981, p. 2.

131. Among them is Sara Ashurbeli, *Gosudarstvo Shirvanshakhov* (Baku: Elm, 1983).

132. Näbi Khäzri, "Dokkuz Qün, Dokkuz Qeje-Iran Täässurati," p. 107.

133. Ibid., p. 109. The author seems to be recounting these stories metaphorically in order to stress Azerbaijani identity versus Turkic identity. At the time, most Azerbaijanis in Iran referred to themselves as *Turks,* and the term Azerbaijani was rarely used.

134. See, for instance, Azäroghlu, "Fäkhr Etmäyä Haglïyïg," *Ädäbiyyat vä Injäsänät,* April 9, 1982, p. 6; and Sirus, "Shähriyar Körpüsü," *Ädäbiyyat vä Injäsänät,* April 2, 1982, p. 6.

culture and language of the ethnic minorities, if not complete cultural autonomy. Thus, most activists pursued all-Iranian goals in the revolutionary period, to achieve their Azerbaijani demands as well.

The failure of the Islamic Revolution to end the ban on the ethnic languages, in addition to the violent crushing of the rebellion in Tabriz and its treatment of Ayatollah Kazim Shariatmadari, the cleric most respected by Azerbaijanis throughout Iran, led to disappointment and caused feelings of deep alienation. Many Azerbaijanis began to explore their identity as Iranians. That the regime had promised an end to the Persian-centered policies associated with the Pahlavi regime exacerbated the Azerbaijani's bitter disappointment. Furthermore, the regime intensified the Azerbaijanis' desire for more freedom of expression by permitting ethnic language publications for a short period, and then canceling that policy. Nevertheless, the Islamic Republic employed a more lenient policy, albeit still strictly limited policy, in relation to non-Persian culture than the Pahlavi regime.

The oppressive undemocratic nature of the Khomeini regime led some Azerbaijanis who had felt primarily Iranian on the eve of the revolution—many of leftist political orientation—to explore the idea of achieving their political goals within an Azerbaijani framework. At the time, direct relations with the Azerbaijanis to Soviet Azerbaijan had been renewed, albeit in a very limited fashion, and Baku was pushing for the renewal of ties. Some Iranian Azerbaijanis stated that they and many of their family and friends toyed with the idea of supporting unity between the two Azerbaijans in this period. Most rejected it; they felt it would make them vulnerable to Soviet oppression.

This process of exploring collective identity accelerated after the nature of the Islamic Revolution became clear, but was abruptly placed on the back burner with the severe crackdown on political opposition in 1982–83, the climax being the repression of the Tudeh in April 1983.[135] Open demands for expanded ethnic rights were not tolerated by the end of this period. These demands resurfaced later, further affected by the war between Iran and Iraq.

In the late 1970s and early 1980s, a trend of asserting Azerbaijani national identity also emerged in Soviet Azerbaijan; there was some exploration of Azerbaijani history and culture, as well as ties with the Azerbaijanis in Iran. Though this trend became more evident from the mid-to-late 1980s, and especially in the period of glasnost in the Soviet Union, its beginning in the 1970s refutes the frequent claim that the Azerbaijanis'

---

135. Many of the activists of the Tudeh and other left-wing movements were Azerbaijanis.

assertion of their national identity in the late 1980s was chiefly a response to challenges from Armenia and the struggle for control over Nagorno-Karabagh.[136] As the next chapter shows, the conflict over Nagorno-Karabagh had an enormous impact on the goals and the intensity of the Azerbaijani national movement in the late 1980s; however, the identity trends were not based on the immediate events in the Caucasus or in Moscow. The exploration of national identity and the heightened expressions of Azerbaijani identity in Soviet Azerbaijan reveals that this trend predated glasnost.

---

136.   See, for instance, Saroyan, "The Karabagh Syndrome and Azerbaijani Politics," pp. 14–29; and Carrere d' Encausse, *The End of the Soviet Empire*, p. 59.

Chapter 4

Between Two Revolutions

During the 1980s, the Azerbaijanis in the Soviet Union and in Iran underwent very different historical experiences. The divergent political climates in these states in this period had an impact on the distinct development of Azerbaijani identities on each side of the Araz.

In Soviet Azerbaijan, the trend of growing Azerbaijani national identity that emerged in the late 1970s and early 1980s gained further momentum. The change in Soviet Azerbaijan's political atmosphere—first with Heydar Aliyev's departure from the republic to Moscow in 1981, and then by Mikhail Gorbachev's inauguration of the policy of glasnost in the beginning of 1986—was conducive to politicization of cultural trends. Challenges from Armenia and Moscow in the second half of the 1980s, especially over the control of Nagorno-Karabagh, contributed to the politicization of issues connected with Azerbaijani collective identity. The small group of people engaged in these issues grew into a mass movement.

Throughout most of the Soviet period, the Azerbaijanis generally stressed their distinctive identity. In the late 1980s, however, many political and cultural groups began to stress *Turkism* as a major component of that identity. For the most part, the focus was on cultural Turkism, and few advocated political unity with Turkic states. Nevertheless, Abulfez Elchibey of the Popular Front of Azerbaijan, who later served as the first democratically elected president of the Republic of Azerbaijan, adopted a clear political orientation toward the Republic of Turkey.

In the mid-1980s, Soviet Azerbaijanis displayed a marked identity with and concern for their co-ethnics beyond the borders of the republic in Iran, the Soviet republics of Armenia and Georgia, and even Iraq.[1] The treatment of the Azerbaijanis in Armenia, as perceived by Baku, served as a catalyst for political action. Calls from Baku for increased ties with co-ethnics in Iran, Armenia, and Georgia, as well as concrete efforts to make connections, became a major theme of the political movements that emerged in the second half of the 1980s, growing throughout the period. A highlight of the drive for renewed contact was the demolition of the border installations between the two Azerbaijans, along a large section of the Soviet-Iranian frontier in December 1989.

In contrast to the political relaxation of Soviet Azerbaijan in the mid-1980s, the Azerbaijanis in Iran were subject to increased political and cultural suppression. Open expressions of separate identity by the ethnic minorities in Iran were extremely limited during Iran's war with Iraq, and strict censorship returned in the wake of the final crackdown on opposition political organizations in 1983. By 1983, all regularly published Azerbaijani-language publications, with the exception of *Varliq*, had been closed down. By mid-1983, opposition political groups in Iran had been completely suppressed. For a large number of Azerbaijanis involved in left-wing organizations, the arrest of most of the leaders of the Tudeh in April 1983 was a turning point in their relation to the regime. Many politically aware Azerbaijanis, even those who were active in all-Iranian politics, chose to emigrate at that time.

The constraints of the war severely restricted the ability of the citizens of Iran to deal with abstract issues like their national identity. Yet, the effects of the war and other developments on that identity became evident later, during the period of limited political relaxation after the end of the war, and after Khomeini's death and Hashemi Rafsanjani's presidency, which allowed some restricted political pluralism.

This chapter chronicles and analyzes the formation of Azerbaijani collective identity from the end of 1983 through the independence of the Republic of Azerbaijan in December 1991, focusing on events in Soviet Azerbaijan.

Continued Exploration of National Identity in Soviet Azerbaijan

Prior to the advent of the policy of glasnost in the Soviet Union under Mikhail Gorbachev in 1986, the Azerbaijanis in Soviet Azerbaijan contin-

---

1.   Among the many examples, see Gäzänfär Pashayev, "Böyük Marag," *Ädäbiyyat vä Injäsänät*, April 13, 1984, p. 7; *Ädäbiyyat vä Injäsänät*, July 6, 1984, p. 8 (UPS-84-106); Räfigä Gasïmova, "Seyid Mehdi E'timad," *Ädäbiyyat vä Injäsänät*, May 18, 1984, p. 8; Vagif Gurbanov, "Poetik Injilär," *Ädäbiyyat vä Injäsänät*, January 25, 1985, p. 6.

ued to explore their collective identity and to express attachment to Azerbaijan. Academic scholarship and literary works remained a major vehicle for such expression. Many of the themes dealt with in the early 1980s continued to be of interest throughout the decade: the nature of the homeland, predominantly referred to in intellectual works as *veten* and *yurd*;[2] Azerbaijani history; and the frequent use of Azerbaijani collective symbols in literary works.

Some of the literary works expressed general love of the homeland, some praised and articulated pride in Azerbaijan and some explored the writer's relationship with his or her country. That so many works with these themes were written and published reflected a general exploration of national identity in the late 1970s and 1980s, and an increased connection to Azerbaijan as a homeland. Quite divergent views of what constituted the homeland and Azerbaijani identity appeared in Soviet Azerbaijani literary and academic journals before the introduction of glasnost, indicating that there was a relative degree of intellectual pluralism, and that some debate of certain controversial issues took place before the advent of the glasnost. Works exploring issues of identity in the Soviet Union appeared almost exclusively in Azerbaijani-language publications, and few references to this issue can be found in Russian-language publications in the republic.

The status and preservation of the Azerbaijani language continued to be an important issue in Soviet Azerbaijan. In February 1985, a conference was held on fostering the use of the Azerbaijani language in the republic. Addressing this issue, Professor Jamal Ehmadov complained publicly that too few hours were devoted to teaching Azerbaijani language and literature in elementary schools.[3] Azerbaijani literary figures advocated "purifying" the Azerbaijani language of foreign elements.[4] In addition, advocacy for direct translations of scientific and literary works into Azerbaijani from other languages continued.[5]

2.   See, for example, Mirvarid Dilbazi, "Anam Ishïglï Dünyam!" *Azärbayjan*, No. 3 (1985), p. 5; Allahverdi Mämmädli, "Sän Yolsan, Män Yolchu," *Azärbayjan*, No. 3 (1985), pp. 161–162; and Bäkhtiyar Vahabzadä, "Taras Shevchenkoya," *Azärbayjan*, No. 8 (1986), pp. 3-4.

3.   Jamal Ähmädov, "Ädäbiyyat Müälliminin Nüfüzü," *Ädäbiyyat vä Injäsänät*, January 27, 1984, p. 2.

4.   See for instance, Mirzä Ibrahimov, "Häyat vä Gurujulug Amili," *Ädäbiyyat vä Injäsänät*, May 11, pp. 1, 7; and Sabir Rustämkhanlï, "She'rimizin Dili," in *Ädäbiyyat vä Injäsänät*, June 15, 1984, p. 6. This trend also appeared in the period analyzed in the previous chapter.

5.   See *Ädäbiyyat vä Injäsänät*, June 1, 1984, p. 6 (JPRS-UPS-84-100).

Toward the middle of the 1980s, a number of books examining various aspects of Azerbaijani culture were published, demonstrating an interest in its investigation. Two examples are, *Azerbayjan Khalk Seneti*, which explores Azerbaijani folk art, and *Azerbayjan Khalchasi*, which examines Azerbaijani carpets.[6] In books on Azerbaijani culture and art forms, works from north and south Azerbaijan were treated as one entity. In discussions of works produced, for instance, in Tabriz or Ardebil, etc., there was no indication that these were from Iran, rather than Soviet Azerbaijan. They were treated as a natural part of Azerbaijan and Azerbaijani culture. In many of the works cultural artifacts from as early as the third century were referred to as "Azerbaijani," illustrating a desire to show ancient roots of Azerbaijani culture, primordial ties among Azerbaijanis, and that a separate Azerbaijani identity existed from early times. Themes of fire and fire temples appear quite frequently in many literary works, alluding to the Azerbaijanis' pre-Islamic Zoroastrian roots which are important in the identity of many in the republic.[7]

THE IMPACT OF GLASNOST

With the change in the political environment of the Soviet Union after 1986, themes that had been confined to intellectual and literary journals were aired by the mass media, and were later adopted by open political movements which emerged in Soviet Azerbaijan. Starting in 1986, a number of unofficial organizations emerged in Azerbaijan, though many did not, or could not, officially register until 1988, when the glasnost policies were in full swing. Most of them expressed their attachment to and concern for Azerbaijani identity at this stage, dealing mainly with matters which were not directly political. Some of these new organizations, such as The Baku Center for the Arts (founded in 1986), dealt with Azerbaijani culture. Others, such as *Yurd* (founded in 1987), sought to preserve historical and architectural monuments in Azerbaijan. Another important public organization formed at this time was *Veten*, which held its founding conference on December 28, 1987. It sought to establish ties with Azerbaijanis abroad. *Veten* was initially formed within the communist apparatus under the leadership of the writer Elchin, who was part of the official Writers' Union and was elected *Veten's* first presidium chair-

---

6. Rasim Äfändiyev, *Azärbayjan Khalg Sänäti* (Baku: Ishïk, 1984); and Lätif Kärimov, *Azärbayjan Khalchasï* (Baku: Yazïchï, 1985), Part II (Baku: Gyandzhlik, 1983), and Part III (Baku: Gyandzhlik, 1983).

7. See, for instance, Mämmädli, "Sän Yolsan, Män Yolchu," p. 161–162.

man.[8] The informal organization *Chanlibel*, which was formally established in the spring of 1987, was especially concerned with expanding research on the history of Azerbaijan and disseminating it on the popular level. Many of the articles that appeared at this time called for study of Azerbaijani contributions to various fields of research. In addition, research on different periods of Azerbaijani history was advocated.[9]

Like other national movements in the Soviet Union, in the initial period of glasnost the Azerbaijanis explored "blank spots" in their history, articulated concern for their natural environment, and requested the return of traditional Azerbaijani names to many places around the republic and the preservation of historical sites.

One of the most important changes was the attitude toward the Sovietization of Azerbaijan in 1920. All officially published Soviet history had treated the fall of the Azerbaijan Democratic Republic and the Soviet takeover as the "liberation" of Azerbaijan; it was described as a voluntary act of the people of Azerbaijan, and the *Musavat* ruling party of the time was condemned as a nationalist-bourgeoisie party.[10] In a shift from this line, a poem written in 1985–86 appeared in the August 1987 issue of the journal *Azerbayjan*. It describes Baku in April 1920, immediately after the Soviet takeover, in very gray terms, and the period following the Soviet takeover is described as "bedlam." The poet predicts that the "Musavat" government may return to Baku, alluding to a return in the contemporary period of a nationalist Azerbaijani government.[11] The poem questions the ability of workers to run a country, saying:

> Do not think that a country can be taken over by
> a worker of an oil field, or by a servant of the bazaar
> The worker is not able to build a state
> He has no idea about laws!
> The nation will be destroyed.
> My heart is breaking for the people.[12]

---

8. "Sozdano Obshchestvo 'Veten,'" *Bakinskii rabochii*, December 31, 1987, p. 3.

9. See, for example, Aghababa Rzayev, *Ädäbiyyat vä Injäsänät*, January 16, 1987, on the importance of the study of Azerbaijani contributions to world science, especially in the medieval period.

10. See, for instance, "Musavat," *Azärbayjan Sovet Ensiklopediyasï*, Vol. 7 (Baku, 1983), p. 130.

11. Azäroghlu, "Häyat Yolu," *Azärbayjan*, No. 8 (1987), pp. 59–67.

12. Ibid., pp. 59–60.

In September 1987, in an attempt to rehabilitate Musavat-era figures, the journal *Ädäbiyyat vä Injäsänät* carried an article entitled, "Nobody Can Deny that. . . ." which expressed a positive opinion about one of the senior diplomats of the Musavat-led Democratic Republic of Azerbaijan.[13] Nizammeddin Shemizade called for the study and rehabilitation of cultural figures who were active before the Soviet takeover of Azerbaijan.[14] In July 1988, Academy of Sciences member Mahmud Ismailov, in an article in *Ädäbiyyat vä Injäsänät*, urged historians to acquaint the public with the accomplishments and history of the sovereign Azerbaijani state (1918–20).[15] In 1990, the historian Nasib Nasibzade published *Azerbayjan Demokratik Respublikasi*, in which he presented the Soviet takeover of Azerbaijan as a military coup that did not enjoy grassroots support, thus challenging the official Soviet historiography.[16] Excerpts of this book were published in Baku newspapers in 1989. The political implications of these historical works were far-reaching. By condemning the Sovietization of Azerbaijan in 1920, the authors were in essence challenging the legitimacy of Soviet rule in Azerbaijan. Through these works some were suggesting the desire for independence from the Soviet Union. In the middle of 1988, revisionist articles on the republic's Stalinist era frequently appeared in the Azerbaijani press, further challenging the base of Soviet rule.[17] Among the accusations leveled against the Stalinist regime was the damage done to mosques throughout the republic, especially in Sheki.[18]

Researchers in Azerbaijan continued to produce research on the ethnic origins of the Azerbaijani people, generally building a picture of their long-standing distinctive Azerbaijani identity. The authors seem to have been trying to address and counter many widely propagated works, especially based on Iranian sources, that fix the appearance of the Azerbaijanis in the eleventh or twelfth century. Intellectuals' concern with the ethnic origins of the Azerbaijani people served as a way to affirm their

---

13. *Ädäbiyyat vä Injäsänät*, September 11, 1987, p. 6 (JPRS-UPA-88-002).

14. Nizammäddin Shämizadä, "Unudulmushlar Haggïnda Uvertura," *Ädäbiyyat vä Injäsänät*, September 18, 1987, pp. 1, 6.

15. Mahmud Ismaylov, *Ädäbiyyat vä Injäsänät*, July 15, 1988, quoted in Annette Bohr and Yasin Aslan, "Independent Azerbaijan, 1918–1920: Call to Reevaluate History of Former Nation-State," *RFE/RL* 377/88 (August 18, 1988), p. 1.

16. Näsib Näsibzadä, *Azärbayjan Demokratik Respublikasï*.

17. See, for instance, *Kommunist* (Baku), June 11, 1988, p. 2; and L. Polonskii, "Hamestnik Vozhdia," *Bakinskii rabochii*, June 15, 1988, p. 3.

18. *Kommunist* (Baku), June 11, 1988, p. 2.

separate identity.[19] Zumgud Quluzade stressed the need for more research on Caucasian Albania, which "could serve as valuable source for research by scholars who are occupied with the Albanian problem and the ethnic origins of the Azeri people."[20] Ziya Buniatov, who headed the Oriental Institute of the Azerbaijan Academy of Sciences, stressed in his writings the common origins of the residents of the Caucasus and Iranian Azerbaijan.[21] Interest in Azerbaijani name origins was also expressed, and in November 1986 an Onomastic Center was established as part of the Azerbaijan Pedagogical Institute to explore this subject.[22] A book on Azerbaijani name origins, published in 1986, claimed that the Azerbaijani language was formed in the fourth and fifth centuries, and not in the twelfth, "as is often wrongly claimed."[23]

The drive to preserve the status of the Azerbaijani language in the republic was one of the most central issues stressed in glasnost's initial period. In the Baku Communist Party daily, *Kommunist*, Y. Ryzayev wrote that "greater attention should be given to publishing more literature and recommendations in the Azeri language."[24] In addition, the head of the Azerbaijan Writers' Union, known as Anar, who was elected in 1987, stated that,

. . . the truth is that proper attention has not always been paid to the national languages. I appreciate and sympathize with the distress and alarm felt by my Russian fellow writers who campaign for the purity, preservation, and clarity of their language. But the concern of national writers, who are no less sensitive, must also be appreciated. After all, literature in these languages, its terminology and the sphere of its use are much more restricted. This also explains the alarm felt by the national intelligentsia concerning the fate of their languages.[25]

19.   See, for example, Aydïn Mämmädov, "Därin Köklär," *Kommunist* (Baku), May 15, 1984, p. 4; S. Mollazade, quoted in *Ädäbiyyat vä Injäsänät*, February 14, 1986, p. 8 (JPRS-UPS-86-023); Zümrüd Guluzade, "Elmi Tädgigatlarïn Näshri," *Ädäbiyyat vä Injäsänät*, November 7, 1986; Mirzä Bala, "Azärbayjan Tarikhinde Türk Albaniya," *Azärbayjan* 10 (1989), pp. 119–166; and A. S. Sumbatzade, *Azerbaidzhantsy- Etnogenez i formirovanie naroda* (Baku: Elm, 1990).

20.   Zümrüd Guluzade, "Elmi Tädgigatlarïn Näshri."

21.   See, for instance, Ziia M. Buniatov, ed., *Istoricheskaia geografiia Azerbaidzhana* (Baku: Elm, 1987).

22.   *Ädäbiyyat vä Injäsänät*, November 21, 1986 and November 28, 1986 (UPS-87-024).

23.   S. Mollazade on Azerbaijan toponymy, reviewed in *Ädäbiyyat vä Injäsänät*, February 14, 1986 (UPS-86-023).

24.   Y. Rzayev in *Kommunist* (Baku), April 2, 1986, p. 2.

25.   *Komsomol'skaia pravda*, October 7, 1987, p. 4.

The poet Bakhtiyar Vahabzade was one of the most vocal proponents of expanding the use of the Azerbaijani language in the republic. He suggested emulating Lithuania's new practice: pupils begin studying Russian only in grade three, rather than first grade, which was the practice in Azerbaijan at the time.[26] There was also open criticism of the compliance of Azerbaijanis with Russification efforts. In an article in *Azerbaijan Qenjleri*, Aydin Mammedov criticized Azerbaijanis who sent their children to Russian-language schools, and denounced the fact that much of the scientific terminology in Azerbaijani was taken from Russian.[27] In his article, he quoted Vahabzade: a person who does not know "his native language should not be provided with a job."[28]

In the early stages of glasnost, some academics stressed the need to teach Arabic and Persian in the republic. This apparently reflected their desire to reconnect with Muslim, though not necessarily religious, aspects of their identity and to communicate with the peoples around them. For instance, *Azerbayjan Muellimi*, the teachers' journal, pointed out that the Ministry of Education hoped to expand the number of schools teaching Persian and Arabic, "which are related to our republic's geographical situation and our people's history."[29]

One important debate, which revealed the different identities of the Azerbaijanis, was over the preferred alphabet for written Azerbaijani. Initially, many prominent historians and intellectuals advocated that the teaching of the Arabic alphabet be expanded in Soviet Azerbaijan and criticized the move to the Latin alphabet in 1924 and to Cyrillic in 1940. In an article in *Elm ve Heyat*, Ziya Buniatov singled out the elimination of the Arabic alphabet as one of the gravest blows imposed on Azerbaijani culture, and declared that it should be taught in the universities, possibly in high schools.[30] In contrast, Aziz Mirakhmedov, a candidate member of the Azerbaijan Soviet Socialist Republic Academy of Sciences, criticized the supplanting of the Latin alphabet by Cyrillic, claiming that the Latin alphabet had "met all the needs of the Azerbaijani language." Nevertheless, Mirakhmedov expressed support for the teaching of Arabic script, in

---

26. Bakhtiiar Vagabzade (Vahabzade), *Bakinskii rabochii*, November 10, 1988.

27. Aydïn Mämmädov, quoted in "Dil Äväzsiz Särvätdir," *Azärbayjan Qänjläri*, October 18, 1988, p. 2.

28. Ibid.

29. *Azärbayjan Muällimi*, August 12, 1987, p. 3. This journal often reflected the desire for unity with south Azerbaijan and for the establishment of links between Soviet Azerbaijan and the Muslim world.

30. Ziya Bünyatov, *Elm va Häyat*, No. 10 (1988), pp. 1–3.

order to communicate with Azerbaijanis in Iran. According to Mirakh-medov, the use of Arabic script would facilitate correspondence and exchange with "our brothers and relatives on the other side of the Araz river."[31]

In November 1988, protests were held in Azerbaijan. The two changes of alphabet that took place under the Soviets were one of the issues. Demonstrators complained that the change from Arabic to Latin and then to Cyrillic had meant that few could read Azerbaijani books printed early in the century, or "even the inscriptions on their grandfathers' gravestones."[32]

TRANSITION TO A MASS MOVEMENT

Toward the end of 1988, large groups of Azerbaijanis began to openly express support for Azerbaijani-based issues, such as the use of the Azerbaijani language in the republic and concern for co-ethnics abroad, and challenged the legitimacy of Soviet rule in the republic. These topics were no longer the sole domain of intellectual circles, and demonstrations and protests began to draw large crowds from diverse socioeconomic groups in Azerbaijan. From the second half of 1988, much of this activity was conducted under the leadership of the Popular Front of Azerbaijan (PFA).[33] The organization was formed as an umbrella group uniting individuals and groups of different political orientations under an agenda that: opposed any change in the republic's borders (chiefly the province of Nagorno-Karabagh); was concerned for Azerbaijanis living outside the republic; and supported the expansion of glasnost and perestroika and greater use of the Azerbaijani language in the republic. The PFA operated in a decentralized fashion, with branches forming throughout Soviet Azerbaijan.

In a major article published in November 1988, Babak Adalatli stated that the question of South Azerbaijan was one of the reasons that he and his colleagues established the PFA. (The Nagorno-Karabagh issue, discussed below, was another). Adalatli called for the enhancement of ties

31. Aziz Mirakhmedov, *Kommunist*, June 25, 1988, quoted in Yasin Aslan, "Azerbaijani Intellectuals Discuss Legacy of Alphabet Reforms," *Report on the USSR*, No. 71 (February 1, 1989), p. 7.

32. *Moscow News*, No. 49 (1988), quoted in William Reese, "The Role of the Religious Revival and Nationalism in Transcaucasia," *RFE/RL* 535/88 (December 5, 1988), p. 1.

33. The first public references to the organization appeared on Radio Baku, November 23, 1988. See also Baku Domestic Service in Azerbaijani, November 28, 1988 (FBIS-SOV-88-230).

with "Southern Azerbaijan" and proposed that the border be opened on certain days of the week for visits with relatives.[34]

Another organization, *Birlik* (Unity), began its political activity around the same time as the PFA, and championed most of the same political goals. Many of its founders and activists were Azerbaijani emigres from Iran, and its main goal was uniting both Azerbaijans under one state.

The Qizilbash Popular Front was also established in this period, on October 30, 1988. In contrast to the PFA, this group clearly stated that its main political goal was achieving sovereignty for Azerbaijan, and independence from the Soviet Union. The Qizilbash adopted an exceptional position and unequivocally called for South Azerbaijan to separate from Iran and join the north to form a united independent state.[35] The name *Qizilbash*—the main military force that assisted Shah Isma'il to establish the Safavid regime in Iran—illustrates the founders' emphasis on the Azerbaijanis in Iran.

One of the most important catalysts for the national movement's transformation into a mass movement in Azerbaijan was Armenia's drive to control the province of Nagorno-Karabagh. From mid-1987 throughout 1988, ethnic Armenian delegations from Nagorno-Karabagh visited Moscow with the aim of convincing officials to transfer jurisdiction over the province to Armenia. In February 1988, two Azerbaijanis were killed in direct clashes between Armenians and Azerbaijanis in Nagorno-Karabagh. This incident triggered intense eruptions of violence in the town of Sumgait, near Baku. On February 27–29, twenty-six Armenians and six Azerbaijanis were killed. These incidents led to the mass flight of Azerbaijanis from Armenia, and Armenians from Azerbaijan, creating immense refugee problems on both sides. The refugee situation made political action seem urgent. The failure of Baku to effectively solve the refugee problems evoked public criticism, and many Azerbaijanis joined the opposition to the Communist regime in Baku, and reinforced their identification as Azerbaijanis and their desire for self-rule. The Sumgait violence was a turning point in the self-identification of many Armenians throughout the region. However, many Azerbaijanis did not cast blame on themselves for the violence perpetrated against Armenians at Sumgait and related the Azerbaijani part in the events as the work of local hood-

34. Babak Adalatli, *Ädäbiyyat vä Injäsänät*, November 25, 1988, quoted in Mirza Mikhaeli, "Formation of Popular Front in Azerbaijan," *RFE/RL* 558/88, December 9, 1988, pp. 1–2.

35. See Leila Iunusova, "Pestraia palitra neformal'nykh dvizhenii v Azerbaidzhane," *Russkaia mysl'*, September 22, 1989, p. 7.

lums. This round of violence did not trigger much soul-searching or significantly affect Azerbaijani collective identity in this period.[36]

Throughout February 1988, large demonstrations in support of the Karabagh Armenians' drive to separate from Azerbaijan were held in Yerevan, Armenia. In March 1988, Gorbachev formed a government commission to investigate the problem and make recommendations about the future status of Nagorno-Karabagh. In May 1988, the heads of the Communist parties of Azerbaijan and Armenia were dismissed, allegedly due to their failure to contain the conflict.

Azerbaijani intellectuals responded to this perceived threat to Azerbaijani control of Nagorno-Karabagh. In February 1988, the poet Bakhtiyar Vahabzade and historian Suleiman Aliyarov coauthored an "Open Letter" rebutting Armenian claims to the disputed province.[37] This letter, which went far beyond confronting the Armenian claims, was also an important treatise on Azerbaijani identity. When collectives are both exploring their identity and in conflict with adjacent peoples, they frequently tend to stress the long roots of their continual primordial identity to boost their claim to rights and land. The authors presented their view that the Azerbaijanis and Karabagh Armenians both emanate from the same ethnic stock: the Caucasian Albanians.[38] They linked this ancient people and the contemporary Azerbaijanis. They drew a connection between the contemporary threat to their lands from Armenia and the 1828 division of Azerbaijan between Russia and Iran:

Since 1828 our people have been divided into two parts. In the Union of Soviet Socialist Republics, the Azerbaijani people were deservingly presented with their own national state, the Azerbaijan Soviet Socialist Republic. The part of our people living in southern Azerbaijan, subordinated to Iran, is deprived of every type of national rights. There, the Azerbaijan language and entire culture of more than ten million south Azerbaijanis are subject to ruthless repression. Under such conditions it is natural that the entire hope of the south Azerbaijan people lies in the Azerbaijan SSR.[39]

The purpose of this letter was to obtain political support for the Azerbaijanis in their conflict over Nagorno-Karabagh; it was not directly

---

36. See, for example, Ziia Buniatov, "Pochemu Sumgait? Situatsionnyi analiz," *El*, No. 19 (1989).

37. Bäkhtiyar Vahabzadä and Suleiman Äliyarov, "Redaksiya Pochtundan," *Azärbayjan*, No. 2 (1988). English translation, Audrey L. Alstadt, *Journal of the Institute of Muslim Minority Affairs*, Vol. 9, No. 2 (July 1988), pp. 429–434.

38. Ibid., p. 432.

39. Ibid., pp. 433–434.

related to the southern question. That the authors raised the issue anyway exemplifies the extent to which the question of Iranian Azerbaijan was important to some Azerbaijani intellectuals.

Many intellectuals stated that the threat from Armenia to what they viewed as Azerbaijani land contributed to their political awakening. In an appeal for support for Azerbaijan in the conflict over Nagorno-Karabagh, staff members of the Institute of Art and Architecture in Baku stated:

Azerbaijani intellectuals can by no means divest themselves of responsibility for the situation created. We blame ourselves for our passivity, for the lack of a clear social position during the period of decline.

Unfortunately, the consolidation of the healthy forces of Azerbaijani society occurred only after the events of Karabagh, but it did occur. And this inspires hope in us for the renewal of our society. In any case, the necessity for restructuring in all spheres of life both in Azerbaijan as well as in our whole country, has become evident to us.[40]

Toward the end of 1988, tension over the control of the province further intensified when the local Nagorno-Karabagh authorities, who were predominately ethnic Armenians, authorized the construction in the Topkhana forest of recreation facilities for an aluminum enterprise headquartered in Armenia. With this act, the Nagorno-Karabagh officials circumvented and directly challenged Baku's authority on behalf of an entity in Yerevan.[41] It is interesting to note that one of the arguments used by the Azerbaijanis in challenging the construction project in the Topkhana forest was that the park was "a national shrine," by virtue of the fact that a battle against Iranian forces had taken place there in the eighteenth century.[42]

For two weeks, starting on November 19, Azerbaijanis held mass protests in Baku. The demonstrations were directed against Yerevan, Moscow, and Baku, because it was felt that Moscow was acquiescing to Yerevan's demands and that Baku was not taking effective action. The Popular Front of Azerbaijan was instrumental in the organization of these rallies. At a mass meeting held on December 4 in Baku, which was forcibly dispersed by security forces, PFA activists were arrested. In the

---

40.   Institute of Art and Architecture in Baku, letter, printed in "Samizdat Armenia-Azerbaijan Conflict," *Central Asian Survey*, Vol. 7, No. 4 (1988), pp. 143–144.

41.   Saroyan, "The Karabagh Syndrome and Azerbaijani Politics," p. 20.

42.   Elizabeth Fuller, "The Nemat Panakhov Phenomenon—As Reflected in the Azerbaijani Press," *Report on the USSR*, No. 70 (January 31, 1989), p. 3.

beginning of December, strikes and protests followed throughout Azerbaijan.

Large demonstrations began at the end of November 1988 and continued throughout 1989; they later became known as the "Maydan" (Square) Movement. The demonstrators included people from various socio-economic strata in the republic. According to a main organizer of the demonstrators, a number of Azerbaijanis from Iran who were associated with the protest leaders attended the first demonstrations.[43]

In January 1989, the Soviet authorities removed Nagorno-Karabagh from Azerbaijan's control, and placed it under direct rule of Moscow. Most Azerbaijanis perceived Moscow as being pro-Armenian, so this strengthened their desire to distance themselves from Moscow.

During the period of glasnost, many groups in the Soviet Union made conflicting claims about the borders they shared. In all these conflicts, Moscow had adopted a policy in this period not to change these borders between republics. The exception was Nagorno-Karabagh, where Moscow was willing to consider a change of jurisdiction. Azerbaijanis were incensed that only with regard to "their territory" was Moscow willing to make a change. Azerbaijanis perceived the Moscow media and intellectual community as being completely biased against them in this conflict. They saw themselves as the victims in this conflict. They felt that Moscow's media generally portrayed them as threatening Muslims, while representing the Armenians as the victims. This perception of bias contributed to the Azerbaijani drive for self-rule, and further weakened the limited identity ties to Moscow. Describing these feelings, Bakhtiyar Vahabzade wrote:

I cannot imagine how long we will have to stand for the biased position of the central newspapers. How long will they write that we are wrong when we are right, and they are right when they are wrong, and how long will they remain silent about our just demands?[44]

As part of the cultural and political trend of distancing themselves from Moscow, many Azerbaijanis decided to drop the Russian name endings, such as "-ov" and "-sky," from their surnames, and replace them with more traditional Azerbaijani endings, such as "-li," "-lu," and "-oglu." In an article in *Azerbaijan Qenjleri*, Logman Nasibzade of the

---

43. Based on a colleague's conversation with a central PFA activist.

44. Bäkhtiyar Vahabzadä, "Yumrug Kimi Birleshmäli," *Ädäbiyyat vä Injäsänät*, October 13, 1989, p. 2.

Azerbaijan Pedagogical Institute in Baku expressed support for this trend.[45]

The threat to Azerbaijani territorial integrity posed by the Nagorno-Karabagh conflict influenced national unity in Soviet Azerbaijan in two ways. First, Azerbaijanis from different sectors of the population, many of whom had relatives in Nagorno-Karabagh and in Armenia who were directly affected by the strife, opposed any change in the status of the province and condemned Moscow's handling of the conflict. Both the opposition and the Communist establishment opposed any change in the status of the province and disagreed with the way Moscow was dealing with the conflict. A Baku Communist official stated:

Like the people of Azerbaijan, we too believe that Nagorno-Karabagh is a land which belonged to our people and will continue to belong to our people. This land has produced great poets, writers . . . scientists, and popular heroes in the past, and it will continue to do so in the future.[46]

Second, since most of the population felt that the Communist leadership of the republic blundered in the Nagorno-Karabagh issue and had failed to maintain control over the disputed province, many joined the opposition forces at this time. The intensification of the struggle over Nagorno-Karabagh also persuaded many Azerbaijanis to participate in political demonstrations and join Azerbaijani national political movements. This activity built on the attachment and the awareness of Azerbaijani identity, which existed prior to this perceived threat.

TURKIC IDENTITY

In 1989, signs of an emerging trend toward increased identity as Turks appeared in Soviet Azerbaijan. This trend was reflected in a shift in the alphabet debate. Before, many had called for readopting the Arabic script, but now most groups and leading figures advocated the adoption of the Latin alphabet.

Most of the major political organizations active in this period, such as the *Yeni Musavat* party, formally stressed the identity of the Azerbaijanis as Turks. The election of Abulfez Elchibey, who for many years had stressed the Turkish component of Azerbaijani identity, as president of

---

45. Loghman Näsibzadä, "Ad, Familiya, Täkhällus," *Azärbayjan Qänjläri*, February 21, 1989.

46. Niyazi Karagashli, Baku Domestic Service in Azerbaijani, November 28, 1988 (FBIS-SOV-88-230).

Azerbaijan in 1992, was a reaffirmation of support for this idea. He supported strong cultural identity as Turks, and also advocated close relations with the Republic of Turkey:

There is no need to debate the direction to be taken. We wish to follow the direction which will give us an opportunity to be Turks, Muslim, and modern. This idea is symbolized by the national flag we have adopted for the Turkish Republic of Democratic Azerbaijan.[47]

Elchibey made it clear that his approach was not Pan-Turkic and that he believed that each Turkic people must control its own political destiny:

Turkey is the window of all the Turkish peoples in Central Asia opening onto the Western world. . . . We believe that economic cooperation will form the basis of our relations with Turkey. Of course, this will lead to a political rapprochement. However, we do not have a pan-Turkic approach. Each side must own its own homeland and territory. The nations must always have the right to determine their own future. We do not want much from Turkey in this difficult struggle. Turkey's moral support will be enough for us. The Turkish Nation of Azerbaijan is strong enough to resolve its problems by itself.[48]

Many of the major PFA activists also emphasized the Turkic element of Azerbaijani identity. For example, Etibar Mamedov, who led at the time the more radical faction in the PFA, underscored both the secular and the Turkic aspects of Azerbaijani identity:[49]

There is not and cannot be any Islamic fundamentalism among us . . . Azerbaijanis want to be modern, to be real Turks and real Muslims . . . maintaining Eastern traditions but keeping what is progressive in Western society, without simply copying it, and set up a real democratic state.[50]

On August 15, 1989, demonstrators in Soviet Azerbaijan protesting Sofia's treatment of the Turkic minority in Bulgaria, forced the cancellation of a Bulgarian music concert in Baku. The protest was organized by the PFA. At the assembly, PFA leader Elchibey stated that the Turks of Azerbaijan were expressing their solidarity with the Turks of Bulgaria

---

47. Abulfez Elchibey, in an interview to *Günaydin* (Istanbul) in Turkish, September 3, 1989, p. 9 (FBIS-SOV-89-173).

48. Ibid.

49. Mamedov's faction formally broke off from the PFA in June 1991.

50. AFP in English, January 25, 1990 (FBIS-SOV-90-018).

through the protest.[51] At the same time, activists in Tabriz reportedly collected money for refugees of Turkic origin who had fled Bulgaria, showing their Turkic identity.[52] These actions may have been coordinated. A further expression of Azerbaijan's Turkic solidarity was Baku's decision to accept Meshketian Turk refugees who had fled Uzbekistan following the incidents of violence there. Some academic works that appeared in this period also highlighted the Turkic roots of the Azerbaijanis.[53]

PROGRESSING TOWARD INDEPENDENCE

In 1989, the Popular Front–led opposition in Azerbaijan became more aggressive in challenging the Communist-associated leadership of the republic and demanded that Baku retain control over Nagorno-Karabagh. At this time, it began to articulate the goal of sovereignty for Azerbaijan. The movement promoted the preservation of Azerbaijani culture and language and voiced concern for Azerbaijanis living outside the Republic, including those in Iran. In January and February 1989, PFA activists began circulating a draft of their political platform. In its final version, the platform stated that the name of the people of Azerbaijan is the "Azerbaijani Turks,"[54] stressing the Turkish component of Azerbaijani identity. It refrained from calling for the independence of Azerbaijan, advocating instead for "sovereignty within the USSR" yet demanding representation in the United Nations. Stressing its belief that Azerbaijani identity is tied to the Middle East, and the need to develop connections "in particular with the peoples who historically formed the cultural region of the Near and Middle East," the PFA program "supports decisive steps toward the development of understanding and cooperation with Islam." The program also emphasized the need to strengthen relations with the Azerbaijanis in Iran, calling for the "abolition of all political barriers to the development of cultural and economic ties with Southern Azerbaijan." The program states:

While recognizing the indisputable nature of the borders between the USSR and Iran, the PFA supports the restoration of the ethnic unity of Azerbaijanis living on both sides of the border. The Azerbaijani people should be recog-

---

51. Abulfez Elchibey, quoted in *Radio Liberty Report on the USSR*, Vol. 1, No. 34 (August 25, 1989), p. 31.

52. Anthony Hyman, "Soviet-Iranian Relations and the Two Azerbaijans," *Report on the USSR*, No. 19 (1990), p. 15.

53. See, for instance, Mirzä Bala, "Azärbayjan Tarikhinde Türk Albaniya," pp. 119–166.

54. Programme of the People's Front of Azerbaijan (Azerbaijani).

nized as a united whole. Economic, cultural and social ties between our divided nation should be restored. All obstacles to the creation of direct contacts (visits to relations and friends) should be abolished.[55]

In addition, it stated that "the PFA supports the broadening of international and cultural ties between Azerbaijanis living in the country and abroad, and considers it essential to create Azerbaijani cultural centers and schools for groups of Azerbaijanis living outside the republic."

The Communist leadership in Azerbaijan, which was affected by Moscow's progressive loss of central control and evidently hoped to preempt the growing support for the PFA, took the lead from the opposition and began to respond in 1989 to demands for increased local Azerbaijani control over the republic and the promotion of Azerbaijani culture. For instance, the official media in Baku announced in March 1989 that "taking into consideration the wish of the people, the Azerbaijan SSR Supreme Soviet Presidium has returned the names of Zhdanov Town and Zhdanov Rayon back to Beylaqan Town and Beylaqan Rayon."[56] In December 1989, the city of Kirovabad reverted to its ancient name, Ganja.

Many articles from all sectors of the Azerbaijani population appeared throughout 1989 demanding expanded use of the Azerbaijani language in the republic and legal guarantees for the upgrading of its status.[57] Other national movements active in the Soviet Union at this time made similar demands. In August 1989, responding to public demands, the Central Committee of the Communist Party of Azerbaijan adopted a decision on measures for "guaranteeing the more active functioning of the Azerbaijani language as a state language in the republic."[58]

From mid-1989, the PFA-led opposition became more aggressive in the struggle over Nagorno-Karabagh. This also increased grassroots support for its political movement and goals. On July 29, and on August 5 and 9, large demonstrations were held in Baku to call attention to the plight of the Azerbaijanis in Nagorno-Karabagh. On August 12, the PFA led a demonstration in Baku that was attended by 200,000 Azerbaijanis.

55. Ibid., p. 9.

56. Baku Domestic Service in Azerbaijani, March 18, 1989 (FBIS-SOV-89-057).

57. See, for example, M. Shiräliyev, "Taleyä Biqanä Olmazlar," *Kommunist* (Baku), January 17, 1989, p. 4; "Häyatdan Qälän Problemlär," *Azärbayjan Muällimi*, January 4, 1989, p. 2; Zulfugar Ähmädzadä, "Ana Dili—Anamïzïn Dili," *Kommunist* (Baku), January 25, 1989, pp. 2–3; "Khalgïn vä Dilin Taleyi Birdir," *Ädäbiyyat vä Injäsänät*, January 27, 1989, pp. 1, 6; and *Bakinskii rabochii*, February 9, 1989, p. 3.

58. Moscow Domestic Service in Russian, August 24, 1989 (FBIS-SOV-89-167).

In mid-August, the opposition-led activities shifted into higher gear, and on August 14, a one-day warning strike involving workers from more than sixty workplaces was held in Baku. Among the strikers' demands was the return to Baku of the administration of Nagorno-Karabagh. That evening, 500,000 protesters gathered for a demonstration. On August 19, another demonstration drew over half a million participants. Events escalated further on August 21–22, when the PFA organized another workers' strike in Baku and Sumgait, involving employees from 101 enterprises.[59] The government failed to respond to their demands, and the PFA called for demonstrations throughout the republic on September 2 and threatened that if its demands were not met, it would initiate a week-long strike on September 4. In addition to the return to Baku of the direct administration of Nagorno-Karabagh, the PFA also sought recognition as a legal political organization and agreement by the Communist establishment in Baku to work for expanded sovereignty of the republic.

On September 2, demonstrations were held throughout Azerbaijan, most of them attended by over 1,000 protesters, and on September 4, a country-wide strike was held. Almost all industries, including defense and oil refining, participated in the strike.[60] Among the most important participants were the railroad workers; traffic throughout the North Caucasus and transport to Armenia was disrupted.[61] By organizing strikes involving workers in most of the republic's sectors, the PFA demonstrated its extensive organizational ability and strength and the scope of its grassroots support.

An interesting change appeared in the symbols used at the protests that took place. Throughout fall 1989, the flag of the Azerbaijan SSR, which had been flown at protests the preceding year, was replaced by the tricolor flag of the short-lived Azerbaijan Democratic Republic, linking the demonstrators to the independent, pre-Soviet state from 1918–20.

Yet, the PFA's attitude toward full independence was ambiguous throughout the intense political activity of fall 1989. In its formal statements, the PFA consistently claimed that its goal was to achieve sovereignty within the framework of the Soviet Union. Yet they described "sovereignty" as including the right to issue passports, conclude interna-

---

59.   Leila Iunusova, "End of the Ice Age: Azerbaijan, August-September 1989," *Caucasus and Central Asia Chronicle*, Vol. 8, No. 6 (1989), p. 10.

60.   Ibid. The only exceptions were essential services, health care, and the oil wells.

61.   Eighty-five percent of all transport to and from Armenia passed along Azerbaijan railways.

tional treaties, and send representatives to international organizations. Moscow's failure to acquiesce to the Azerbaijani demands for the return of control over Nagorno-Karabagh prompted the PFA activists to expand their concept of sovereignty to include the right to veto any legislation emanating from the Soviet capital.

On September 10, 1989, the PFA announced that it would halt the strikes and protests after an agreement had been reached with the republic's leadership: It included formal recognition of the movement and the convening of a parliamentary session to discuss the expansion of the republic's political and economic sovereignty.

On September 23, the parliament of Soviet Azerbaijan formally declared the republic "sovereign within the USSR." The government, though, delayed the publication of the content of the declaration of sovereignty until October 5. The formal statement asserted that "the competence of Azerbaijan is limited only in matters which have voluntarily been delegated by the republic itself to the USSR," that it "retains for itself the right to withdraw freely from the USSR," and that it "has the right to enter into direct relations with foreign states."[62] The Nagorno-Karabagh conflict's impact on the declaration was clear: It emphasized "the sovereignty of Azerbaijan extends over all its territory, including the Nakhchivan Autonomous Republic and the Nagorno-Karabagh Autonomous Oblast that are inalienable parts of the union republic. The territory of the republic, declared, cannot be changed without Azerbaijani's agreement, expressed in a referendum of the whole population conducted by a decision of the Supreme Soviet. Frontiers with other union republics can be changed only by mutual agreement."[63] The law stated that "the land, its soils, forests, waters, and other natural resources are national riches and the property of the republic, and belong to its people," and that the Azerbaijani language is declared the state language. However, the free use and development of Russian and other languages used by the population is ensured.[64]

Escalation of Confrontation

Despite the PFA's recognition by the authorities in Baku and the formal declaration of the republic's sovereignty, confrontation between the Azerbaijani PFA-led opposition and the communist establishment contin-

---

62. Moscow Television Service in Russian, October 5, 1989 (FBIS-SOV-89-193).

63. Ibid.

64. Ibid.

ued through the fall and winter of 1989. Crippling strikes and demonstrations demanding true sovereignty and the return of Nagorno-Karabagh to Azerbaijani rule persisted through the end of 1989. Violent confrontations surged in a number of locations between Armenians and Azerbaijanis; the worst was on the weekend of January 13–14, 1990 in Baku, which left up to ninety Armenians and a number of Azerbaijanis dead.[65]

Debates continued within the PFA over the directions of its policies. In December 1989, some of the major activists left after a number of clashes with the main PFA leadership. These included Leila Yunosova and Zardusht Alizade, who joined forces with the Social Democratic Party of Azerbaijan.

BORDER INCIDENTS AND 'BLACK JANUARY'

In the beginning of December 1989, the issue of connections and unity with the Azerbaijanis in Iran became a focal point of PFA activity. Different branches of the decentralized PFA adopted varying stances regarding the question of how to improve relations between the Azerbaijanis. Some activists felt that ties to the Azerbaijanis in Iran should be strengthened by expanding direct cultural and trade links, while others adopted a more militant approach and sought to directly confront Iran over control of south Azerbaijan.[66]

In early December 1989, local PFA activists gathered along the frontier with residents of towns and villages of Nakhchivan, a region near the border between the Soviet Union and Iran. During the first two weeks of December, the protesters held ongoing rallies at the border, lit bonfires, and attempted to communicate with the Azerbaijanis on the other side of the border. Many of them called for "the unity of Northern and Southern Azerbaijan." The atmosphere was somewhat party-like. The demonstrators were particularly active on December 12, the date that symbolizes for many Azerbaijanis the independence of Iranian Azerbaijan. According to some journalists, on December 12 the PFA's Nakhchivan chapter submitted an ultimatum to the border guards demanding that obstacles to free travel be removed by December 31, or the demonstrators would destroy the border installations.

Throughout December, the number of demonstrators along the border gradually grew to several thousand. On December 31, the tone of the

---

65. The violence against the Baku Armenians led to their mass exodus from the city. In Armenian minds, "Black January" refers to these violent events, while in Azerbaijan the term refers to the subsequent violence by Moscow against the Azerbaijanis.

66. Interview with PFA activist Leila Iunusova in AFP (Paris), January 2, 1990 (FBIS-SOV-001).

demonstrations changed; protesters began to burn and tear down several frontier stations and sections of the fence that divided the Soviet Union and Iran in a symbolic attempt to unite the two Azerbaijans.

A participant in the demonstrations explained to an *Izvestiia* reporter his motivations for participating in the actions at the border:

For decades barbed wire has cut us off from our homeland—south Azerbaijan—which is situated on Iranian territory. For decades we have been unable to see our relatives. And, you know, many people have sisters and brothers on the other side of the Araz. We wish the border troops no ill, but why have they forbidden us to walk on our land and make use of it—after all, there beyond the barbed wire there are 17,000 hectares of land, land which our stony Nakhchivan so lacks! It has been extremely difficult for us to visit our forebears' graves and see our ancient monuments—they too, you see, are also in the border strip.[67]

At the same time that the actions at the border were intensifying, more than 150,000 protesters gathered in Baku on January 4, 1990, demanding the opening of the border between Azerbaijan in Iran in the area of Nakhichivan, and expressing solidarity with the demonstrators at the border. A large number of Soviet Azerbaijanis illegally crossed the border into Iran.[68]

According to one PFA activist, the movement's activists in Baku supported and encouraged the actions taking place at the border.[69] A group of Baku activists sent a letter in support of these actions to the Moscow Politburo and the Presidium of the Supreme Soviet. They compared the partition of Azerbaijan in 1828 to the division of Vietnam and Korea, and called for the "relaxation of the frontier regulations in existence between the two parts of our homeland."[70] Some PFA activists compared the Soviet-Iranian frontier with the Berlin Wall, which had just been torn down.[71]

Iran and the Soviet Union agreed to allow a number of direct meetings between residents on both sides, evidently to "release steam." On January 7, 1990, a meeting was held between "friends and relatives,"

67.   *Izvestiia* (Moscow), January 9, 1990, p. 1, 6.

68.   AFP (Paris), January 5, 1990 (FBIS-SOV-90-004).

69.   Based on an interview with a senior PFA activist.

70.   "Ob istoricheskom edinstve severnoi i iuzhnoi chastei Azerbaidzhana," *Azerbaidzhan* 1, No. 11 (1990) quoted in Swietochowski, *Russia and Azerbaijan: A Borderland in Transition*, p. 203.

71.   Reuters (Moscow), December 30, 1989; and Samad Oghlu, *Washington Post*, January 3, 1990.

from Soviet and Iranian Azerbaijan.[72] According to the Tehran International broadcasting service, the participants "talked for four hours with relatives in Iran who had gathered at the border in the piercing cold," and one of them delivered a speech in which he praised Ayatollah Khomeini and stated that the Soviet Azerbaijanis want to spend the upcoming Novruz holiday with their relatives in Iran "and have free economic and cultural exchanges."[73] Some Azerbaijanis crossed the freezing waters of the Araz river that marks the border in order to participate in the encounters that were taking place on the Iranian side.

Despite the organized meetings, demonstrations and illegal border crossings continued; many traversed the river by swimming or in small boats. IRNA reported that the Iranian Azerbaijanis went to the border area and joined the Soviet Azerbaijanis: "Iranian border residents also gathered on the southern bank of the river and responded to the enthusiasm of the Soviet Muslims."[74]

According to the Iranian Press, on January 12, for instance, 1,000 Soviet Azerbaijanis gathered at the border, many of them chanting Islamic prayers. They "sent messages in Azeri to their relatives across the Aras River in Iran" and "roughly the same number of people of this border town stood on the Iranian side of the river, cheering and responding to their brethren from the Soviet Union."[75] An Iranian reporter described the interaction between the Azerbaijanis from both sides of the border:

They also exchanged messages with their Iranian relatives standing on the other side of the river. The information included addresses, phone numbers and identities, written on scraps of paper and wrapped around small stones which were thrown across the river. Those who managed to trace their relatives after more than fifty years were so overcome by emotion, that they beat their chests and heads out of joy.[76]

It is quite significant that despite over seventy years of separation, many Azerbaijanis had information about their relatives from the other side of the border.

---

72. Baku Domestic Radio Service in Azerbaijani, January 8, 1990 (FBIS-SOV-90-006); and Tehran International Service in Arabic, January 8, 1990 (FBIS-SOV-90-007).

73. Ibid.

74. IRNA (the official Iranian news agency) in English, January 7, 1990.

75. IRNA in English, January 13, 1990.

76. IRNA in English, January 14, 1990.

Many Iranian Azerbaijanis who went to the border area to meet their co-ethnics greeted them with fruit and rice and other symbols of celebration. The atmosphere at the frontier was often very emotional and festive. IRNA reported that "people on the Iranian side of the river also gathered together and cheerfully began responding to the Soviet Azeris, with whom many share family ties."[77] According to IRNA, some Azerbaijanis from Iran also crossed into Soviet Azerbaijan.[78]

A number of Iranian media reports acknowledged the common background of the Azerbaijanis from both sides of the Araz River. For example, one stated that "the people of Azarbayjan Province of Iran and its corresponding Soviet republic speak the same language and share the same religion and culture."[79] Initially, Iran seemed to take a positive view toward the Soviet Azerbaijani desire for ties with co-ethnics in Iran, considering this an opportunity for expanding Iranian influence among the Soviet Muslims.[80] The international version of the Iranian newspaper *Keyhan Havai* began publishing an Azerbaijani-language section, evidently hoping to extend their influence among the Soviet Azerbaijanis during this turbulent period.

On January 13, Iranian Foreign Minister Ali Akbar Velayati went to Tabriz to establish procedures for receiving visitors in cooperation with the local authorities in the province. Velayati proclaimed that "Iran has no difficulty in receiving Muslims from the Soviet republic of Azerbaijan who want to come to the Islamic Republic to visit its holy shrines, or relatives."[81] An editorial in *Tehran Times* endorsed the idea of an agreement on free border crossings that would "help alleviate the seething emotions of people who wish to see their ancestral land and visit long lost relatives," concluding that this could "only enhance the cultural relations between the two neighbors."[82]

In response to the demands of the demonstrators, officials from the Soviet Foreign Ministry and from Iran held a number of meetings in January 1990 to determine procedures that would simplify the process of meetings between Soviet Azerbaijanis and their relatives in Iran. In the meantime, both legal and illegal crossings continued throughout January

---

77. Ibid.

78. IRNA, January 27, 1990 (FBIS-NES-90-019).

79. IRNA in English, January 6, 1990.

80. See, for instance, *Jomhuri-ye Eslami*, January 22, 1990, pp. 1, 2 (FBIS-NES-90-022).

81. IRNA in English, January 13, 1990.

82. *Tehran Times*, January 6, 1990, pp. 2, 7.

1990, reaching a peak on January 18, when more than 5,000 Soviet Azerbaijanis crossed the border into Iran.[83] The local government of East Azerbaijan Province in Iran organized accommodations for many of the arrivals and a "special headquarters" was established by the local government for this purpose.[84] According to the Iranian press, some of the visiting Azerbaijanis "took up lodging in their relatives' houses."[85]

Throughout December 1989 and January 1990, the Soviet border guards were extremely mild and restrained, especially considering that the actions were one of the most brazen challenges to Soviet authority in the Gorbachev era. There is some indication that the border guards had been ordered to respond with moderation, so that Moscow could take advantage of these occurrences.

On the evening of January 19, Soviet troops began a massive operation in Azerbaijan. On entering Baku on January 20, Moscow declared a state of emergency in the republic. During the military takeover, 132 Azerbaijanis were killed, most of them bystanders. Moscow's military capture and occupation of Baku caused immediate public outcries, and both the PFA and the communist government declared a period of mourning throughout the republic.

"Black January," as the Soviet military takeover became known, had a profound effect on the rate at which Azerbaijani national identity was adopted in the republic, and dramatically accelerated the support for independence. Many Azerbaijanis rejected Russian culture and language. After this incident, there seemed to be a further rise in the attraction to Turkism as part of the Azerbaijani identity. One of the first responses was growth in the trend of replacing Russian name endings with Turkic ones. Support for supplanting the Cyrillic alphabet with the Latin now became extensive.[86]

The Soviet military takeover sparked a major crossing of Azerbaijanis into Iran. An Iranian official reported that on January 20–21, over 20,000 Soviet Azerbaijanis crossed the border "to visit relatives in Iran."[87]

Forty days after the "Black January" operation, a mourning day was observed throughout Soviet Azerbaijan. In Baku, a million people report-

---

83. IRNA in English, January 19, 1990.

84. IRNA in English, January 20, 1990.

85. IRNA in English, January 19, 1990.

86. In contrast, articles against the proposed change appeared in the Iranian *Varliq*, instead advocating the adoption of the Arabic alphabet. See Abas'Ali Javadi, *Varliq* (July–September 1991), pp. 88–96.

87. IRNA in English, January 21, 1990.

edly participated in public ceremonies to mark the events.[88] After the "Black January" events, opposition groups became more aggressive in their demands for full independence. Even the official bodies of the republic began to work toward achieving independence from Moscow. For the first time, on May 28, 1990, the anniversary of the Azerbaijan Democratic Republic was officially celebrated with the flags and symbols of the defunct republic officially in place of those of the communist era. The platform of the Azerbaijan Communist Party submitted at its June conference now asserted the goal of achieving independence.[89]

Nevertheless, until Moscow's power clearly began to crumble, it was difficult for most of the Azerbaijanis in the Soviet Union to believe that full-scale independence was attainable. In contrast to their neighbors in the Caucasus in Georgia and Armenia, the majority of the Soviet Azerbaijanis participated in and approved Gorbachev's March 1991 referendum on preserving the union. In the autonomous republic of Nakhchivan, however, most of the population boycotted the referendum. As in the other Soviet republics, the drive toward independence was greatly accelerated by the progressive breakdown of Soviet power throughout 1990 and 1991, and especially by the failed coup attempt in August 1991 and the subsequent decline toward the fall of the Soviet Union.

During the annual conference of the PFA in June 1991, the movement officially split into two groups: the national-patriots, headed by Etibar Mamedov, and the liberal-democrats, commonly known as the Radicals and the Democrats. One of the main issues that divided the camps was the relationship between Azerbaijani ethnic identity and the identity of the republic. They were also split over the issue of the appropriate means of achieving independence.

Following the failed coup attempt against Gorbachev in August 1991, the Azerbaijan Communist Party declared itself independent of the Communist Party of the Soviet Union. On September 14, 1991, the Azerbaijan Communist Party disbanded, and on October 18 the Azerbaijani parliament unanimously adopted the draft law "On the Restoration of State Independence of the Azerbaijan Republic." According to this act, Azerbaijan was declared the legal successor of the Azerbaijani Democratic Republic of May 1918–April 1920. The law was formally approved on November 7, 1991. After the fall of the Soviet Union, independence of the

---

88. AFP, March 1990 (FBIS-SOV-90-043), and confirmed by PFA activists.

89. Moscow TASS in English, June 8, 1990.

republic was ratified by 95 percent of the voters in a referendum on December 29, 1991.

Oppression in Iran

In contrast to the increasing leniency of the political atmosphere in the Soviet Union, from 1983 the political surroundings in Iran grew more and more oppressive, and severely limited open expressions of Azerbaijani collective identity. Despite the constraints, Azerbaijani intellectuals continued to explore and express their identity, often in poetry and other art forms, although most were not published in this period.

THE IMPACT OF THE IRAN-IRAQ WAR ON AZERBAIJANI IDENTITY

The Iran-Iraq War affected the development of Azerbaijani identity in Iran in a number of ways. The major Azerbaijani cities in Iran, especially Tabriz and Urmiya, were frequently bombarded during the war, although they were not occupied by Iraqi forces; there was little opportunity for political and cultural activity. For some, especially villagers, induction into the armed services in the war provided their first intensive contact with Persians, as they often trained in predominantly Persian cities before going to the front.[90] This interaction made some realize how different they were and made them aware of their minority status in Iran. Some recruits were the butt of frequent jokes about their accents in Persian and their ethnic origin, and this discrimination reinforced in some their identity as Azerbaijanis and as Turks. In contrast, it has been claimed that participating in the war strengthened some Azerbaijanis' connection to the regime and to Iran.[91]

To generate support for the war effort, the Islamic Republic at times reverted to Iranian nationalist rhetoric. Iranians were now asked "to die for their country," not just for Islam. This provoked some Azerbaijanis to question what the meaning of "country" was for them. A number of Azerbaijanis recounted how relatives would often openly curse Khomeini and the regime at funerals of Azerbaijanis who were killed during

90. According to Cottam, in the Pahlavi period the Azerbaijani garrisons were composed mostly of recruits and officers from Azerbaijan, primarily because of the language difficulties recruits would face if they served outside Azerbaijan and the expense of transport. See Cottam, *Nationalism in Iran: Updated Through 1978*, p. 130.

91. This assertion is made in H. E. Chehabi, "Ardabil Becomes a Province: Center-Periphery Relations in Iran," *International Journal of Middle East Studies*, Vol. 29 (1997), p. 235.

the war.[92] Nevertheless, many Azerbaijanis still supported the regime at this time, and it is difficult to assess the relative sizes of these two groups.

INTEREST IN AZERBAIJANI LANGUAGE AND LITERATURE

During the war, few works in Azerbaijani were published in Iran, but toward the end of the war and in the period of relative political relaxation that followed, a number of volumes of Azerbaijani poetry and works on the Azerbaijani language did appear. This indicates that research and writing took place during the war, while publication was probably delayed until the political climate was more favorable.

In 1987, the Azerbaijani writer Reza Baraheni received permission to publish his novel, *The Mysteries of My Land*. Written in Persian, the narrative opens on Savalan mountain, which is symbolic of the beauty of the land of Azerbaijan, and ends in Tehran. The land that the author refers to is both Azerbaijan and the country of Iran. For him, the novel symbolizes the dichotomy of identity experienced by many Azerbaijani-Iranians: pride in their birthplace and native language, but also a sense of belonging to the culture of Tehran and Iran. This novel was attacked several times by the regime, and one official criticism was that it represents a form of Azerbaijani "nationalism."

Among the major poetic works published in the Azerbaijani language in Iran in this period is *Edebiyyat Ujaghi*.[93] An anthology of Azerbaijani poetry, it is organized geographically by the poets' places of origin in the Azerbaijan provinces. In 1989, Mohammad Dayhim published a collection of mostly contemporary Azerbaijani poems, some of which were written in the traditional Azerbaijani folk style or as folk stories.[94]

In the mid-1980s, many Iranian Azerbaijani poets continued to produce Azerbaijani-language poems, although few were officially published in Iran. Some of these poems discussed themes that were also being aired by intellectuals in Soviet Azerbaijan. The most important was the use and status of the Azerbaijani language. In his "Mohabbat Mahnisi" ("Love Song"), the poet Barez wrote about his mother tongue:

Never do the tears in my eyes get dry
Always is tumultuous my fortune,
When I meet brother shepherd in the mountain,

---

92.   Based on conversations with Azerbaijanis who were living in Iran at the time.

93.   Yayda Shaida, *Edebiyyat Ujaghi* (Tabriz, 1987).

94.   Mohammad Dayhim, *Tazkireh-ye Shu'ara-ye Azerbaijan*, four volumes (Tabriz, 1989), quoted in Javadi, "Research Note: Azeri Publications in Iran," p. 87.

I firmly hold truth and honesty in my hands
'Barez'! I am infatuated with my beloved,
That which is my true culture, my mother tongue,
When I have a friend's hand in my hands,
It is as though with the entire nation I shake hands.[95]

The poet Heydar Abbasi, who writes under the pen name Barishmaz, published a number of literary works in the mid and late 1980s.[96] According to two Tabriz University scholars, these works are a reflection of Azerbaijani thought and folklore: they "show the poet's full cognizance of Azerbaijani folklore, and it is because of this knowledge that his verse is replete with fascinating metaphors and maxims representing the common people's beliefs."[97]

In 1991, a volume of Azerbaijani poetry, *Dinlah Mani*, was published in Iran using a revised Persian alphabet that included markings for the different Turkic vowel sounds.[98] The book opens with a thorough explanation of the system of vowel markings used by the author, which were based on the Latin character representation of the Azerbaijani-language vowels. The effort to produce a revised version of Azerbaijani in Arabic script demonstrates that Azerbaijani scholars in Iran were interested in the evolution of their language and sought to adapt it so that it could be read by more people.

Many Azerbaijani poems written in Iran in the mid-1980s refer to the geography and the historical sites that have symbolic meaning for the Azerbaijanis, such as Mount Savalan and the citadel in Tabriz, known as the Ark.[99] In addition, many poems published at this time refer to "pain" and "dryness" in the mouth, which is apparently an allegorical reference to the inability to use one's mother tongue.[100]

---

95. Barez, "Mohabbet Mahnisi," unpublished poem, referred to in Hariri-Akbari and Aazbdaftari, "A Brief Review of Contemporary Azerbaijani Poetry," *Critique* (Fall 1997, No. 11), p. 101.

96. Barishmaz (Heydar Abbasi), *Naghmeh Daghi va Estimar* (Tabriz: Nashr-e Talash, 1984–85); *Chaghirilmamish Qonaqlar* (Tabriz: Ketabforushi Laleh, 1984–86); and *Oudomlu Dirak* (Tabriz: Chap-e Shafaq, 1988–89).

97. Hariri-Akbari and Aazbdaftari, "A Brief Review of Contemporary Azerbaijani Poetry," p. 103.

98. Aziz Muhsini, *Dinlah Mani* (1991).

99. See, for instance, Naser Merqati, "Yad Torpaghim," and Mohammad Ali Nahavandi, "Sultan Savalan," both quoted in Hariri-Akbari and Aazbdaftari, "A Brief Review of Contemporary Azerbaijani Poetry," p. 110, 114.

100. See, for instance, Sonmez, "Manizlamisham," *Varliq*, Nos. 73–74 (May–July

Some Azerbaijani poets published works outside Iran criticizing the oppression of their culture. One of these poets, Piruz Dilanchi, emigrated from Iran, settling in Baku. In 1987, his poem "Dumanli Vetenden Guneshli Vetene" ("From the Foggy Fatherland to the Sunny Fatherland") was published in Baku's *Ädäbiyyat vä Injäsänät*.[101]

Many grammars and dictionaries of the Azerbaijani language were published in Iran toward the end of the 1980s and beginning of the 1990s. Behzad Behzadi, who published an Azerbaijani-Persian dictionary in 1990, wrote that he believes "that good dictionaries will facilitate the development of the Azeri language and hopes that his work has further watered the blossoming branch of Azerbaijani language."[102] Other Azerbaijani dictionaries such as *Azeri Turkcensinde Benzer Sozcukler*, which contains a section on Azerbaijani grammar, also appeared at this time in Iran.[103]

After the conclusion of the Iran-Iraq War, there were some open calls for expanding the use of the Azerbaijani language in Iran. In an article entitled "Some Suggestions for the Strengthening of the Azeri Language," which appeared in *Keyhan* in June 1988, the author proposed a number of ideas for augmenting the use of Azerbaijani in Iran:

Attention to the language, literature and culture of Azerbaijan is of great importance. Taking into consideration that Iran's Radio and TV Authority is the largest propaganda institution of the Islamic Revolution, it is proposed that this organization, with the permission of the Supreme Council of the Cultural Revolution, conduct activities for the development of the Azerbaijani language, for instance establishing a department in this language in the university, creating of an academy of the language, publishing a newspaper and magazine in Azeri. . . .

The establishment of an Azeri newspaper and magazine under the guidance of the above-mentioned academy will be very useful for the development of local Azeri culture, is a reflection of local events, to propagandize the achievements of the Islamic Revolution, and for the cultural revival of the Azerbaijani people.

. . . Iran Radio and TV Authority . . . must do everything possible to take into consideration that there are in Iran different origins and different lan-

---

1985), p. 65, referred to in Hariri-Akbari and Aazbdaftari, "A Brief Review of Contemporary Azerbaijani Poetry," p. 98.

101.   Piruz Dilänchi, "Dumanli Vätändän Qunäshli Vätänë," *Ädäbiyyat vä Injäsänät*, September 18, 1987, p. 8.

102.   The dictionary is Behzad Behzadi, *Azarbayjani-Farcha Sözlük* (Tehran, 1990). This quote is taken from Javadi, "Research Note: Azeri Publications in Iran," p. 86.

103.   ʿAli Ismaʿil Firuz, *Azeri Türkcensinde Benzer Sözcükler* (Tehran, 1989).

guages and conducting propagandist activities in such languages is very important and more effective.[104]

The author also advocated expanding local Azerbaijani language broadcasting in the Azerbaijani provinces.

Many Azerbaijanis wanted to view television broadcasts in their native language. An interviewee recounted that in this period it was very common for Azerbaijanis to gather in homes that had satellite dishes and watch television broadcasts from Baku. Often twenty or so people would watch together, often giving these gatherings a festive atmosphere.

Many of the main political clerics of Azerbaijani origin continued to speak openly in Azerbaijani, especially when discussing the events that occurred in Soviet Azerbaijan in the beginning of the 1990s.[105] These clerics, such as Ayatollah Musavi-Ardebili, clearly possessed strong Islamic and Iranian identity. However, their concept of Iranian identity was not equated with Persian identity, and they felt—often to the chagrin of their Persian associates—that as Iranians they could openly speak Azerbaijani. Ayatollah Musavi-Ardebeli reportedly helped facilitate the invitation of Azerbaijani cultural figures from Baku to Iran. The public use of their native language by Azerbaijani members of the ruling elite continued to give many of their co-ethnics the feeling that its use was legitimate. On January 24, 1990, two deputies addressed the Majlis (parliament) in Azerbaijani, in speeches that condemned the "Black January" events and expressed sympathy with the Azerbaijanis killed in Baku. This drew strong condemnation in Tehran. An editorial in *Ettela'at* entitled "Speech in Azeri?" declared:

If we accept deputies being authorized to speak in other languages at the Islamic Majlis as a norm, then there will be no end to this. For example, deputies from the Arabic-speaking areas will address the oppressed people of the occupied areas in Arabic, Kurdish deputies will speak in Kurdish, and so on. This attitude is objectionable from the political point of view, as well as with regard to national unity. It is also opposed to the Constitution of the Islamic Republic of Iran.[106]

---

104. "Chand Pishnahad Bara-ye Taqviyat-e Zaban-e Azeri," *Keyhan*, June 15, 1988, p. 2.

105. In some of his Friday sermons in January 1990, at the end of his presentations in Persian, Ayatollah Musavi-Ardebeli stated that instead of giving a sermon in Arabic, he would speak in Azerbaijani. At times during the Azerbaijani sermons, he addressed the Azerbaijanis in the Soviet Union, expressing sympathy with their plight.

106. *Ettela'at*, January 24, 1990, p. 2.

In his comments on the "Black January" events in Baku to the Majlis, the representative from Shabestar in East Azerbaijan Province raised grievances about the government's policy of economic discrimination toward the province:

The Province of Azerbaijan was a target of the disfavor of the tyrant.[107] The conditions resulting from the war over the past ten years and after the revolution did not lead to any significant steps being taken to eradicate deprivation in the province. An examination of the available statistics reveals that this province has lower than average standards in many respects in terms of resources, and even in some areas such as literacy, industry, employment, mines, and roads, it is at the bottom, but it is first in terms of providing migrants. Now, considering the goals of the Five-Year Plan, we expect that by ratifying and allocating the necessary funds, special attention will be paid to eradicating deprivation from this province, so that at the end of the Five-Year Plan it shall enjoy at least the conditions that exist in today's thriving provinces.[108]

By discussing the unrest in Baku while condemning Tehran's policies toward the province, the speaker could have been hinting that the continuation of these policies could led to turmoil in East Azerbaijan as well.

Ties between the Azerbaijanis

From the mid-1980s until the independence of the Republic of Azerbaijan in December 1991, Soviet Azerbaijanis frequently expressed concern and support for their co-ethnics in Armenia, Georgia, and Iran. This identification with brethren outside the republic reflects an ethnically based sense of identity as Azerbaijanis that goes beyond their territorially based identity within the borders of the republic.

Cultural figures as well as political organizations expressed a desire for increased ties and even unity with their co-ethnics in Iran, some even calling for the independence of south Azerbaijan. Though their activities were strictly limited under the political constraints that were imposed in Iran from 1983, some Iranian Azerbaijani writers and cultural figures continued to engage in a cultural dialogue with their co-ethnics in Soviet Azerbaijan, and some published their works in Baku. Direct cultural and economic cooperation was established and developed between the local government of East Azerbaijan Province in Iran and Soviet Azerbaijan in the late 1980s and early 1990s.

---

107. The "tyrant" is a reference to Mohammad Reza Shah of Iran.

108. Hasan Aminlu, *Resalat*, January 29, 1990, p. 5.

In mid-1983, some articles attacking the Islamic Republic's restrictions on Azerbaijani culture and language began to appear in Baku's press. By 1984, a significant change occurred in the way the Soviet Azerbaijani press depicted the Iranian Revolution, and in 1984 there was an upsurge in the number of articles in the Soviet Azerbaijani press attacking the limitations imposed by the regime in Iran on the Azerbaijani minority there. Mirza Ibrahimov wrote:

Recently bad news has come from Iran once again. Black clouds are gathering on the horizon, reaction has spread its wings, progressive forces are under fire, writers and poets who sing of patriotism, even those composing lyric verses on the love, truth, and faithfulness of the human heart are being persecuted. Why? Because they write in the mother tongue—in Azeri.[109]

Many articles condemned the severe restrictions on the Azerbaijanis' ability to study in their native language and to learn about its literature. In August 1985, *Ädäbiyyat vä Injäsänät* carried an article which maintained that "at Tabriz University teachers have been categorically forbidden to give their students any information about modern Azerbaijani literature," and condemning the fact that writers and poets from Iranian Azerbaijan were excluded from the 1984 Congress of Muslim Writers held in Iran.[110]

Many journals in Baku published literature written by or about Azerbaijanis in Iran. Some of the periodicals carried regular columns featuring literature and news from south Azerbaijan, such as the "Horizons of Our Literature" column featured in *Ädäbiyyat vä Injäsänät*. In December 1986, *Ädäbiyyat vä Injäsänät* announced the establishment of the Southern Azerbaijan Literature Council by the secretariat of the Azerbaijan Writers' Union, due to the need for "the wide dissemination and study of the works of Southern Azeri authors who write of their love for the motherland and their concern for the defense of the mother tongue."[111] In September 1987, Radio Baku started broadcasting a new program, entitled "Kopru" (Bridge), featuring letters from Azerbaijanis abroad, chiefly from Iran.

---

109.   *Azärbayjan* 2 (1984), pp. 165-167. For additional articles from the Azerbaijani press condemning the Islamic Revolution and the regime in Iran, see M. Sadïgzadä, "Iran Islam Respublikasï Hara Qedir," *Kommunist*, October 7, 1984; *Ädäbiyyat vä Injäsänät*, February 20, 1987 (UPS-87-036); and *Ädäbiyyat vä Injäsänät*, January 20, 1989, p. 8 (UPA-89-035).

110.   *Ädäbiyyat vä Injäsänät*, August 9, 1985, p. 2 (UIA-85-014).

111.   *Ädäbiyyat vä Injäsänät*, December 26, 1986 (UPS-87-034).

The division of Azerbaijan was a major theme in hundreds of works published in literary journals in Baku throughout the mid-1980s and early 1990s. In a speech to the Eighth Congress of Azerbaijani Writers in Baku, first secretary of the board of the Azerbaijani Writers' Union, Ismail Shukhlu, stated:

One of the major themes of our literature, especially our poetry, is the longing, the craving for Southern Azerbaijan. This, by need, is turning into a turbulent river, the flow of which sometimes surges forth, and sometimes recedes. We do not conceal it; our wound festers. We look at the Araz; we castigate the Araz; we spit out our heartache, the bitterness on our tongues into the Araz.[112]

The literary journal *Azerbayjan* published a poem that refers allegorically to the separation between Azerbaijanis by describing the joint burial of an Azerbaijani from Baku and one from Tabriz:

It was impossible to separate them
Those who were strangers above the ground
Now lie as one underground.[113]

Love for the land of south Azerbaijan, and especially for Tabriz, was a constant theme in the literature published in Baku.[114] The teachers' journal, *Azerbayjan Muellimi*, ran a number of articles on this theme. In August 1985, it published a short story entitled "Tabriz," and instructed teachers to read it to their students. In the story, a pupil named Tabriz explains the meaning of his name to the students in the class. The children all cry out that they want to go to Tabriz. Their "teary-eyed" teacher responds: "My dear children, we all want to see Tabriz free."[115]

In some literary works, authors called for the political independence of Iranian Azerbaijan:

Zaire has a government, Chad has a government
We don't have an Azerbaijani government
Such a large nation, such a large people
Does not have freedom, does not have unity.

---

112. *Ädäbiyyat vä Injäsänät*, May 30, 1986, p. 3.

113. Azäroghlu, "Häyat Yolu," p. 66.

114. For instance, ibid., pp. 59–67.

115. Nazim Huseynov, "Täbriz," *Azärbayjan Muällimi*, August 2, 1985.

To Tehran, fifty ambassadors are sent
In Tabriz, there isn't one embassy.[116]

Soviet Azerbaijanis conducted extensive academic work on south Azerbaijan.[117] In June 1986, the Azerbaijan SSR Writers' Union and the Nizami Institute of Literature held a joint conference on "Modern Southern Azerbaijani Literature and the Struggle for Freedom, Democracy and Peace." In 1989, a major study, *Jenubi Azerbayjan Tarikhi Meseleleri* (published in Baku), dealt with different aspects of Iranian Azerbaijan.[118] The works of Samad Behrengi continued to be the focus of many articles by authors in Baku.[119]

In the mid-1980s and early 1990s, many of the political organizations and parties took active stands regarding the rights of their co-ethnics abroad and the desire to increase direct ties with their brethren, especially in Iran. In their platforms, most of the opposition political organizations operating in the republic at this time, such as the PFA and the Azerbaijan Rebirth Party, clearly stated their desire to increase direct ties with the Azerbaijanis in Iran, and their commitment to defend the interests of their co-ethnics abroad.[120]

In October 1989, a delegation from the semi-official Veten Society visiting in the United States reportedly registered a complaint with the authorities at the Metropolitan Museum of Art in New York over the fact that in the Muslim art section, works created in Tabriz in the Safa-

---

116.   Eldar Bakhïsh, "Balïg Ölümü," *Azärbayjan*, No. 7 (1988), p. 16.

117.   Examples include: Nasib Nasibzade, "Puti i formy ideologicheskogo vozdeistviia shakhskogo rezhima na Azerbaidzhanckoe azerbaidzhanskoe naselenie Irana (60-70-e gody)," *Ideologiia i politika*, Part II (Moscow: Oriental Institute, 1986); Nasib Nasibzade, "Territoriia rasseleniia i vopros o chislennosti azerbaidzhantsev v Irane," *Aktual'nye problemy stran Blizhnego i Srednego Vostoka* (Moscow: USSR Academy of Sciences, 1986), pp. 130–140; S. Z. Bairamzade, "Osnovnye izmeneniia sotsial'no-klassovoi struktury Iranskogo Azerbaidzhana v 1947-1962 gg," *Aktual'nye problemy stran Blizhnego i Srednego Vostoka* (Moscow: USSR Academy of Sciences, 1986), pp. 80–88; and V.K. Mustafaev, "Nekotorye aspekty kontseptsii natsii v obshchestvennoi i mysli Irana (konets XIX – I polovina XX v.)" History, Philosophy and Legal Series, No. 2 (Baku: Academy of Sciences, Azerbaijan SSR), 1989.

118.   *Jänubi Azärbayjan Tarikhi Mäsäläläri.* (Baku: Elm, 1989).

119.   See, for instance, Bakhïsh, "Balïg Ölümü"; Magsud Hajïyev, "Ölümü Ilä Doghulan Insan," *Azärbayjan* 12 (1986), pp. 120–124; and Magsud Hajïyev, "Sämäd Behränqinin Häyat vä Yapadïjïghïna Dair," Azerbaijan SSR Academy of Sciences, *Khäbärli* (Literature, Language and Art Series), No. 3 (1988).

120.   Iunusova, "Pestraia palitra neformal'nykh dvizhenii v Azerbaidzhane," p. 7.

vid Period were presented as Iranian exhibitions, and not as Azerbaijani.[121]

Some Azerbaijani cultural figures in Iran engaged in a dialogue with their co-ethnics in Soviet Azerbaijan. Expressing his longing for ties with the north, the poet Sonmez dedicated his work "I Am Weeping" to "my friends on the other side."[122] His poem "It Appears that in the South there is Also a Poet" was written in response to "In Twoness," by the Soviet Azerbaijani poet Nebi Khezri, which metaphorically refers to the ties between the two Azerbaijans. Sonmez wrote to Khezri, "When I finished reading your poem 'In Twoness,' I was inspired to write an imitation of it and response to it which I dedicate to you."[123]

In the late 1980s, direct contacts and cooperation between East Azerbaijan Province in Iran and Soviet Azerbaijan were developed in a number of spheres. The province's activity initially seemed to receive support from Tehran. On September 18, 1989, East Azerbaijan Province invited two hundred Soviet Azerbaijanis to a ceremony in honor of Shahriyar, an Iranian Azerbaijani poet from Tabriz, a year after his death.[124] The East Azerbaijan Province authorities hosted the guests from Soviet Azerbaijan. Governor-General Akbar Parhizkar announced the province's willingness to receive pilgrims from Soviet Azerbaijan on their way to visit shrines in Iran.[125] According to IRNA, Azerbaijanis in Iran "expressed pleasure" over the easing of restrictions at the border in January 1990.[126] As mentioned earlier, during the Novruz holiday in March 1990, the border was opened by Iran and the Soviet Union as a special gesture to allow relatives to spend the holiday together. According to IRNA, 3,500 Azerbaijanis from the north crossed officially into Iran and 2,500 Azerbaijanis from Iran visited the north during the holiday in 1990.[127]

At the height of these exchanges, Governor-General Parhizkar announced the intention of setting up barter trade on the borders with So-

---

121.   *Kommunist*, October 1, 1989, p. 4.

122.   *Ädäbiyyat vä Injäsänät*, June 15, 1984, p. 4.

123.   Excepts from Sonmez's letter (dated October 25, 1986) and the poem were published in *Ädäbiyyat vä Injäsänät*, December 12, 1986, p. 4.

124.   Shahriyar is the author of the poem "Heydar Babaya Salam."

125.   IRNA in English, July 15, 1989.

126.   IRNA in English, January 7, 1990.

127.   IRNA in English, March 27, 1990.

viet Azerbaijan.[128] As part of the direct contacts between the leadership of the Azerbaijani provinces in Iran and representatives from Baku, East Azerbaijan Province held a trade fair in Baku in November 1990. Seven hundred representatives from the Iranian province attended, headed by a high-level political delegation, including the Governor-General and Dr. Said Mohammad Bolabi, the rector of Tabriz University. During the visit, the representatives of East Azerbaijan Province met with the leadership of the Azerbaijan SSR and discussed the establishment of economic, technical, and cultural cooperation.

Direct bilateral cooperation took place on the provincial level as well. In November 1991, a delegation from East Azerbaijan Province visited Nakhchivan. The two sides signed a number of bilateral cooperation agreements, which included the establishment of a joint marketplace in the border area at Jolfa, and an education agreement, which included exchanges of teachers and students.[129]

Bilateral contacts between Baku and Tehran were often conducted by officials of Azerbaijani origin. Ayatollah Musavi-Ardebeli, for instance, was a member of the major delegation from Iran to Baku in the pre-independence period, during the Novruz holiday in March 1991.[130]

Conclusions

In the 1980s and early 1990s, an extensive outpouring of desire among the Soviet Azerbaijanis for ties with their co-ethnics in Iran served as a major focal point for expressing their own sense of Azerbaijani national identity and pride in their culture. The drive for expanded cultural and political contacts increased as restrictions were lifted in the Soviet Union and as Moscow's control eroded. The popular drive for the renewal of ties culminated in the winter 1989–90 border incidents. The enthusiastic reception of the Azerbaijanis by their co-ethnics in Iran illustrates that despite the great differences in national identity, mentality, and lifestyle, most Azerbaijanis still possessed a feeling that they belonged to the same people as those from the other side of the Araz. The fact that many relatives from both sides of the border looked for each other and were able to find each other after almost seventy years of separation throughout the periods of repression in the Soviet Union and in Iran demonstrates that

---

128. Tehran Domestic Service in Persian, January 12, 1990 (FBIS-NES-90-009).

129. Tehran Voice of the Islamic Republic of Iran in Persian, November 15, 1991 (FBIS-NES-91-225).

130. TASS (in English) March 22, 1991 (FBIS-SOV-91-058).

within families, stories of relatives "on the other side" and information about them had been passed down from generation to generation. The value of family ties is strongly emphasized in Azerbaijani culture, and many Azerbaijanis have relatives on the other side of the border; these family ties seem to have played an important role in preserving the self-perception of belonging to one people despite the differences that evolved between the two communities.

This chapter analyzed the development of Azerbaijani identity in the period between the Islamic Revolution in Iran and the collapse of the Soviet Union. After the initial period of the Islamic Revolution, political developments in Iran and in the Soviet Union proceeded in very dissimilar directions. In Iran, after the consolidation of the new regime, political and cultural limitations sharply increased, and outward expressions of Azerbaijani identity and political activity connected with that identity decreased significantly. These manifestations of Azerbaijani identity resurfaced during the period of relative political relaxation at the beginning of the 1990s. In contrast, in Soviet Azerbaijan, expanding political tolerance and the erosion of Moscow's power facilitated the increase of expressions of Azerbaijani national identity and the expansion of the sectors of society actively dealing with issues of national identity.

The different political climates under which the separate Azerbaijani communities lived affected the rate at which that identity developed, the extent of the articulated political goals, and the possibility of realizing the goals. Yet, in neither country did the political climate or the regimes create or eliminate these identities. In Soviet Azerbaijan, a trend of rising Azerbaijani identity had already begun to emerge in the late 1970s and early 1980s, and it accelerated under Gorbachev. In Iran, despite the extreme restrictions and suppression of the opposition, a separate Azerbaijani identity continued to develop among some of the Azerbaijanis in the period after the revolution, as illustrated by the writings discussed in this chapter. The restrictions imposed on literary and political activity make it impossible to gauge the extent and pattern of these developments among the Iranian Azerbaijanis at the time; however, the fact that signs of distinct Azerbaijani identity reemerged in Iran in the subsequent period of political relaxation indicates that a distinct sense of identification as Azerbaijanis continued to exist and develop during the period of oppression.

The extent of Azerbaijani nationalist sentiments in Soviet Azerbaijan as described in this chapter and in Chapter 3 undermine many of the commonly accepted ideas about the magnitude of the role played by glasnost and Gorbachev in some of the developments in the Soviet Union. Before the inauguration of glasnost a diversity of opinions had emerged in intellectual circles in Azerbaijan, and the model of identity fostered by the regime was rejected by many Azerbaijanis. For most intellectuals, the homeland was not the Soviet Union, but Azerbaijan. Glasnost and the changes that Mikhail Gorbachev wrought, as well as the erosion in Moscow's power that came about as a result of those changes, provided the opportunity for the politicization of ideas that predated glasnost; it did not create them.

Chapter 5

The Republic of Azerbaijan's Independence

Following the establishment of the Republic of Azerbaijan in December 1991, Azerbaijanis in the new republic and in Iran took part in intensive political, cultural, and intellectual activity that expressed different forms of collective identity. The founding of the new state led the Azerbaijanis to explore and define their national identity. In the north, the decisions and policies that the newly independent state had to make and the institutions that it set up demanded the formalization of the republic's state identity, spurring public debate and activity. Few Azerbaijanis in Iran were indifferent to the establishment of the Republic of Azerbaijan. Viewpoints became entrenched (and more extreme): those who identified primarily as Iranians and Muslims felt a need to express that view, while the establishment of the Azerbaijani Republic gave rise to heightened Azerbaijani identity. Few among this group expressed support for the secession of the Azerbaijani provinces from Iran and their attachment to the new republic, yet many of them articulated demands for expanded linguistic and cultural rights in Iran.

In Iran, the period following the independence of the Republic of Azerbaijan saw the emergence of open, coordinated political activities and the founding of organizations that brought together Azerbaijanis from all over the country, from widely varying sectors, and with diverse viewpoints. For example, Majlis members of Azerbaijani origin formed a caucus to promote Azerbaijani interests, while some student groups sought fundamental change in the government's policy toward the country's ethnic minorities. The intensity of political activity during the first five years of independence of the Republic of Azerbaijan was facilitated by the removal of many political restrictions in the post-Soviet Republic of Azerbaijan and in Iran.

In the last decade of the Soviet period, limited communication took place between the Azerbaijanis from both sides of the border. By the eve of the new republic's independence, mutual visits had become frequent, social ties were reestablished, and economic cooperation flourished between the Azerbaijanis. This chapter examines the extent to which interactions among Azerbaijanis in the two states affected Azerbaijani identity. An additional factor that influenced the rapid chain of events was influences from outside Azerbaijan, such as the introduction of television transmissions from the Republic of Turkey into both Iran and the Republic of Azerbaijan.

The Beginning of Independence: A Charged Ideological Atmosphere

After a series of carryover and caretaker governments, a Popular Front–led government, under the leadership of Abulfez Elchibey, was elected in May 1992 in the first democratic elections in the new state. The period from independence to the fall of the Elchibey government was highly charged ideologically. The new regime imposed few restrictions on freedom of expression, and debates abounded in the media on the identity of the new state and its citizens. Independent Azerbaijan had no honeymoon period in which to determine its creeds and national priorities. Instead, it was born into a war with Armenia, an extensive refugee population, tense relations with most of its other neighbors, and a collapsed social welfare system.

The ideological debates over the identity of the new state were fueled by the urgent need to make policies. For instance, the new state had to determine state symbols and language. It faced challenges that demanded that it prioritize its values—such as stability versus civil liberties; the conflict of interests between the new state and the Azerbaijani ethnic group; defining who is a citizen; designating the rights of the non-Azerbaijani citizens, both individually and collectively; determining the relations between religion and state; resolving the problem of how to consider historical lands outside the jurisdiction of the new state; and relations between the new state and co-ethnics beyond its borders.

Once in power, the PFA activists needed to find a balance between Azerbaijani ethnic identity and Azerbaijani state civic identity, and to formulate a state identity that could encompass the Azerbaijani ethnic group as well as other ethnic groups in the new state. This created many dilemmas. Years of cultural oppression had instilled in the new government a drive to create a state that was a manifestation of Azerbaijani ethnic culture. Yet, the liberal values and practical considerations of the new ruling elite motivated them to search for accommodation with the non-Azerbaijani ethnic groups in the republic. Before their rise to power, the mainstream of the PFA leadership had emphasized Azerbaijani ethnic-based identity; upon assuming power, they attempted to formulate an additional territorial-based civic and state identity that would encompass all the citizens of the new state. For example, the terms Azerbaijani and Azerbaijanism were used to refer to citizens of the state and patriotism toward it, while "Turk" or "Azerbaijani Turk," were used to designate ethnic Azerbaijanis. Tension persisted between territorial versus ethnic-based identity in the new state, as well as the balance between civic and ethnic identity. These topics were debated throughout the post-independence period. This debate was complicated by the fact that the majority of the ethnic Azerbaijanis lived outside the borders of the new state.

The situation in the new state challenged many of the tenets of PFA ideology that it had espoused while in opposition. For instance, the movement and especially its leader, Elchibey, were committed to campaigning for expanded ties with the Azerbaijanis in Iran and championing their cultural and language rights. This cause severely complicated Azerbaijan's relations with Iran. During the war with Armenia, and given the complicated relations with Russia, the new republic could hardly afford hostile relations with its neighbor to the south; thus Elchibey, when serving as president, toned down his south Azerbaijan campaign.

THE REPRESENTATION OF HISTORY

As part of the process of state-building, an official view of Azerbaijani history was formulated for school textbooks, official commemorations of historical events, and state museums and institutions. In many ways, this official account of history reflected the state's view of Azerbaijani identity. However, this process in actuality was conducted in Azerbaijan in a very rushed fashion in order to create new books for schools in the post-independence period, not allowing time for wide debate involving various segments of society.

Groups involved in strengthening collective identity typically formulate and disseminate a shared view of history. It is frequently a part of the state-building process, and it is intended to foster collective memories among members of a group or citizens of a new state. Newly politicized nations often try to reach far back into the past to display ancient roots of their collective existence.[1] For many groups, these ancient foundations form part of their claim to the legitimacy their state. Many of the historical accounts published in the post-independence period portray the Azerbaijans' origins as an ancient Turkic-speaking people with long-established native roots in the Caucasus.[2] Some of these accounts also attempted to discredit the long-standing separate existence of other peoples in the Caucasus, especially the Armenians, evidently as a way to dismiss their claims to disputed territories.

Throughout this period, state museums emphasized the Azerbaijani ethnic group rather than the history of all the ethnic groups within the territory of the republic. The exhibits highlighted the secular culture of the Azerbaijans, and few displays were connected to Muslim identity. At the same time, most of them presented the history and culture of the Azerbaijanis in Iran as an integral part of their people's general history. For instance, in the Nizami Museum of Azerbaijani National Literature, authors, historical figures, and literary works from the south were presented as part of Azerbaijan's literary heritage. Authors such as Nizami, who were of Azerbaijani ethnic origin but wrote most of their works in Persian, were presented as Azerbaijani authors and their works as part of its national literature. No distinction was made between figures from the north and those from Iranian Azerbaijan, and the maps showed both parts as integral components of Azerbaijan. For example, the maps of Azerbaijan in Baku history museums included territories in Iran, and presented them as part of Azerbaijan. As in the Soviet period, in the National Carpet Museum, carpets from Tabriz are labeled as products of Azerbaijan. Continuing the trend that began in the Soviet period, many archaelogical studies were conducted in Azerbaijan.[3] In his work, *Antichnaia Kavkazskaia Albaniya*, Kemal Aliyev pointed out "the importance of conducting archaeological research in the republic, claiming that the study of material and ancient culture operatively sheds light on the ethnic uniqueness of the population of ancient Azerbaijan."[4]

Indeed, many Azerbaijani activists emphasized the new independent state's links to Azerbaijani history. The Azerbaijan Republican Party pub-

---

1. Eric Hobsbawm, *Nations and Nationalism Since 1780* (Cambridge: Cambridge University Press, 1990), p. 76.

2. See, for instance, Kemal Aliev, *Antichnaia Kavkazskaia Albaniia* (Baku: Izdatelstro Azerbaidzhan, 1992).

3. In Iran, as well, in this period material on archaeological sites in the Azerbaijani provinces was published.

4. Aliev, *Antichnaia Kavkazskaia Albaniia*, p. 4.

lished an appeal to maintain national unity in order to "safeguard and maintain our freedom, and hand down to future generations a national territory inherited from our forefathers."[5] The newly-independent Republic of Azerbaijan claimed to be the heir of the Democratic Republic of Azerbaijan (1918–1920). The regime employed many of its symbols and readopted its slogans. Elchibey stated that "The religious and ethnic policy of the leadership of Azerbaijan will follow the traditions of the Azerbaijani Democratic Republic of 1918–1920, traditions laid down by its founder, Muhammad Amin Rasulzade."[6] Azerbaijan celebrates republic day on May 28, the day on which the previous republic had been established. Street names were changed in Baku and other cities, replacing figures and values associated with the Soviet era with new names commemorating personalities and events associated with the first Azerbaijani republic, such as "Rasulzade" and "May 28."

One of the subjects of debate among Azerbaijani intellectuals in this period was the contemporary relevance and meaning of one of the slogans of the Pan-Turkism movement, "Turkify, Islamicize, Europeanize." This slogan had been adopted by Rasulzade and the republic that he headed, and was later reactivated by Elchibey. *Musavat* Party leader Isa Gambar stated that after independence the meaning of the slogan was only symbolic. In relating to its three terms, he said that today, in terms of "Islamization,"

we mean spiritual freedom and equal rights. As for Turkization, this should not be understood literally. The people of Azerbaijan are of Turkic origin: for example, until 1936, the identity cards carried the word 'Turk' in the rubric depicting one's nationality. Therefore, we are talking here about a return to our historical roots and identity. However, among the aforementioned three slogans, I regard 'modernization' as the most important one, and we will focus our attention on this.[7]

NEW MEANINGS OF AZERBAIJANI IDENTITY

Prior to the independence of the Republic of Azerbaijan, many Azerbaijani activists and cultural figures referred to Azerbaijani identity as an ethnic-based identification. After independence, however, the state leadership attempted to use this term for a state identity common to all the

5.   Radio Baku Network in Azerbaijani, January 7, 1992 (FBIS-SOV-92-009).

6.   Moscow Ostankino Television First Program Network, July 5, 1992 (FBIS-SOV-92-130).

7.   Some activists translate the term "Europeanize" as modernize, which was the original intent of the slogan. Interview with Isa Gambar in Budapest, *Magyar Hirlap*, May 26, 1992, p. 8 (FBIS-SOV-92-104).

citizens of Azerbaijan, regardless of ethnic background. Since Azerbaijan needed a state identity that encompassed all its citizens, debate emerged over the correct balance the new state should strive for among the supra-ethnic state identity, the identity of the Azerbaijani Turks, and the degree of collective rights for other ethnic minorities in the republic. All the mainstream political organizations supported the adoption of a state identity that encompassed all the citizens; the granting of equal individual civic rights to non-ethnic Azerbaijanis; and cultural autonomy on a collective level. However, they differed regarding the extent to which the state should serve as a manifestation of ethnic Azerbaijani Turkic culture.

Elchibey's regime endorsed the idea of full cultural autonomy for the minorities.[8] In the platform he presented for the May 1992 presidential elections, Elchibey declared:

We shall make special efforts to build up trust and promote mutual understanding in our multi-ethnic society. We are convinced that our multi-ethnic population represents the guarantee of our society's stability and that it will promote our development.

However, to ensure the attainment of our goals, all citizens of Azerbaijan, irrespective of their ethnic origin and religion, should have equal rights and opportunities for preserving and developing their ethnic identity.[9]

Polemics waged during Elchibey's tenure on the appropriate balance between Azerbaijani state identity and Azerbaijani ethnic identity in the new state were illustrated by the discussions in December 1992 concerning the name of the republic's official language. The lack of resolve over this issue of the relationship between state identity and ethnic identity was reflected in the fact that initially the new state failed to formulate a comprehensive citizenship law, due to the lack of consensus regarding the question whether ethnic Azerbaijanis from outside the republic— such as in Turkey, Iran, or refugees from Armenia— should be granted citizenship. The lack of accord on the issue of criteria for citizenship is indicative of the lack of consensus with respect to the relations between the state and co-ethnics abroad, and the rights of ethnic Azerbaijanis vis-a-vis the state, versus the rights of native citizens, regardless of their ethnic ori-

---

8.   Due to the conflict with the Armenians over Nagorno-Karabagh and the political activity of other non-Azerbaijani minorities, Azerbaijani intellectuals were forced to form views on minority-majority relations, even though Azerbaijan had a small non-Azerbaijani ethnic population.

9.   Election manifesto of Elchibey, *Interfax* in English, May 11, 1992.

gin. Elchibey supported the granting of citizenship to Turkish military officers of Azerbaijani descent and granting the right to Azerbaijani citizens to hold dual citizenship;[10] he even appointed a Turkish citizen, Jemil Unal, as a minister in the government he led. In addition, some Azerbaijani national activists from Iran found refuge in the Republic of Azerbaijan, and many continued their political activities in Baku.[11]

Many of those who emphasized that the Azerbaijani state was a manifestation of the Azerbaijani ethnic group held that the new state must champion the cause of cultural rights for the Azerbaijanis outside the republic, and especially those living in Iran, and believed that the population of the new state was incomplete without its co-ethnics abroad. The next section will discuss the competing and sometimes parallel trends in Azerbaijan which emerged in the post-independence period in the Republic of Azerbaijan.

IDENTITY AS TURKS

In the Elchibey period, the governing elite and leading intellectuals stressed their identity both as Azerbaijanis and as Turks. In this period, Turkic identity was equated with Azerbaijani ethnic identity, while state identity was promoted as supra-ethnic.

As in the pre-independence period, few equated Turkic identity with a desire for political unification with the Republic of Turkey or other Turkic countries. For most, identity with other Turks was restricted to the cultural sphere. Even the political forces with the strongest pro-Turkey orientations, such as the PFA, Musavat, and the National Independence Party, advocated political cooperation among the Turkic states, and rejected the notion of a single Turkic state.[12]

One of the first major decisions of the newly independent Republic of Azerbaijan was the official adoption on December 25, 1991, of the Latin alphabet. It is significant that this decision was made before the PFA-led government rose to power. The initially approved version of the Latin alphabet was more similar to the one used in Turkey than the final form

---

10.   *Hurriyet* (Istanbul), June 28, 1992, p. 15 (FBIS-SOV-92-128).

11.   For example, Piruz Dilanji, who wrote for *Varliq* under the name 'Ali Ismail Tamrin in 1984–88, moved to Baku, where he became active in political efforts on behalf of the Azerbaijanis in Iran.

12.   Some authors mistakenly term these political organizations, and especially the PFA, as Pan-Turkist. These organizations stressed their cultural links with other Turks and their desire for political cooperation with the Republic of Turkey, but did not call for political unity.

adopted a few months later.[13] The government immediately published and disseminated materials for teaching the Latin alphabet to the country's residents.[14] Members of the Islamic movement, who preferred the Arabic alphabet, opposed this decision, and some members of Islamic religious circles started courses for teaching Arabic script.[15] These courses were phased out in 1993–94. When the Islamic groups saw that there was little support for the adoption of Arabic script, they joined forces with the communists and others who wished to keep the Cyrillic alphabet. In September 1992, the first school textbooks in Latin characters were introduced for use by the first graders. From the fall of 1992, new publications for use in schools were produced in Latin characters.

Though the language of the republic had officially been called "Azerbaijani" since 1938, it was almost always referred to on the popular level as "Turkish." One of the most significant expressions of the Turkish component of Azerbaijani identity was the parliamentary decision of December 22, 1992, to call the official language of the Republic *Türkce Dili* (The Turkish language). Extensive debate in the parliament and the media preceded this decision. Polemics revealed different, complex opinions on the national identity question and the change that had taken place in the meaning of the term *Azerbaijani* since independence. Some activists objected to the official use of the term *Türkce Dili* and other uses of "Turk," claiming that they gave disproportionate importance to the republic's ethnic Azerbaijanis. They asserted that the term Azerbaijani, which in this period officially described all the citizens of Azerbaijan, should be used instead. Among those who opposed calling the state language the "Turkish language," were the leaders of the Social Democratic Party of Azerbaijan (SDPA). The first deputy chairman of the Azerbaijan parliament, Tamerlan Karayev, justified the decision to name the state language "the Turkish language," stating that "our return to the appellation of Turkish language also implies the re-establishment of the historical name of the nation—Azerbaijani Turks."[16] Karayev maintained that the decision would not lead to a split or estrangement between ethnic groups in Azerbaijan:

---

13. For instance, the "ae" sound was initially represented by ä, and not by the ə later adopted. The initial version did not contain q and x, which are not in use in the Republic of Turkey.

14. See, for instance, "Latïn Grafikalï Azärbayjan Älifbasï" (Baku: Azärnäshr, January 28, 1992).

15. Tamam Bayatly, "Alphabet Transitions: The Latin Script: A Chronology, Symbol of a New Azerbaijan," *Azerbaijan International*, Vol. 5, No. 2 (Summer 1997), p. 24.

16. *Turan* in English, December 26, 1992.

Having re-established their historical name, the Turks equalized themselves in civil rights with all ethnic groups living within Azerbaijan. And in this case, all nations and nationalities may call themselves the Azerbaijanis to convey the idea of not national but civil belonging . . . If we do really wish to build the democratic state we have the only way—all citizens of Azerbaijan are the Azeris, and the USA's experience shows a brilliant example of it.[17]

Wide consensus existed on the need to institute the use of Azerbaijani and phase out Russian throughout the state. The December 1992 law on the official language of the Republic of Azerbaijan stipulated that Azerbaijani Turkish would be in use in all the country's official bodies and organs. Yet in the initial period after independence Russian remained for many Azerbaijanis the language of prestige. Many educated Azerbaijanis continued to speak it among themselves, especially when dealing with academic and political topics, despite their support for elevating the Azerbaijani language's legal status. However, from the mid-1990s, Azerbaijani has reemerged as the prominent language among Azerbaijanis in the republic.

In late 1991 and early 1992, Turkey began broadcasting television programs into the Republic of Azerbaijan. These broadcasts gained an immediate and vast following, becoming the most popular programs in the republic. In the long run they could have a significant impact on the Azerbaijanis' perception of themselves as part of the larger Turkish world, and on the intermeshing of Azerbaijani Turkish and Anatolian Turkish. While the languages are mutually understandable, many expressions are different, and Azerbaijani contains many more Arabic and Persian words than the Turkish in use in the Republic of Turkey. Azerbaijanis began to incorporate many expressions used in Turkey, and it seems that if these the broadcasts continue, the languages will become even more similar. Some intellectuals, such as many associated with the Musavat Party, began replacing Persian words in Azerbaijani with Turkic ones, such as using *evet* for yes, versus the Persian-origin *bäli*.

SECULAR MUSLIM IDENTITY

A unique view of Islam that is consistent with the Azerbaijani secular tradition was widely adopted in the Republic of Azerbaijan. Many Azerbaijanis in the new republic valued their identity as Muslims and expressed their desire to develop ties with other states whose inhabitants were Muslim. Most of the proponents of Muslim identity viewed it in a secular context and as a secondary component of Azerbaijani identity. To

---

17. Ibid.

most, Islam is a form of culture and social relations, but not a religious mandate. The leaders of the new state continually emphasized that the Republic of Azerbaijan was to be a secular state, whose people retained pride in their identity as Muslims.[18]

Information Minister Sabir Rustemkhanli stressed the need to form relations with the Arab world, which he described as related to the Azerbaijanis "culturally and historically." However, he emphasized that the Azerbaijanis reject the use of religion in political activity.[19] Isa Gambar, the leader of the Musavat Party and prominent PFA activist, stated that "religion is one of the factors that contribute to the normal moral condition of a society"; however, "Islam should not play a political role in the country."[20] Elchibey asserted that "Islamic fundamentalism can be understood in two senses: There is the study of Islam's history and culture, which is not dangerous; it is another matter to use the ideas of Islamic fundamentalism, used by fanatics who want to raise it to the rank of state policy."[21]

However, a small group of people, many associated with the Islamic Party of Azerbaijan, advocated a more prominent role of Islam in the Republic. The Islamic Party of Azerbaijan was officially formed on December 6, 1992. It has a very strong pro-Iranian orientation.

On the grassroots level, there were frequent expressions of Shi'i identity, such as displays of pictures of Imam 'Ali in taxis, homes, and at religious shrines in the post-independence period, often observed among highly secular people. Nonetheless, anti-Iranian sentiments run high in the Republic of Azerbaijan, and the connection to Shi'a has little political manifestation. In addition, Shi'i and Sunni followers can be found praying together in many mosques, as well as studying together in the same *madrasas* in the Republic of Azerbaijan.

FOREIGN ORIENTATION

Throughout the post-independence period, many Azerbaijanis stressed the identity of their people as a special balance between East and West, or "Europe and Asia." Some perceived themselves as playing a special role as a bridge between these two cultural worlds. In his election platform,

---

18. See remarks of Elchibey, *Milliyet* (Istanbul), May 31, 1992, p. 19 (FBIS-SOV-92-109).

19. *Al-Sharq Al-Awsat* (London), February 1, 1992, p. 2 (FBIS-SOV-92-025).

20. Interview with Isa Gambar in Budapest, *Magyar Hirlap*, May 26, 1992, p. 8 (FBIS-SOV-92-104).

21. Moscow Ostankino Television First Program Network, July 5, 1992 (FBIS-SOV-92-130).

Elchibey professed that: "Azerbaijan, a state located at the junction of Europe and Asia, has every right to participate in the newly-born Asian process and in the well-developed European mechanism of peaceful cooperation and maintenance of international security."[22]

In the first years after independence, many Azerbaijanis expressed admiration for and cultural affinity with some foreign states, first and foremost the Republic of Turkey. However, almost all firmly rejected any new foreign domination or political unification with foreign states. Information Minister Sabir Rustemkhanli stated that Azerbaijan's supreme ambition is independence: "We know that many states want to control Azerbaijan in one way or another, but independence is one of the ideals of the Azerbaijani people's fight."[23]

In contrast, members of the Islamic movement in Azerbaijan were oriented toward Iran and ardently supported it. For example, the Islamic Party of Azerbaijan advocated the conclusion of major oil development contracts with Iran, and in April 1994 demanded the return of Iranian television broadcasts.[24]

As part of a policy of rebuffing any foreign domination, under Elchibey Azerbaijan rejected joining any rigid political unions. Azerbaijan did not join the CIS during Elchibey's term, and refused to concede to Russian pressure to sign agreements allowing the continued presence of Russian military bases in the republic.[25] The policy of refusing to allow the stationing of Russian soldiers in Azerbaijan was continued under President Heydar Aliyev.

RETURN TO EMPHASIS ON STATE IDENTITY

In June 1993, Elchibey's rule was challenged by an armed uprising. During the insurrection, Elchibey fled Baku and power was assumed by Aliyev, who served as speaker of the parliament. His presidency was later consolidated in elections. Although debate on national ideology and identity continued both on the elite and popular levels after Aliyev reassumed power, the regime concentrated on the day-to-day running of the republic, focusing much less on ideological issues. Furthermore, the government passed legislation that imposed censorship and restricted public discussion.

---

22.   Interfax in English, May 11, 1992.

23.   *Al-Sharq Al-Awsat* (London), February 1, 1992, p. 2 (FBIS-SOV-92-025).

24.   *Turan* in English, April 15, 1994; and *Azadliq*, November 1, 1994, pp. 1, 3.

25.   The only exception is a small force in the Qabala station, which is an integral part of the Russian monitoring system for ballistic missiles.

Much of the ideological fervor and excitement of the initial period after independence was dampened, especially due to the military defeats by Armenia, lack of unity in the country, and collapse of the social welfare system. Literary works of this period often reflected the disappointment and difficulties of the time.[26] A strong split occurred between the views on identity published by the regime and those of many independent intellectuals. Aliyev tended to stress the identity of the state as opposed to that of the Azerbaijani ethnic group:

Azerbaijan is the homeland of all those living in Azerbaijan regardless of their nationality, religion, language, and origin; including Armenians living in Nagorno-Karabagh.[27]

In the new constitution, published in November 1995, the language of the country was again called by its Soviet-era name, the Azerbaijani language, annulling the PFA-era decision to call it Turkish. [28] Nevertheless, an official atlas prepared for use in the republic's middle schools and high schools and approved by the Historical Institute of the Academy of Sciences of the Republic of Azerbaijan emphasized the Azerbaijani ethnic group. The school atlas contained an ethnographic map of the Azerbaijanis that displays the Azerbaijanis living outside the borders of the state and not just the population within the territory of new republic.[29] The map defines many Turkic tribal groups in Iran as Azerbaijanis, including those located northwest of Mashad and southwest of Shiraz. In addition, the maps of Azerbaijan showing the territory up to the nineteenth century defined northwest Iran as part of Azerbaijan.[30] However, in the maps that illustrate the situation after the division of Azerbaijan in 1828, only the territories that were part of Russia and later the Soviet Union were shown as part of Azerbaijan.

---

26.   See, for instance, Anar, *Otel Otagi* (Baku: 1995), cited in Shouleh Vatanabi, ed., "Azerbaijan," *World Literature Today*, Vol. 70, No. 3 (Summer 1996), p. 497.

27.   Baku Azerbaijan Radio Television Network, November 12, 1995 (FBIS-SOV-95-219).

28.   *Azärbayjan Respublikasïnïn Konstitusiyasï* (Baku: Azärbayjan Press, 1996), paragraph 21.

29.   This ethnographic map encompasses part of Eastern Turkey, all of northwest Iran, including the area south of Zenjan, extending to the environs of Tehran, and includes Tehran itself, and designates these areas as being populated by ethnic Azerbaijanis.

30.   Ziya Bünyatov, *Azärbayjan Tarikhi Khäritäläri* (Baku: Azärbayjan Ensiklopediyasï, 1994).

Intellectuals, mainly those who opposed the government, continued to debate the desired balance between the state identity of Azerbaijan and the Azerbaijani ethnic-based nation. An exchange between top thinkers in the *Musavat* movement over drafts of their party program illustrates this dispute. Emphasizing state identity as the national identity in the Republic of Azerbaijan, Hikmet Hajizade wrote in his proposed draft:

Human rights must be a new basis for national unity. Azerbaijan is not only the state of the Azeri Turks, but also of representatives of all ethnic groups living here, of all the citizens of the country.

Nation is not an ethnic, but a political notion. The following notion is applied: the Azerbaijan nation is a voluntary nation of all citizens of the country, regardless of ethnic origin, religion, or any other parameters.[31]

In contrast, Nasib Nasibzade's proposed platform stated that national identity should be based on the identity of the Azerbaijani ethnic Turkic group. Nasibzade advocated

formation of a strong democratic state, nationalism (patriotism) as a factor strengthening the statehood.

Azeri Turks have created their own state—the Azerbaijan Republic, but here, the rights of ethnic minorities must be protected. The reason for the Karabagh war is separatism on the one hand and lack of patriotism among us, on the other. In the period of reform, the nation must espouse the idea of solidarity, different social groups must live in harmony with each other and should be guided by the concept of national morality. Azerbaijan must be the political and moral center for the Azerbaijanis throughout the world. Since Azerbaijan is part and parcel of the Turkic world from the political, ideological, and economic points of view, the integration with that world agrees with our national interests.[32]

Intellectuals and official publications continued to project the view of the Azerbaijanis as an ancient Turkic people and to stress primordial ties. For example, in an introduction to *Ilk Azerbayjan Kitabi*, which chronicles the history of manuscripts in Azerbaijan, the author refers to "the ancient Azerbaijanis" as "ancestors of Turkic nations" who produced literature during the first centuries of the common era.[33] In this book, Azerbaijani culture and history in the north and south are treated as one entity. For instance, the book concentrates on manuscripts produced in Tabriz in the thirteenth century.

---

31. *Azadliq*, March 16, 1995, pp. 2–6, 15.

32. Näsib Näzibzadä, *Yeni Musavat*, April 17, 1995.

33. Aydin Khalilov, *Ilk Azärbayjan Kitabï* (Baku: Sharq-Qärb, 1995), p. 9.

Consistent with its predecessor's position, the *Constitution of the Republic of Azerbaijan*, drafted and adopted under the Aliyev regime, clearly declares the separation of religion and state.[34] Under Aliyev, Azerbaijan joined the Commonwealth of Independent States, reversing the anti-CIS policy of the previous government, and showing its more pragmatic approach, as well as the erosion of ideological considerations.

The Impact of Independence on Iranian Azerbaijan

The Republic of Azerbaijan achieved independence during a period of relative political laxity in Iran that allowed the expression of many responses to this event. It led to the radicalization or entrenchment of views and positions concerning different forms of primary identity of the Azerbaijans in Iran, whether as Iranians, Muslims, or Azerbaijanis, and many people responded to the establishment of a new state. In the early 1990s, increased articulations of heightened Azerbaijani identity became noticeable in Iran. However, not all who reacted to the advent of the new state viewed it as a positive event, neither did they all articulate a heightened Azerbaijani identity. Some who held primary identity as Muslims or as Iranians expressed that identity; they seemed to be saying "count me out."

Many Azerbaijanis responded to the gap they perceived between their structural status and their social status. By the early 1990s, Azerbaijanis comprised a large proportion of the governing elite in the country and dominated important business sectors. For example, the spiritual leader Ayatollah Khamane'i is Azerbaijani. Nonetheless, Azerbaijanis continued to be ridiculed in Iranian society, and many felt they had to assimilate and Persianize in order to advance and succeed. The first half of the 1990s was marked by many expressions of indignation over a low social status that contrasted with their extensive political and economic success. Many Azerbaijanis challenged public and media sources that ridiculed their accents and portrayed the "Turk" as uncultured. Azerbaijani activists frequently put this treatment, which they perceived as "humiliating," on the same plane as demands for expanded tangible rights. This seems to have been due to heightened ethnic pride and assertiveness that emerged in this period. The establishment of the Republic of Azerbaijan—a state based on their ethnic culture—and the introduction of the Turkish television broadcasts seem to have contributed to their enhanced ethnic self-esteem.

---

34. *Azärbayjan Respublikasïnïn Konstitusiyasï*, paragraph 18.

One of the first major trends that emerged among the Azerbaijanis in Iran after the establishment of the republic was their tendency to refer to themselves as "Azerbaijanis," or "Azeris." Previously, most had called themselves "Turks." This term, almost universally used up to the early 1990s, had a slightly negative connotation for some since it had been employed by the Shah's regime, and because "Turks" had been the brunt of so many jokes in Iran. In literature as well, Azerbaijanis in Iran began to refer to their language as "Azerbaijani," "Azeri," the "language of Azerbaijan" or "Turki-Azerbaijani," in contrast to "Turki," as had been customary in the past.

RENEWED LITERARY REVIVAL IN IRAN

In the first half of the 1990s, a major Azerbaijani literary revival took place in Iran, encouraged by the relative political freedom at that time. Many of the works appeared in the Arabic script with Turkic vowel markings. Many new Azerbaijani grammars and dictionaries appeared in this period as well, including *Azerbayjan Dilinin Grameri*, which was published in 1992 in Tabriz.[35] It is a transcription of a grammar produced in Cyrillic in Soviet Azerbaijan, and its publication demonstrated the existence of academic cooperation between the Azerbaijanis and their sense of sharing one language. In this work, the language is referred to as the "language of Azerbaijan." Another noteworthy book is an extensive Azerbaijani-Persian conversational "phrase guide."[36] The book, written in Arabic script, contains comments in both Azerbaijani and Persian and a table for transcribing Arabic characters into Latin and Cyrillic. The inclusion of the Cyrillic table indicates a desire to facilitate the reading of texts from the Republic of Azerbaijan.

Many books published in this period dealt with Azerbaijani literature, poetry, and proverbs.[37] One notable example is *Azerbayjan Edebiyyat Tarikhinden Qizil Yarpaqlar*, which discussed some of the major works of Azerbaijani literature.[38] One interesting Azerbaijani language book is a collection of "Kind Words."[39] In this period, such self-help books became

---

35. Qasam Hasanov, Kamil Aliyov, and Faridun Khalilov, *Azarbayjan Dilinin Grameri* (Tabriz, 1992).

36. 'Abed Alkarim Manzuri Khamena, *Mukalemat-e Ruzmarah-e Turki-Farsi* (Türkche-Farsche Me'amuli Danishiqlar) (Tehran, 1993).

37. See, for instance, 'A. Zafarkhah, *Ata Babalar Diyiblar* (Tabriz: Entesharat-e yaran, 1991–92).

38. Eziz Mohseni, *Azerbayjan Edebiyyat Tarikhinden Qizil Yarpaqlar* (Tehran: Neshar, 1995).

39. Vahdat Shabistari, *Dadli Sözler* (Tabriz, 1992).

very popular among the general population in Iran, appealing especially to the less-educated strata. The publication of such a book in Azerbaijani illustrates a desire by non-intellectuals for written works in the Azerbaijani language. In the past, generally only intellectuals in Iran had been interested in reading in Azerbaijani.

Many books and articles dealt with Azerbaijani culture and folklore.[40] One example is a series of volumes on different aspects of Azerbaijani folklore. In addition, many books on Azerbaijan and Azerbaijani history and culture appeared in Persian.[41] One of these, *Aras dar Gazargah-i Tarih*, that deals with many questions connected to the Araz River.[42]

Some Azerbaijanis from Iran published books and articles in the Republic of Azerbaijan. For instance, Javad Heyat, the editor of *Varliq*, published a number of books on the history of the Turkic peoples and the literature of Azerbaijan in Cyrillic script, evidently for readers in the republic. In his works, Heyat often stressed the common origins of the Azerbaijanis in the north and in Iran.[43]

Starting in 1991 and 1992, many of the major Iranian newspapers, such as *Keyhan*, *Ettela'at*, and *Jomhuri-ye Islami*, included an Azerbaijani language page. The editors of these Azerbaijani-language supplements sometimes included articles whose themes would probably have been censored in the Persian-language press. For instance, in January 1993 an article entitled "President of the Republic of Azerbaijan: Azerbaijanis of All the World Unite," appeared in *Keyhan Havai*. It reported:

Abulfez Elchibey, the president of Azerbaijan, said: If we unite with the Azerbaijanis living abroad, we will be able to support their rights. According to a report from "Bakinsky Rabochi" newspaper, Elchibey said during the world-wide Azerbaijanis' Congress in Baku: Our noble and eternal goal is to

---

40. For example, Mir Hidayat Hasari, "Azerbayjan Folklorunden Numunahlar," *Varliq* (January–April, 1992), pp. 67–71; Zahareh Vafasi, *Folklor Ganjinahsi, Oyunlar* (Entesharat-e yaran, written 1991).

41. For example, Behruz Khamachi, *Tavaf-e Saha* (Tabriz: Zougi Research Institute and Publication Centre, 1991), on the tribes in the Mount Sahand area of Azerbaijan; and Rahim Raisnia, *Azarbayjan dar Masir-e Tarikh-e Iran*, 2 vols. (Tehran, 1991), cited in Javadi, "Research Note: Azeri Publications in Iran," p. 87.

42. Muhammad Hafizzadah, *Aras dar Guzargah-e Tarikh* (Aztasharatniye, 1995).

43. See, for instance, Javad Heyat, "Origins of the Name and Boundaries of Azerbaijan."

assist to unify all the Azerbaijanis residing in foreign countries on the basis of common national, cultural, and spiritual life.[44]

In a sophisticated manner, this article, which was written as a regular informative news article and seemingly attributed the idea of unity to President Elchibey, conveyed the idea that unification could assist the Azerbaijanis in Iran, and that Baku was interested in joining with the Azerbaijanis in Iran.

Toward the end of 1991, the regime allowed the publication of a regular magazine, *Yol*, in the Azerbaijani language. Each edition of *Yol* contained a "Sözlük" page that translated Azerbaijani terms into Persian in order to spread their use, illustrating the fact that *Yol*'s authors read books and articles published in Soviet Azerbaijan and were familiar with many of the terms coined there for modern academic use. In addition, the magazine contained many articles on historical sites in the Azerbaijani provinces. *Yol* often included special children's supplements, with games and stories intended to teach and encourage the younger generation to read Azerbaijani. While the magazine expressed many official views, it also contained many sophisticated nationalist Azerbaijani messages. For instance, the magazine often printed articles seemingly condemning the activities of Azerbaijani nationalist organizations operating in Europe. Yet, through these denunciations the messages of these organizations were disseminated. In one edition the symbol of *Ana Dili*, an Azerbaijani nationalist newspaper published in Germany, appeared on a full page.[45] *Yol* was popular among Azerbaijanis in Iran; the regime, evidently threatened by this popularity, closed it down after two years.

These Azerbaijani publications were primarily for the elite; a large number of those living in the Azerbaijani provinces are illiterate.[46] According to professors at Tabriz University, Azerbaijani is used as a native language by the peasants and urban poor, who constitute a large portion of Iran's Azerbaijani population.[47] Azerbaijani folk poetry is very popular among these people, and poets continued to reflect the experience and language of the common Azerbaijani people in new poems. Thus, many Azerbaijani poets disseminated their works without actually publishing

---

44. "Azerbayjan Jumhuriyet Reis: Dunyanin Butun Azerbayjanlari Birlash-mehlidirler," *Keyhan Havai* (Azerbaijani section), January 20, 1993, p. 4.

45. *Yol*, December 22, 1991, p. 2.

46. Hariri-Akbari and Aazbdaftari, "A Brief Review of Contemporary Azerbaijani Poetry," p. 96.

47. Ibid.

them. In this period, poems dealt with the theme of the land of Azerbaijan and its beauty.

In the early 1990s, Azerbaijanis took issue with the status and use of the Azerbaijani language in Iran. Compared with the Pahlavi regime, the Islamic Republic was unquestionably more lenient in allowing public use of Azerbaijani: Azerbaijani clerics often spoke publicly in Azerbaijani, and Friday (*Juma*) prayer addresses in cities with large Azerbaijani provinces were often delivered in the language. In recognition of the importance that Azerbaijanis attach to their language, when Iranian leaders of Azerbaijani origin, such as Ayatollah Khamene'i, spoke in the provinces, they often delivered their addresses in Azerbaijani. However, the content of official statements was still strictly controlled, and official broadcasts in Azerbaijani in Iran were read by non-Azerbaijanis and highly assimilated Azerbaijanis. In *Varliq*, Husein-Quli Salimi criticized the language used in Radio Tabriz broadcasts, calling it "pidgin Azerbaijani." He asserted that these so-called Azerbaijani-language broadcasts used a Persian sentence structure, with a mix of Azerbaijani and Persian vocabulary.[48] An Azerbaijani author from Iran recounted,

It is a humiliation. My mother could not understand these broadcasts. This is a humiliation of the language. This chauvinistic policy spurs other chauvinistic policies.[49]

Yet, many Azerbaijani intellectuals still perceived Persian as the language of status in Iran. For example, an Azerbaijani medical student from Tehran recounted in an interview how he would go to great lengths to hide his Azerbaijani accent and try to sound like a Persian when he was trying to make a good impression on a girl.

Demands for expanded use of the Azerbaijani language were made in a number of publications. Many activists anchored their demands in Article Fifteen of the Constitution of the Islamic Republic. In an open letter sent to the Iranian leadership as part of a coordinated letter-writing campaign, Azerbaijani students wrote:

It is time to pay attention to such important items as the realization of a bilingual educational system on the basis of clause fifteen of the Iranian constitution. This does not contradict our unity, because we are united by Iranian Muslim duties, but not by the Persian language. We must take into consider-

---

48. Husein-Quli Salimi, "Tabriz Radiosunun ve Erilishlanishlarineh Bir Bakhish," *Varliq* (January–April, 1992), pp. 38-48.

49. From interview conducted in 1998 with an Iranian Azerbaijani author who was outside Iran and has spent most of his life in Iran.

ation that if we do not realize necessary issues in the sphere of native language, culture and other demands, some undesirable phenomena may occur. Persons producing cultural and educational programs at present must immediately give importance to the non-official languages and particularly to the Turkic [Azerbaijani] language.[50]

The students participating in the letter-writing campaign also called for the establishment of local broadcasting in Azerbaijani from the radio and television stations of Tabriz, Urmiya, Zenjan, Ardebil, and Hamadan and labeled the absence of such broadcasts a "constitutional violation." This demand for the expansion of local Azerbaijani language broadcasts was echoed in a letter written by university students from Meshkinshahr (and that illustrates the coordination of the student groups' political activity). Moreover, while praising the increased use of non-Persian languages since the fall of the Shah, the Meshkinshahr students complained that the Azerbaijanis in Iran were still deprived of the right to read and write in their native language, as stipulated by Article Fifteen of the Constitution.[51]

All the Azerbaijanis from Iran interviewed in this study who were born to two Azerbaijani parents remarked that they were strongly attached to their mother tongue. Even though Persian was their primary language for reading and writing, almost all expressed an affinity for Azerbaijani and many called it a "beautiful language." Many related that their mothers' practice of telling them stories in the Azerbaijani language was a very positive childhood memory and an important factor in making the Azerbaijani language dear to them. In both the north and the south, many Azerbaijanis have mentioned the importance of the tradition of elaborate storytelling—the domain of Azerbaijani women—in instilling in them an affection for their language and culture, as well as respect for Azerbaijani women. This tradition has been depicted in many cultural works, such as those of Reza Baraheni and Bakhtiyar Vahabzade.[52] At the same time, most Iranian Azerbaijanis, especially those above age forty, expressed appreciation for and attachment to the Persian language. However, many asserted that they were offended by Persian attempts to di-

---

50. Letter of the Azerbaijani Students Studying in Tehran Universities to the Azerbaijani Deputies of the Iranian Majlis (Persian), June 1994 (unpublished).

51. "Letter of the Meshkinshahr Students Studying in the Universities of the Country to the Government of the Islamic Republic of Iran," *Varliq* (April–June, 1994), pp. 93–96 (originally published in the weekly *Omid-e Zenjan*).

52. See, for instance, Bakhtiyar Vahabzade, "Autobiography," in Hadi Sultan-Qurraie, ed., *Selected Works of Bakhtiyar Vahabzade*, p. 26.

minish the status of their language and disregard for a language the Azerbaijanis respect very highly.

IMMENSE IMPACT OF TELEVISION FROM TURKEY

Iranian television programming held little interest for the public at large because of their predominantly religious character. Thus, many in Iran chose to watch foreign television by means of satellite, when available.[53] In 1992, the price of home windowpane satellite devices fell dramatically in Iran, making them accessible to many households. This seems to have produced important social consequences. Azerbaijanis, who can easily understand Turkish, chose overwhelmingly to view television from Turkey. Broadcasts from Turkey became much more popular than those from Baku. Azerbaijanis from Tehran and the provinces recounted that Turkish television was regularly watched in Azerbaijani homes since 1992. Many of those interviewed stated that this had an extremely important impact on their self-identity as Azerbaijanis and as Turks. Many pointed out that for the first time they saw the "Turk" portrayed in a positive light—educated, successful, wealthy—in contrast with the image presented in the Iranian media, which is predominantly that of the "Turkish donkey," the menial laborer, the uncultured peasant.

In 1994, at the university in Urmiya, a demonstration was held protesting the "image of the Azerbaijani" in the Iranian media. The protestors called for the expansion of television broadcasting in the Azerbaijani language and demanded that Azerbaijani be taught in both schools and universities. The trigger for this demonstration, according to some interviewees, was the introduction of television broadcasts from Turkey, with its positive image of the Turk, which made a great contrast with the image in the Iranian media.

PROVINCE GERRYMANDERING: RESPONSE OF ESTABLISHMENT AZERBAIJANIS

In the 1990s, Tehran frequently changed the boundaries of its provinces (*iyalat*) to reflect demographic trends and to adjust the governing of certain populations in response to different challenges.

In October 1992, Tehran decided to split East Azerbaijan Province, creating a new province in the Ardebil area.[54] The names Sabalan, Sahand

---

53.   In the 1960s and 1970s, television from Baku was frequently watched in the border towns that had good reception.

54.   See Chehabi, "Ardebil Becomes a Province: Center-Periphery Relations in Iran," pp. 235–253, for an in-depth discussion of the author's views of the motivations for the creation of the new province, and the processes involved.

and Ardebil were proposed for the new province.[55] The debates on this decision revealed that many Azerbaijanis were willing to openly criticize the regime concerning this issue, and that even those who identified with Iran strongly supported the preservation of the name Azerbaijan for this territory in Iran. Mainstream ethnic Azerbaijanis, who as Majlis members in the early 1990s could not be considered in any sense radical or oppositional, vigorously and openly struggled to prevent the removal of the name Azerbaijan from the province and illustrated that some of the Iranian Azerbaijanis who are strongly connected to the regime maintain special identification with the Azerbaijani provinces and ethnic identity. The debates over naming this province also revealed that the policy process in Iran at times is quite open and wide debate takes place over different policies.

The idea of the split itself produced only limited opposition from some Azerbaijanis, and many residents of the Ardebil area evidently supported the idea, expecting it to bring added resources to the region and create additional positions with the establishment of another provincial government. However, the decision to remove the name "Azerbaijan" from the new province generated indignation. Letters opposing the elimination of the name "Azerbaijan" began to appear in the press. Many suggested that the new province be called East Azerbaijan and that the Tabriz-centered province be known as Central Azerbaijan. A letter written by a resident of Ardebil, published in *Varliq*, stated:

Is it logically correct to give any other name to the new *ostan* except the name of our motherland—Azerbaijan? It is correct that Sabalan is the highest mountain of Azerbaijan and one of the nicest mountains of the world. Yet, is it nice that the name of one mountain will replace the name of such a glorious and famous country as Azerbaijan? The name of Ardebil, the historical center of Azerbaijan, cannot be a substitution for Azerbaijan. The new province consists of such towns like Sarab, Meshkinshahr, Astara, Khalkhal. Their residents are not Ardebilis but Azerbaijanis. Thus, taking the name of East Azerbaijan for a new province with the center in Ardebil is more logical. Removal of the word of Azerbaijan from the name of the province with the center in Ardebil—the eldest son of our motherland—for us Ardebilis is like struggle and oppression with ourselves and with our mother, is it not?[56]

---

55. Sabalan and Sahand are two mountains in the Ardebil area. Azerbaijanis refer to Sabalan as Savalan.

56. Letter from 'Ali-Reza Hamide Khoo about the formation of Ardebil Province (Persian), *Varliq* (October–December, 1992), pp. 109–110.

On October 15, 1992, the government announced its decision to establish the new province and name it Sabalan.[57] However, as opposition to the name change continued, the final wording of the Internal Affairs Committee of the Majlis in January 1993 stated that the new province was to be called East Azerbaijan, and the province of East Azerbaijan, with Tabriz as its capital, was to be changed to Central Azerbaijan.[58] A member of the commission in charge of making these changes presented the bill and remarked that:

In the bill it presented the government chose Sabalan Province as the new province name, but in view of the discussions that took place in the commission and in view of the fact that the name Azerbaijan is associated with the luminous history of the brave uprisings of the valiant, self-sacrificing, believing, and committed people throughout Azerbaijan and that this name has always held memories for the noble people of this land, to preserve this epic memory, the name Azerbaijan was given to the new province. Consequently, the Islamic Republic of Iran will have three provinces with the name Azerbaijan: West Azerbaijan with Urmiya as its center, Central Azerbaijan with Tabriz as its center, and East Azerbaijan, with Ardebil as its center.[59]

However, the government remained adamant about removing the name Azerbaijan from the province, and various Azerbaijanis continued to oppose this action. Hasan Aminlu, a deputy from Shabestar in East Azerbaijan, stated in the Majlis:

Despite the fact that Sabalan and Sahand are two beautiful names for two beautiful mountains in Azerbaijan, Azerbaijanis have preserved their own identity and purity under the name of Azerbaijan and Azerbaijanis over the centuries and ages as the guardian of our dear homeland Iran and the protector of the world of Islam.[60]

In the end, and in the final legislation approved on April 11, 1993, the new province was declared Ardabil Province, and the name East Azerbaijan was retained in the Tabriz-centered province.[61] It seems that the choice of the name was a last-minute decision. Some officials and

---

57. IRNA in English, October 15, 1992.

58. *Resalat*, January 13, 1993, p. 5.

59. Ibid.

60. *Resalat*, March 11, 1993, p. 5.

61. *Resalat*, April 12, 1993, p. 5.

agencies were unaware of this change, and mistakenly called the new province East Azerbaijan or Sabalan.[62]

In support of the final approval of the legislation, Nur-eddind No'i-Eqdam, a Majlis deputy from Ardebil, linked the establishment of the new province to a desire to combat the political influence of the Republic of Azerbaijan. He commented that one of the "political fruits" of the final decision on the new province is that it "disrupted the criminal and lifeless dream of Pan-Turkism, an ugly phenomenon . . . which took shape across the border," referring to the Republic of Azerbaijan.[63] This statement illustrates that the decision to split East Azerbaijan, and evidently the government's tenacity regarding the removal of all onomastic links to Azerbaijan was partly based on its desire to preempt potential ties between the Iranian provinces and the Republic of Azerbaijan.

After the name change, some Azerbaijanis continued to express indignation over the removal of the name "Azerbaijan" from the new province. In a 1994 letter-writing campaign by Azerbaijani students, this issue was again aired. In an open letter addressed to the Majlis deputies from the Azerbaijani provinces, a group calling itself "The Azerbaijani Students of Tehran Universities," complained that the new province's name did not include the name "Azerbaijan."[64] In an open "Letter from the Meshkinshahr Students Studying in the Universities of the Country to the Government of the Islamic Republic of Iran," which was originally published in the Zenjan local weekly *Omid-e Zenjan,* the students, who are from a city which is part of the new province, expressed total disagreement with the removal of the name Azerbaijan from the new province:

In our opinion changing the name of the new province to the name of one town is a historic error, which will become more acute after a few years. In the history of Iran, we have such a precedent in the province of Bakhtaran, formerly named after the Pahlavi dynasty.[65]

---

62.   IRNA, for instance, reported on April 13, 1993, that "Majlis deputies from Iran's West, East and Central Azerbaijan Provinces" attended a protest against Armenian actions. Even Ahmed Hemmeti, deputy from the city of Meshkinshahr in the new province, referred to the new province as "the province of Sabalan when praising the Majlis decision." *Resalat,* April 19, 1993, p. 5.

63.   Ibid.

64.   "Letter of the Azerbaijani Students Studying in Tehran Universities to the Azerbaijani Deputies of the Iranian Majlis."

65.   "Letter of the Meshkinshahr Students Studying in the Universities of the Country to the Government of the Islamic Republic of Iran."

The students declared that the government's decision to split East Azerbaijan province has "caused anxiety and worry among all our people." They responded with cynicism to the supposed benefits to be reaped by the declaration of the new province, even refusing to recognize the new name:

Under the conditions of the rapid economic, social and cultural development and progress of other regions and provinces, this part of Azerbaijan, named Ardebil Province, lives in conditions of poverty and hardship. The province, once ranked as the third most successful, is now located in the seventeenth place. Of course, our leadership knows the situation in the newly formed province. Reality is the following—our towns are now like big villages. There is a real shortage in the fields of education, public health, culture, etc. [66]

The split did not change the people's perception that together the three provinces formed part of Azerbaijan. Despite their official status as distinct provinces, Majlis representatives from the three provinces often operated as a united bloc attempting to deal with issues affecting "Azerbaijan" as a whole.

Changes in other provincial jurisdictions also elicited responses. Riots broke out in Qazvin in August 1994 over the proposal to grant the city of Qazvin provincial status. Qazvin's population is ethnically mixed, composed mainly of Azerbaijanis and Persians. Some Azerbaijani activists interpreted the attempt to separate this city from the predominantly Azerbaijani-populated city of Zenjan as part of a policy of dispersing the Turkic-speaking population among Persian dominated units. The Iranian newspaper *Resalat* reported the appearance of "nationalist sentiment" during the incidents in Qazvin.[67]

NO LONGER THE "TURK-E KHAR"

Azerbaijanis are one of the most frequent objects of ridicule in Iranian society. Their distinctive accents are often mocked, and the Azerbaijanis are frequently referred to as "Turk-e khar" ("Turkish donkey"). This degrading term was used particularly during the later years of the Pahlavi regime. At that time, it seems that most Azerbaijanis tolerated these jokes: those holding a primary Iranian identity may have seen them as a natural part of Iranian society that mocks all the different regional groupings. In the early 1990s, however, derogatory remarks against Azerbaijanis often provoked extreme reactions. Many of the statements issued by Azer-

---

66. Ibid.

67. *Resalat*, August 8, 1994.

baijanis in this period not only demanded the expansion of their language and cultural rights, but also addressed what they termed cultural "humiliation." They asserted their refusal to tolerate further slurs and "dishonorable treatment." The feeling of being humiliated by the regime, and especially its media, was expressed in the open "Letter of the Azerbaijani Students Studying in the Tehran Universities to the Azerbaijani Deputies of the Iranian Majlis." The authors claimed that Iranian media had a policy to "mimic and defame the culture and language of the Azerbaijan Shi'i," and asked, "When will it be possible to give an effective answer to all this humiliation and mockeries?"[68]

In spring 1995, a survey conducted by the Iranian Broadcasting Authority revealed widespread prejudice among Persians toward the Azerbaijanis. The questions in the survey and its results outraged many Azerbaijanis and prompted vehement, open reactions. According to a letter distributed by the South Azerbaijani Front for Independence (GAMIC), close to 2,000 Azerbaijani students participated in an antigovernment demonstration at Tabriz University on May 9 in response "to the racist questionnaire distributed by the official Radio/Television Center of the Islamic regime." This letter stated that the demonstration was dispersed by the police. The participants reassembled in a hall at the university, where the governor of East Azerbaijan Province, Abdol-'Alizadeh, met them and they agreed to disband after talking with him. According to the letter, which claimed that GAMIC activists had participated in the demonstration, the offensive survey was conducted in order to incite inter- ethnic tension and thus "to divert our national struggle from its main course by reducing it to 'Fars/Turk' issues and conflicts."[69]

Salam newspaper reported that on May 21, 1995, a group of students from Tabriz University, together with Azerbaijani-speaking students from Tehran University, demonstrated in Tabriz to protest the survey. According to the *Salam* report, the demonstrators claimed that the survey was an affront to the honor of the Azerbaijani community in Iran.[70] Ten days after the publication of the survey, the Broadcasting Authority denied any connection to it, maintaining that its research center had merely published the results. After the denial, Azerbaijani students sent letters to the offices of the president, the Majlis, and the Friday sermon leaders,

---

68. "Letter of the Azerbaijani Students Studying in Tehran Universities to the Azerbaijani Deputies of the Iranian Majlis."

69. "GAMIC Announcement Regarding Azerbaijani Students' Demonstration," May 1995 (unpublished).

70. *Salam*, May 21, 1995.

and to the heads of the provinces of Azerbaijan, Zenjan, and Ardebil, calling for support for the use and study of the Azerbaijani language in Tabriz University and condemning the survey.

The extreme reaction of many Azerbaijanis to this survey may point to the formation of increased Azerbaijani self-pride. Furthermore, if this survey accurately reflected commonly held attitudes among Persians in Iran, prejudice and widely held anti-Azerbaijani stereotypes were apparently prevalent in Iran and may have reinforced separate Azerbaijani identity.[71]

In summer 1995, some Azerbaijanis protested against the frequent Iranian Broadcasting Authority programs in which jokes about Azerbaijani accents were made. Moreover, ethnic sentiments entered the sports arena in Iran. Both western and Iranian witnesses to sports events in Iran stated that when soccer teams from Tabriz came to Tehran, Azerbaijani fans thronged to the sports stadiums, rooting for them with cheers and songs in Azerbaijani, often to the chagrin of Persian-speaking opponents.

In this period, some changes occurred in the way many Azerbaijanis saw their history. Interviews revealed that many Azerbaijanis, including those who saw themselves primarily as Iranians, were now willing to say positive things about the Pishaveri period, praising its success in the field of strengthening Azerbaijani culture, language, and education.

POLITICAL ACTIVITY

The first half of the 1990s saw the formation of many Azerbaijani political forums and organizations and increased political activity by Azerbaijanis in Iran. These bodies represented a wide range of opinions; some worked within the Iranian parliament, while others called for the Azerbaijani provinces to secede from Iran. One of the most important political developments was the formation in 1993 of a faction in the Majlis—The Assembly of Azerbaijan Majlis Deputies—composed of delegates from the Azerbaijani provinces; it focused on issues concerning the Azerbaijani provinces and the fostering of relations with the Republic of Azerbaijan.[72] In addition, Azerbaijani members of the Majlis openly aired their opinions about problems affecting all Azerbaijanis, and not just those living in their provinces. For instance, in July 1993, one representative, Ibrahim Saraf, openly criticized Tehran for appointing many non-Azerbaijani

---

71. For instance, according to the survey, most Persians answered that they would not like to have an Azerbaijani neighbor, or have their daughter marry an Azerbaijani.

72. The first published reference to this body is from April 1993. See *Resalat*, April 7, 1993, p. 3.

officials to the Azerbaijani provincial government bodies, and for central government discrimination against Azerbaijanis.[73]

The press in the Republic of Azerbaijan and Azerbaijani nationalist organizations based outside Iran often reported about the existence of several Azerbaijani nationalist organizations in Iran, among them the Azerbaijan Feda'iyin Organization, the South Azerbaijan Popular Front, and the Azerbaijan Liberation Organization.[74] It is difficult to assess the extent of the activities and the following that these organizations commanded in Iran.

Many of these organizations pointed to the breakup of the Soviet Union and the establishment of the independent Republic of Azerbaijan as having influenced their political course of action. The founding statement of GAMIC, a front encompassing a variety of organizations working toward the independence of "South Azerbaijan" that was established in 1995, declared:

The worldwide struggle of the subjugated nations coupled with the support that they receive from the international community for their cause is one of the salient characteristics of the contemporary era. The formation of a number of independent nation states from the ruins of Soviet imperialism testify to the above stated fact.[75]

The Azerbaijan Feda'iyin Organization, made a similar statement:

The economic and political developments in the newly independent states of the former Soviet Union—in the Republic of Azerbaijan, Ukraine, and others—are very attractive for Iran and in particular for Azerbaijan. Such trends and political events are like awakening factors for the Azerbaijani people and intelligentsia and such reality forces them to compare their economic, cultural, political and social position with the position of the residents of Isfahan, Shiraz, etc. This comparison has led to the formation of a new political outlook in Azerbaijan and in Iran and the establishing of the new wave of progressive nationalism.[76]

---

73.   Reuters World Service, July 27, 1993.

74.   *Turan*, April 7, 1995.

75.   Güney Azärbaycan Milli Istiqlal Jäbhäsi (The South Azerbaijan National Front for Independence) founding statement, 1995 (Azerbaijani, unpublished).

76.   Azerbaijani activists outside Iran claim that this document was composed and circulated in Iran. *Rafsanjani Dar Azerbayjan Bedumbale Che Bud?* Teshkilat-e Feda'iyin-e Azerbayjan (Azerbaijan Feda'iyin Organization), July 13, 1995 (Persian, unpublished).

In discussing President Rafsanjani's July 1995 visit to Tabriz, the Azerbaijan Feda'iyin stated,

He has not said why the Iranian government did not answer the more than fourteen petitions and appeals sent by thousands of Azerbaijani students. He does not explain the reasons for such official negative attitudes toward the Azeri language and literature. The Iranian president cannot explain the reason for the unjust policy toward Azerbaijan.[77]

Another organization founded in Iran that supports the independence of "South Azerbaijan" is the AQT, Azerbaijan Liberation Organization (Azerbayjan Qurtulush Teshkilati). According to the organization's constitution, its strategic goals are: independence for South Azerbaijan; unification of the two Azerbaijans; promotion of national and democratic principles; facilitating common economic, political, and cultural endeavors and cooperation with all Turkic nations; and the promotion of a free market economic system with a modern technological basis.[78]

One of the most dramatic events of Azerbaijani political activity, in this period took place during the spring 1996 elections for the Majlis. In Tabriz, Dr. Mohammad Chehregani ran on a platform that called for strengthening the use of the Azerbaijani language in East Azerbaijan and for concentrating efforts on the economic development of Azerbaijan. Among the goals enumerated in his platform:

Constant activities for the revival of the Islamic national culture, and particularly—strengthening and reviving of the literature, traditions, and native language (Azerbaijani-Turkic).[79]

This statement is quite striking—Chehregani defines the strengthening of the Azerbaijani-Turkic language as part of "Islamic national culture."

Chehregani's election platform contained additional items that were quite unusual in Iran. On the cover page of his election material, Chehregani addressed the voters as Azerbaijanis, calling them "the patriotic and brave children of Sheikh Mohammed Khiyabani and Sattar Khan," two Iranian heros of Azerbaijani origin. Under his own picture, he included a phrase in Azerbaijani: "Heydar Baba raise truthful chil-

---

77. Ibid.

78. Constitution of the Azärbayjan Qurtulush Teshkilati (Azerbaijani, unpublished).

79. Muhammad Chehregani's election platform, 1996. It was widely distributed as part of his campaign materials.

dren," referring to the hill enshrined by the poet Shahriyar. The inclusion of any Azerbaijani was an extraordinary act. With this phrase he was attempting to appeal to the electorate's sentiments as Azerbaijanis, telling voters to continue to bring up their children in the spirit of their people. In addition, the Ark of Tabriz, a symbol Iranian Azerbaijanis cherish, also appeared on the cover page. When describing his background, Chehregani stressed the work he had done to expand the use of the Azerbaijani-Turkic language in Iran. He noted that his doctoral dissertation was on the influence of Turkic words in the Persian language, and that one of his findings was that modern Persian contains 4,000 Turkic words. Chehregani thus challenged both the frequent claims by Persians that their language is more developed and the higher status accorded to Persian. Chehregani pointed out his contribution to establishing research and studies in the Azerbaijani language. Throughout his campaign literature he referred to the language as "Azerbaijani-Turkic." Nevertheless, in his official literature he stressed his loyalty to Iran and the goals of the Islamic revolution.

In the April 1996 elections, Chehregani received the overwhelming support of the electorate. But security services detained him for two weeks, until he agreed to resign from the parliamentary race. The announcement of his resignation led to large demonstrations in Tabriz on May 12. Many participants were arrested, and according to various press reports, five Azerbaijanis were executed following the demonstrations. Tehran claimed that the five men were executed on the charge of drug trafficking. However, their bodies were hung in public from construction cranes, a very unusual practice in recent years, and evidently a warning to the public. Dr. Chehregani claimed that the executions dampened the demonstrations that had been taking place almost daily since he was forced to resign from the parliamentary race. He agreed to withdraw from the race because his arrest had led to a "volatile" situation in Tabriz, and he wanted to avoid the involvement of Azerbaijanis in political violence.[80] After his release from jail, Chehregani was frequently summoned for interrogations by the Iranian security services, and in September 1996 he was again held for sixty days.

Chehregani attempted again to submit his candidacy for the 2000 parliamentary elections in Iran, but in January 2000 his application was denied by the authorities. A demonstration reportedly broke out in Tabriz after Chehregani's candidacy was blocked by authorities. Iranian officials

---

80.   Telephone interview with Muhammad Ali Chehregani, July 27, 1996, cited in *Human Rights Watch/Middle East*, Vol. 9, No. 7 (E) (September 1997), p. 28.

acknowledged the existence of the demonstration but attempted to dismiss its importance, stating that there were only fifty participants.[81]

Like Chehregani, other Azerbaijanis also felt that the prosperity of Tabriz and Azerbaijan had been neglected. They openly expressed indignation over the Azerbaijani provinces' lack of development and the need for more resources. In letters the Azerbaijani students sent to the leadership of Iran in 1994, they pointed out the decline of economic development in those provinces, and called on the Azerbaijani delegates to the Majlis to obtain more resources for them. Azerbaijanis in Tehran also protested over their economic situation. In April 1995, violent demonstrations against the regime took place in the Tehran suburb of Islam-Shar, which is predominantly inhabited by Azerbaijanis. The demands of the demonstrators were chiefly economic, but the fact that it was Azerbaijanis who reacted violently to regime policy may indicate their increased alienation from the regime.

The coordinated letter-writing campaigns of the Azerbaijani students in the early 1990s was a political manifestation of a rise in Azerbaijani identity. Their letters contained many common demands, which indicates that they are the result of a joint effort. They also reflect a sense of self-empowerment, since they claim that the number of Azerbaijanis in Iran is 27 million.

The authors of the letter from the "Meshkinshahr Students Studying in the Universities of the Country," refer to Azerbaijan as "our land," yet before introducing their political demands, they state:

We point out that we are forever Iranians and as people of Azerbaijan as a part of Iran, we will struggle for our independence and the territorial wholeness of our Islamic motherland.[82]

One of the demands in the letter was that regional officials be elected by local residents. The students criticized the fact that the new governor appointed to Ardebil province was not "selected from among the local residents," and that he did not even speak Azerbaijani:

Unfortunately, after waiting for some months we said 'Welcome' to our governor (*ostandar*) who does not understand our language. This took place despite the fact that half of our population does not understand Persian. Indeed, is it not a matter for regret, or is it impossible to elect a governor from

---

81. *Tehran Times*, January 11, 2000.

82. "Letter of the Meshkinshahr Students Studying in the Universities of the Country to the Government of the Islamic Republic of Iran."

the residents of the native town of Ayatollah Meshkini and among the Ardebilis?[83]

The students also reproached the new administration for bringing non-locals who were not versed in the Azerbaijani language and culture to work in the new provincial bureaucracy. They described this policy as "a kind of insult to the able local figures":

At the same time with the assignment of the new governor, some very active, devoted and revolutionary figures were dismissed from their administrative posts and they were replaced by non-local persons who do not have sufficient experience in our region. They don't know our cultural and geographical peculiarities, our language, etc. We are sure that such steps will cause the continuation of failures in the spheres of education and the environment.[84]

TEHRAN AND THE AZERBAIJANI CHALLENGE

One of the most significant indicators of the existence of an "Azerbaijani problem" in Iran is the behavior of Tehran and its policies; Tehran showed that it is very sensitive to expressions of Azerbaijani ethnic identity and that it fears Baku as a potential object of attraction for the Azerbaijanis in Iran. The internal Iranian Azerbaijani ethnic factor had an immense impact on the state-to-state relations between the Republic of Azerbaijan and Iran, and affected Tehran's policies in the Caucasus. For instance, Iran feared that the establishment of a strong and attractive Republic of Azerbaijan could lead to a rise in identity of its own Azerbaijani minority, and so adopted a policy of de facto cooperation with Armenia in the conflict with Azerbaijan for Nagorno-Karabagh. Evidently, Iran preferred that the Republic of Azerbaijan be involved in a conflict, making it less attractive to Iran's Azerbaijanis.[85] Despite its rhetoric of neutrality in the Karabagh conflict—which was inconsistent with the official ideology of a state that portrays itself as the protector and champion of the Shi'i in the world—throughout most of the post-independence pe-

---

83. Ibid.

84. Ibid.

85. Examples of Iran's assistance to Armenia include its establishment of diplomatic relations with Armenia in February 1992, and that it signed a number of economic agreements at one of the heights in the battles between Azerbaijan and Armenia. In April 1992, at one of the most crucial points in the confrontation between Azerbaijan and Armenia, Iran agreed to supply natural gas and oil to Armenia, and transportation links were improved between the sides, breaking Baku's blockade on Armenia. See Interfax (in English), April 15, 1992.

riod, Iran cooperated with Armenia. Even in all-Muslim forums, such as the Economic Cooperation Council, Tehran refrained at that time from criticizing Armenia.[86] In relating the causes of the conflict, Iranian representatives and official media criticized "colonial powers" and other external agents, such as Russia, Turkey, the United States and occasionally the "Zionists." They even blamed Azerbaijani President Elchibey for the conflict, while seldom pointing at Yerevan. Tehran's lack of action on behalf of Azerbaijan in this period was so pronounced that hard-liners in Iran criticized the official policy as not a proper reflection of Iran's "religious and ideological responsibilities."[87] Iran's Deputy Foreign Minister, Mahmud Va'ezi, pointed to internal considerations as one of Iran's major factors in its policy toward the Nagorno-Karabagh conflict.[88] Perhaps the best indication of Iran's tilt toward Armenia was that Yerevan and the Nagorno-Karabagh Armenians repeatedly praised Iran's role in the negotiation process and expressed their preference for Tehran over many other foreign mediators.[89]

Evidently fearing a permanent Azerbaijani presence in the center of Iranian Azerbaijan, Tehran did not allow the Republic of Azerbaijan to open a consulate in Tabriz, though the two countries had signed an agreement in August 1992 permitting each of them to open one, and Tehran had already established its own consulate in Nakhchivan. The Islamic Republic conducted a flagrant media campaign against Elchibey, evidently due to his consistent campaigning for the rights of the Azerbaijanis in Iran.[90] The Islamic Republic also welcomed the return of Aliyev in June 1993.[91] Since the end of 1992, Tehran attempted to minimize the direct connections between Azerbaijanis on both sides of the border. In contrast to its policy toward refugees from Afghanistan and Iraq, Iran turned back

---

86. For example, the communiqué issued at the end of the first ECO summit in Tehran (February 16–17, 1992) does not even mention the Nagorno-Karabagh conflict. In contrast, it makes a clear statement supporting the "restoration of the inalienable rights" of the Palestinian people and respecting the rights of the people of Kashmir. See, IRNA (in English), February 17, 1992.

87. *Jomhuri-ye Islami*, March 2, 1992, p. 2.

88. Mahmud Va'ezi in Interfax (in English), March 25, 1992 (FBIS-SOV-92-059). See, also, *Tehran Times*, March 10, 1992, p. 2, for reference to the internal Azerbaijani and Armenian factor as affecting its suitability to mediate in the conflict.

89. See, for instance, TASS, February 28, 1992 (FBIS-SOV-92-040).

90. *Abrar*, June 28, 1992; *Tehran Times* also stated that the election of Elchibey was "not good news for Iran," quoted in IRNA in English, June 8, 1992; IRNA in English, June 28, 1992; and *Salam*, June 25, 1992, p. 10 (FBIS-NES-92-130).

91. See, for instance, IRNA, June 16, 1993.

Azerbaijani refugees fleeing the areas of hostility with Armenia, sending them to refugee camps inside the Republic of Azerbaijan. Another illustration of Tehran's fear of potential Azerbaijani nationalism was that speeches given by senior Iranian officials visiting in the Azerbaijani provinces often stressed the ethnic unity of the country and praised Azerbaijan's role in defense of the territorial integrity of Iran. The fact that the leaders feel compelled to mention and praise "Iranian unity" when visiting Azerbaijan shows that the question of Azerbaijani loyalty and ethnic relations was on Iran's agenda.[92]

ASSERTION OF IDENTITY AS IRANIANS

Many Azerbaijanis in Iran asserted their loyalty to Iran and the regime and their identity as Iranians, apparently in response to the question of self-identity that arose after the establishment of the Republic of Azerbaijan and the subsequent interaction between the two co-ethnic populations.

Fatema Homayoon Moghaddam, a Majlis deputy from Tabriz, insisted that Baku should not think about annexing the Azerbaijani provinces; rather, it should realize that Azerbaijan should return as an integral part of Iranian territory. She stated, "Azerbaijan is part of the territory of Iran and must return to Iran in order to fulfill the dream of... Azerbaijanis in Iran."[93] In addition, she supported an attempt to block the reception of foreign television by satellite in Iran, believing that the television broadcasts from abroad are intended to "destroy our Iranian, national, and Islamic identity."[94]

The difference of attitudes between Azerbaijanis in Iran and those in the Republic of Azerbaijan was displayed in protests regarding the status of Islam in the new state. On November 12, 1995, in response to the publication of the draft Constitution of the Republic of Azerbaijan, Friday worshippers in Tabriz protested against the clause on the separation of religion and state and the fact that the constitution did not declare Islam as the official religion of the republic. According to *Keyhan*, the organizers of the demonstration said that the "people of Tabriz" called upon their "dear Azeri brothers" to reject the constitution.[95]

---

92. See, for instance, Khamenei's visit in Tabriz, Tehran IRIB Television First Program, July 27, 1993 (FBIS-NES-93-143); Khatami's visit in Tabriz, IRNA, November 21, 1998; IRNA, July 24, 2000; and Khatami's speech in Urmiya, *Financial Times*, September 18, 2000.

93. Quoted by French News Agency from Tehran, March 1, 1995.

94. *Resalat*, June 1, 1994, p. 5.

95. *Keyhan*, quoted by Reuters News Agency, November 12, 1995.

The *Imam Juma* (Friday Prayer Leader) of Tabriz, Ayatollah Mohsen Shabestary, remarked in May 1996:

The Azerbaijan Republic once was ours. So if there is any talk of unification of the two Azerbaijanis, it is they who should come back to Iran. Some agents of world arrogance are trying to damage our national unity by spreading secessionist sentiments in our region. Unfortunately some of their mercenaries in Tabriz repeat these words, and talk of Pan-Turkism. The policy of the Islamic Republic is to avoid such polemics. We do not want to create a hue and cry. But if we are faced with these satanic plots, we should remind everyone, including the people of the Azerbaijan Republic, that we have lost some Azeri cities, and we could one day claim them back.[96]

This statement reveals that the issue of relations with the republic was being debated in Tabriz; Shabestary condemned of activists in Tabriz, which indicates that Azerbaijani nationalist activity was taking place there.

Many Azerbaijanis asserted that demanding Azerbaijani rights did not contradict being loyal Iranians. A letter that appeared in *Varliq* declared that for Iranian Azerbaijanis "our flag is the same as the flag of Iran."[97] Yet, the author adds that "it is impossible to feel content in Iran and to praise it when Azerbaijanis are constantly being offended and humiliated."[98] The author continues:

At present, in Tehran University there are departments of English, French, German, Russian, and Arabic, but it is impossible to teach one Turkic word to students and graduates who are studying in different departments and who after their studies are sent to Azerbaijan to hold important posts in its towns.

There is a small town in Sweden called Linshopnag and in the library of this town there is a collection of books in Turki, in Kurdi. In contrast, in Iran's libraries it is very difficult to find any sources for learning or researching the local and tribal languages.[99]

Like the students from Meshkinshahr, the author condemns Tehran's practice of sending governors and administrators to the Azerbaijani provinces who do not speak the language of the inhabitants.

---

96. "Ayatollah Shabestary Addresses the Seminary Students in Tabriz," *Sobz*, May 28, 1996, cited in Human Rights Watch/Middle East, Vol. 9, No. 7 (E) (September 1997), p. 27.

97. Letter from Nosarat Khavani, *Varliq*, p. 92.

98. Ibid, pp. 92–93.

99. Ibid, p. 94.

The students' letter campaign stressed that Iran's Constitution stipulated their right to use their language, so their demand did not conflict with their status as loyal citizens of Iran. In a letter to President Rafsanjani, the students demanded the realization of Articles Fifteen and Nineteen of the constitution, declaring:

We are the people who enriched the history of Iran by offering highly memorable heroes and further enhanced Iran's dignity and glory. We are well aware of our national duty in protecting and maintaining the territorial integrity of this country.[100]

The students also criticized those Iranians who try to delegitimize their efforts to "revive their mother tongue," by calling these activities "separatist and non-Iranian."[101]

An interesting comment on the question of autonomy for the Azerbaijanis in Iran by Iran's ambassador to the Republic of Azerbaijan reflected a different view:

There is no problem of autonomy in Southern Azerbaijan. You can ask if we want autonomy for South Azerbaijan. No, we don't. The spiritual leader of Iran, many ministers, and ambassadors are Turks, I personally and my deputies too. Why do we need autonomy for Azerbaijan if we run Iran?[102]

Those interviewed for this study have made revealing comments about the Iranian Azerbaijanis' self-identity. Some pointed out that in the 1960s and 1970s, the Azerbaijanis overwhelmingly supported "universalistic" answers to their problems, such as communism and Islam. Many claimed that the new generation was seeking particularistic solutions, such as nationalism. One interviewee pointed out that while in the past Shi'a served to bind Persians and Azerbaijanis, it now serves as a divisive force after having been "dragged through the mud" by this regime. A majority of the Azerbaijanis hoped to achieve expanded cultural autonomy in Iran, and expressed pride as Azerbaijanis. Nonetheless, most saw themselves as Iranians as well, viewed Iran in a supra-ethnic sense, and did not equate it with Persian identity or language. For some interviewees, Iranian identity was symbolized by the Safavid dynasty, when Azerbaijani Turkish was the predominant court language and the capital of Iran was in Azerbaijan during much of the time.

---

100. *Akhbar*, June 8, 1996, p. 2.

101. Ibid.

102. *Zerkalo*, June 1, 1996.

Relations: From Contacts to Interaction

Following the independence of the Republic of Azerbaijan, dramatic changes took place in the nature of the contacts and relations between the Azerbaijanis on both sides of the border. In the early and mid-1980s contacts were limited. However, on the eve of independence and after the establishment of the state, these loose ties were transformed into intensive interaction.

Among the Soviet Azerbaijanis, an extensive outpouring of desire for ties with their co-ethnics in Iran served as a major focal point for expressing their own sense of Azerbaijani national identity and pride in their culture in the 1980s and early 1990s. This drive for expanded cultural and political contacts increased as restrictions were lifted in the Soviet Union and as Moscow's control eroded. Western researchers generally portray the "longings" for ties with the Azerbaijanis in Iran during the Soviet period purely as part of Moscow's "campaigns" for gaining influence in Iran.[103] While Moscow often encouraged Baku's activities when this served its interests, the growth of this desire after the disintegration of Soviet power demonstrates that the yearning for ties was also based in local and deeply rooted sentiments that had existed in Soviet Azerbaijan. The interest of the Azerbaijanis in the new republic in Iranian Azerbaijan is illustrated by the fact that Baku's museums presented the history and culture of the Azerbaijanis in Iran as an integral part of their people's general history.

As just before independence, many visits took place. According to Hasan Reza'i, the governor of Astara, at the Astara border crossing alone an average of 400 families a week from Iran and the Republic of Azerbaijan visited one another in 1992.[104] In addition, during the height of the Armenian conquests in the fall of 1993, tens of thousands of refugees from the Republic of Azerbaijan crossed into Iranian territory to escape the progressing Armenian forces.[105]

Visits and interaction became so frequent that the Foreign Ministry of Iran opened an office in Tabriz in December 1993 to take care of the increasing volume of visits and trade. Iranian Foreign Minister Velayati commented that

---

103.   For example, Alexandre Bennigsen and S. Enders Wimbush, *Muslims of the Soviet Empire: A Guide* (Bloomington: Indiana University Press, 1986), p. 144.

104.   IRNA in English, February 26, 1993.

105.   IRNA in English, November 2, 1993, reported that in the last week of October 1993, 37,027 refugees crossed the Araz seeking refuge in Iran.

With the establishment of the Foreign Ministry office in Tabriz, all consular, student, cultural, economic and travel affairs of the provinces of East Azerbaijan, West Azerbaijan, and Ardabil will be tended to on the spot and people will no longer have to apply to Tehran for these transactions.[106]

Relatives searched for one another and many family ties were renewed. Azerbaijanis on both sides of the border advertised in Iranian and Baku newspapers in search of relatives with whom they had lost contact during the Soviet period. Azerbaijanis from the two sides married, and these marriages became an important means for regenerating the links between the Azerbaijans. Azerbaijanis in Iran and in the republic who shared the same professions established relations and cooperation. For instance, in October 1992, the First Tabriz-Baku Conference of Foreign Language Teaching was held in Tabriz.[107]

Improvements also took place in communications and transportation. On July 11, 1993, direct flights were inaugurated between Tabriz and Baku. In addition, regular daily bus service was established between various cities in the Azerbaijani provinces and the Republic of Azerbaijan.

One of the most momentous developments was the establishment of formal, direct cooperation and interchange between the local government of the Azerbaijani provinces in Iran and the Republic of Azerbaijan, circumventing Tehran. Delegations from all three Azerbaijani provinces visited Baku and established formal direct cooperation in many fields, including trade, education, and scientific research. For instance, representatives of the Iranian Azerbaijani provinces and the republic signed protocols and agreements for direct bilateral technical and economic cooperation.[108]

In 1992–93, most of the humanitarian and refugee assistance from Iran to the Republic of Azerbaijan was organized directly from the Azerbaijani provinces.[109] Beginning in the summer of 1992, many Azerbaijanis wounded in the Nagorno-Karabagh war were treated in Tabriz hospitals. Throughout 1992–93, convoys of supplies and other aid were sent directly from the Azerbaijani provinces to the needy and to refugees

---

106.   Voice of the Islamic Republic of Iran First Program, December 8, 1993 (FBIS-NES-93-234).

107.   The logo of the conference (as published in *Varliq*, October–December 1992, p. 9), appeared in many languages—Azerbaijani in Cyrillic script, French, and English—but Persian was not among them.

108.   See, for instance, IRNA in English, February 22, 1993.

109.   See, for instance, IRNA in English, August 31, 1993.

in the republic; initially Azerbaijani representatives from the Iranian provinces had coordinated these convoys.[110]

For instance, in June 1992 a delegation from Urmiya set up a refugee center in Nakhchivan, and the East Azerbaijan Province opened a refugee camp within the territory of the republic in September 1993.[111] While this humanitarian assistance may have fostered direct ties, it apparently did not make the new republic attractive to the Azerbaijanis in Iran, since they had been exposed to the harsh conditions produced by the war.

The republic focused its cooperative activities on Tabriz rather than on Tehran. In August 1992, the Republic of Azerbaijan opened a trade fair in Tabriz. In 1992, cooperation and regular exchanges were inaugurated between Tabriz University and the Azerbaijani Academy of Sciences and two of Baku's leading universities—Khazar University and Baku State University. In January 1996, a decision was made to establish a permanent joint market at the border town of Bilasuvar; it was meant to handle an estimated annual $10 million worth of goods.[112]

Some of the exchanges were conducted directly on the provincial level between the Iranian Azerbaijani provinces and the Nakhchivan Autonomous Republic, especially during the period when Aliyev headed Nakhchivan's government before he returned to power in Baku. For instance, in May 1993, the governor of Iran's West Azerbaijan Province visited Nakhchivan.[113]

Iranian Majlis deputies from the Azerbaijani provinces were especially active in facilitating Iran's relations with the Republic of Azerbaijan. Members of the Assembly of Azerbaijani Deputies caucus conducted visits and initiated cooperation projects with members of parliament from the Republic of Azerbaijan. Assembly members issued protests against Armenia, and deputies from the Azerbaijani provinces led campaigns pressuring Tehran to minimize its relations with Armenia. In the Majlis, they openly called for Tehran's assistance to Azerbaijan and participated in demonstrations against Armenia.[114] On April 13, 1993, Kamel Abedinzadeh, the Azerbaijani deputy from Khoi, even spoke

110.   Voice of the Islamic Republic of Iran First Program Network in Persian, June 11, 1992 (FBIS-NES-92-114); and IRNA in English, April 22, 1993.

111.   IRNA in English, September 7, 1993.

112.   Voice of the Islamic Republic of Iran First Program Network in Persian, January 21, 1996 (FBIS-NES-96-016).

113.   Voice of the Islamic Republic of Iran in Azerbaijani, May 12, 1993 (FBIS-SOV-93-092).

114.   *Resalat*, April 19, 1993, p. 5; and IRNA in English, April 13, 1993.

in Azerbaijani in the Majlis when he condemned Armenian actions against Azerbaijan. In addition, he issued press releases for publication in *Hamshahri* and other journals on this issue.[115] On April 6, 1993, Mohammed 'Ali Nejad-Sarkhani, a deputy from Tabriz, read a resolution in the name of the Assembly of Azerbaijan Majlis Deputies condemning Armenia's attacks on Azerbaijan and calling for Iranian support for the Republic of Azerbaijan. In this statement to the Majlis, which showed his knowledge of the history of the Azerbaijanis in the north, the deputy drew a parallel between the "Russian-assisted Armenian attack on Azerbaijan" and the "crimes committed in 1920 by the Ninth Regiment of the Red Army in Azerbaijan."[116] Due to their special interest in fostering relations with the Republic of Azerbaijan, Majlis representatives from the Azerbaijani provinces participated in special discussions in the parliament on Iran's ties with the states in the Caucasus and Central Asia. They also made proposals during these discussions for expanding Iran's "cultural and economic activities" with these countries.[117]

In addition to the role they played in facilitating relations between Tehran and Baku, the Azerbaijani Majlis members encouraged cooperation and contacts between the Azerbaijani provinces in Iran and the Republic of Azerbaijan. Many of them visited the Republic of Azerbaijan and hosted their counterparts in return. During a visit to Baku in August 1996, Ahad Kaza'i, a Majlis deputy from Ardebil and member of the Azerbaijani parliamentary group, expressed the hope that the strengthening of interparliamentary relations with the Republic of Azerbaijan would contribute to the expansion of trade and economic relations between the republic and the Azerbaijani provinces in Iran.[118] In 1993, an interparliamentary friendship group was established between Iran and the republic. The majority of the participants from Iran were Azerbaijanis.[119] In addition, Ibrahim Saraf, Majlis deputy from Marand, was active in coordinating assistance from East Azerbaijani Province to Nakhchivan.

These direct interchanges and cooperation efforts seem to have contributed to an increased desire for more local control over affairs in the Azerbaijani provinces, especially in East Azerbaijan Province. The direct bilateral cooperation with the Republic of Azerbaijan served as a prece-

---

115. *Resalat*, April 14, 1993, p. 5.

116. *Resalat*, April 7, 1993, p. 3.

117. *Resalat*, November 18, 1992, p. 5.

118. *Turan* (English), August 5, 1996

119. *Azärbayjan* (newspaper), December 9, 1994, p. 4 (FBIS-SOV-95-028-S).

dent, and the Azerbaijani provinces expanded their independent activities with foreign countries, especially with other Turkic peoples. For instance, on May 8, 1996, the governor of East Azerbaijan Province visited Istanbul, where he conducted talks on trade activities and the exchange of technical information between Turkish industrialists and their counterparts in East Azerbaijan. In addition, West Azerbaijan Province signed a trade agreement with the Tatarstan Autonomous Republic on February 14, 1996.[120] One of the most significant challenges to central authority was the request by Majlis Deputy Saraf for more independent authority for officials in East Azerbaijan province to organize assistance to the Republic of Azerbaijan without the interference of Iranian customs authorities.[121]

The contracts and cooperation between the Azerbaijani provinces and the Republic of Azerbaijan raised the importance of these provinces, whose economic position had deteriorated compared to other parts of Iran throughout the Pahlavi period and under the Islamic Republic. These provinces' foreign trade increased dramatically, and they became an important transit point for the expanding exchange between Iran and the newly independent republics of the former Soviet Union. The total non-oil exports from March 1991–March 1992 were worth over 4,400 billion rials, up 450 percent over the preceding year.[122] Azerbaijani Majlis representatives in Iran often stressed the role of the three Azerbaijani provinces in building links with the Republic of Azerbaijan to underscore their own importance and to justify their requests for resources.[123]

Initially, Iran welcomed the interchange between its Azerbaijani citizens and their co-ethnics in the Republic of Azerbaijan, and saw it as an opportunity to spread Iran's influence in the new Muslim republics and build economic and other types of cooperation with them. However, toward the end of 1992, Tehran saw that influence could flow two ways, and that the interaction could contribute to a rise in Azerbaijani identity in Iran. Iran tried to regain control over the connections and put them under central control, and toward the end of 1992 began to create obstacles to direct contacts between the Azerbaijanis. For example, Iranian authorities ordered that anyone wishing to marry citizens of the Republic of Azerbaijan must obtain a special permit, and declared all marriages car-

---

120. IRNA in English, February 14, 1996.

121. *Resalat*, March 8, 1993, pp. 5–6.

122. IRNA in English, June 16, 1992. This period corresponds to the year 1370 on the Iranian calendar

123. *Resalat*, December 23, 1992, pp. 5-6.

ried out without the permit illegal and invalid under the laws of the Is-
lamic Republic.[124] Iran prevented high-level officials from the Republic of
Azerbaijan from making official visits to Tabriz and other cities in the
Azerbaijani provinces. The Iranian Ministry of Foreign Affairs barred
Azerbaijani Ambassador Nasibzade from official visits in Tabriz, and
from traveling there in the embassy car displaying the Azerbaijani flag.[125]
On the eve of a planned visit to Iran in March 1994, Aliyev stated publicly
that he planned to visit Tabriz and other cities in the Azerbaijani provinces. This visit was delayed a number of times because Iran refused to
allow Aliyev to visit Tabriz, though he had been invited by the governor
of East Azerbaijan Province.[126] The visit to Iran, excluding Tabriz, was
eventually held in July 1994, but in a very tense atmosphere. Tehran refused to allow President Aliyev to include Tabriz in his state visits a number of times throughout the decade, and this often caused tension surrounding potential visits.

On the grassroots level, many Azerbaijanis in Iran expressed their
solidarity with the Republic of Azerbaijan in its struggle with Armenia
over the control of Nagorno-Karabagh, and criticized Iran's cooperation
with Armenia during this conflict. On May 25, 1992, 200 students demonstrating at Tabriz University chanted "Death to Armenia." They pointed a
finger at Tehran when they condemned the "silence of the Muslims"
in the face of the Armenian "criminal activities" as "treason to the
Koran."[127] According to *Salam*, the Azerbaijani demonstrators in Tabriz
urged Tehran to support the Republic of Azerbaijan in this struggle during a march marked by "nationalist fervor and slogans." *Salam* reported
that the demonstration was held "despite the opposition of the authorities."[128] On April 13, 1993, Tehran University students held a demonstration in front of the Armenian Embassy to show their support for the
Republic of Azerbaijan in its struggle with Armenia.[129] Azerbaijani language publications in Iran showed a special interest in the Nagorno-
Karabagh conflict and carried many articles that expressed solidarity
with the plight of the Azerbaijanis there. In the spring of 1994, an impas-
sioned article by Javad Heyat in *Varliq* was addressed to President

---

124. *Jomhuri-ye Islami* quoted by *Keyhan* (London), December 24, 1992, p. 1
(FBIS-NES-93-007).

125. From an interview with Ambassador Nasib Nasibzade.

126. *Tehran Times*, June 28, 1994, and conversation with Ambassador Nasibzade.

127. *Salam*, quoted by Reuters, May 25, 1992.

128. *Salam*, as quoted by Agence France Presse, May 25, 1992.

129. IRNA, April 13, 1993.

Suleiman Demirel of Turkey; it pleaded for Turkey to assist Azerbaijan in the Nagorno-Karabagh conflict.[130] *Varliq* frequently carried articles about Azerbaijani victims of this conflict, as well as poems written in memory of the fallen Azerbaijani soldiers.[131] Ayatollah Musavi-Ardebeli, an Azerbaijani, often mentioned the conflict in his Friday sermons, and was more assertive than other clerics in supporting the Republic of Azerbaijan. Musavi-Ardebeli also visited the republic after independence. Some claim that Azerbaijanis, prompted by the conflict in Karabagh, made threats against Armenians in Iran.[132]

These expressions of solidarity are an indication of the extent of the Azerbaijanis' special identity with the north. In addition, for some of the Azerbaijanis in Iran, Tehran's lack of support for Baku in the conflict seemed to create tension between their Azerbaijani and Iranian identities.

Azerbaijani language publications in Iran frequently carried news about events in the Republic of Azerbaijan and about cooperation between Tabriz and Baku, as well as articles by Azerbaijanis from the republic, including the ambassador to Iran.[133] A letter published in *Varliq* in spring 1991 discussed the culture of the Azerbaijanis, and mentioned cultural figures from both Baku and Iran.[134] Following the independence of the Republic of Azerbaijan, *Varliq* published a poem by Barez entitled "Baku."[135] It even published articles by writers from the north, such as Nebi Khezri, who had been very outspoken in his support for the rights for the Azerbaijanis in Iran and the establishment of ties between the two sides. However, the editor of *Varliq* stressed that the Azerbaijanis in Iran reject the calls from Baku to separate from Iran and join "northern Azerbaijan."[136]

---

130. Javad Heyat, in *Varliq* (April–June 1994), pp. 25–30.

131. For instance, "Khujali," *Varliq* (April–June 1992), pp. 31–33; and "Shahidlar," *Varliq* (January–May 1995), pp. 135–136.

132. Based on a conversation with an Armenian official. In the Azerbaijani provinces in Iran, there are approximately 5,000 to 6,000 Armenians, concentrated mostly in Tabriz, Salmas, Urmiya, and surrounding villages.

133. See, for instance, *Varliq* (October–December 1992).

134. Letter from Khavani, *Varliq*, p. 95.

135. El Barez, "Baki" (Azerbaijani), *Varliq* (July–September 1992), p. 125.

136. Javad Heyat, Telegram from *Varliq* to Azerbaijan's Prime Minister on the Occasion of His Interview to Baku TV (Persian), *Varliq* (October–December, 1991), pp. 134–136.

THE NORTH'S YEARNING FOR THE OTHER HALF

Following the independence of the Republic of Azerbaijan, individuals and representatives from all parts of the political spectrum expressed interest in ties with their co-ethnics in Iran, and concern for their cultural rights. Most mainstream politicians in the Republic of Azerbaijan thought of the Azerbaijanis in Iran as the same people. Opinions diverged over the manner and timing for building those relations and campaigning for their rights. Some Azerbaijani activists stressed that independence in the north was only the first stage of the Azerbaijani national movement, and that unification with an independent south Azerbaijan was necessary to acheive the goals of the movement.[137] However, on the grassroots level many felt that given the difficult circumstances of the new republic, unification of the south must remain an emotional, non-operative aspiration.

Elchibey raised the issue of campaigning for the rights of the Azerbaijanis in Iran to the level of state policy. Many of the PFA political elite saw unity with their co-ethnics in Iran as a way to build a strong and independent Azerbaijan. On the eve of his election, Elchibey stated that if elected he would strive for the independence of south Azerbaijan, adding that:

The twenty million Turks living in South Azerbaijan do not even have one school. Iran's attempt to help us is not very convincing especially when you consider that they deny the most basic rights to people living on their territory.[138]

Yet, in his official platform and at his inaugural ceremony, Elchibey did not mention the subject of south Azerbaijan, evidently aware of the probable political consequences. Nevertheless, in August 1992, Elchibey appointed Nasib Nasibzade to serve as the Republic of Azerbaijan's first ambassador to Iran. Nasibzade, a former student of Elchibey, had written many academic studies about the Azerbaijanis in Iran, and his views supporting the unification of north and south Azerbaijan were well known. By appointing Nasibzade, Elchibey was making a clear statement about his intent to work for unification.[139]

The various governments that have been in power in the Republic of Azerbaijan since independence have all marked December 31 as World

---

137. For example, Elchin Arifogly, *Muxalifat*, December 20, 1995, p. 4.

138. *Turkiye* (Istanbul), May 28, 1992, p. 13 (FBIS-SOV-92-108).

139. Nasibzade was removed from his post in January 1994.

Solidarity Day for Azerbaijanis. It was observed for the first time in 1989, when it served as the trigger for border incidents. Since independence, both the communist-era leaders and the opposition have expressed support for increasing ties with the Azerbaijanis in Iran. When asked about the Azerbaijanis in Iran, Mutalibov, the head of the transitional government head, remarked,

That problem is like a bleeding wound. We have many relatives in northern Iran. It is natural that we remain in touch with them. We are moving to adopt the Latin alphabet; they are using the Arabic script. Of course, we want to unite with them, but this is a very difficult problem. We have to consider political matters related to this problem.[140]

On Solidarity Day in 1993, President Aliyev remarked, "On this symbolic day, I congratulate all the Azerbaijanis in the world and wish for stronger solidarity among them in the future."[141] However, in 1999 his statement was much stronger:

millions of Azerbaijanis live in different countries of the world. It is Azerbaijan's historic mission to become a unifying factor for them. All Azerbaijanis should know that independent Azerbaijan is their homeland. The fate of our Republic, our Homeland should be the fate of every compatriot.[142]

In the Aliyev period, a third of all the newspaper articles on Iran published in the Republic of Azerbaijan in spring 1995–spring 1996 dealt with the theme of south Azerbaijan. The official government press was cautious in dealing with the issue of south Azerbaijan, while the independent and opposition press carried many articles in support of their co-ethnics and on the theme of "united Azerbaijan."[143] However, President Aliyev also mentioned the topic of divided Azerbaijan during major national speeches and documents. In an official decree, Aliyev stated:

The dismemberment of the Azerbaijani people and the division of our historical lands began with the treaties of Gulistan and Turkmanchay, signed in

---

140.   *Milliyet* (Istanbul), January 26, 1992, p. 5 (FBIS-SOV-92-023).

141.   Radio Baku in Azerbaijani, January 1, 1994 (FBIS-SOV-94-002).

142.   Statement published in Newsletter of the Embassy of Azerbaijan in Washington, D.C., December 30, 1999.

143.   *Azerbaijan-Iranian Relations,* (Baku: FAR Centre for Economics and Political Research), May 1996, pp. 7, 33.

1813 and 1828. The national tragedy of the divided Azerbaijani people was continued with the occupation of its lands.[144]

Following independence, some publications were produced in the Republic of Azerbaijan in the Azerbaijani language for distribution in Iran. Among them was a tri-lingual (Azerbaijani-Persian-English) children's primer, *Shekili Sözlük*, written by Hafiz Pashayev, in which the Azerbaijani words are written in both Latin and Arabic characters.[145] It seems that one of the purposes of the book was to teach Latin script to Azerbaijani children in Iran and Arabic script to children in the north. During the Aliyev era, a television series called "Shahriyar" on the culture of the southern Azerbaijanis was periodically broadcast by Baku television and was picked up in Iran. Apparently Baku broadcast it especially when relations with Iran were tense, such as at times when Iran closed its border with the republic, as a way of warning Tehran that Baku could also make threats.

Scholars in the Republic of Azerbaijan continued to produce numerous works on the culture and history of south Azerbaijan, including the fourth volume of Mirza Ibrahimov's collection of literature from south Azerbaijan.[146] The republic published many works of Azerbaijani authors from Iran, including additional works by the editor of *Varliq*, Javad Heyat.[147]

Following independence, many place names were changed, and names connected to south Azerbaijan were often adopted. For instance, the Lieutenant Schmidt plant became the Sattarkhan machine-building plant,[148] while streets throughout Azerbaijani towns and villages were named Tabriz. Azerbaijanis in the republic took an interest in cultural monuments in Iran. For instance, Anar Arzayev, chairman of the parliamentary Standing Commission on Cultural Affairs, condemned Tehran's

144.   Decree of the President of Azerbaijan, issued on March 26, 1998.

145.   Hafiz Pashayev, *Shäkilli Sözlük* (Ushaq Kitabï, Baku: Azärbayjan Publishers, 1992).

146.   See Mirzä Ibrahimov, ed., *Jänubi Azärbayjan Ädäbiyyatï Antoloqiyasï*, Vol. 4 (Baku: Elm, 1994); Nisä Mustafeyeva, *Jänubi Azärbayjan Khanlïglarï* (Baku: Azerbaijan Government Publishers, 1993); *Täbrizdän Dörd Däftär* (Baku: Azerbaijan State Publishers, 1994).

147.   See, for example, Mähämmäd Hüseyn Shähriyar, *Yalan Dünya*. See also Javad He'yät, *Türklärin Tarikh vä Mädäniyyätinä Bir Bakhïsh* (Baku: Azerbaijan State Publishers, 1993); and idem, *Azärbayjan Ädäbiyyatïna Bir Bakhïsh* (Baku: Yazïchï, 1993). A book about Heyat, *Doktor Javad Hey'at* was also published in this period, (Baku: Azärbayjan Publishers, 1995).

148.   *Turan* in English, January 4, 1993.

intent to destroy the Ark fortress in Tabriz and sent a denunciation to the Iranian parliament.[149]

After independence, many political parties and organizations, including the PFA, *Musavat,* and the *Himmet* Party, declared that one of their goals was the strengthening of ties with the Azerbaijanis in Iran, and many of these groups established connections with activists in Iran. At their congress in February 1993, *Yurddash* activists remarked that the party intended to become a representative of the Azerbaijani diaspora.[150] At the third congress of the PFA in June 1995, after his fall from power, Elchibey stated that joint efforts by Azerbaijanis in southern and northern Azerbaijan toward achievement of independence for the Azerbaijani state are one of the basic aims of the party.[151] In a protest held in front of the Iranian Embassy in Baku, Fuad Guliyev, deputy chairman of the National Emancipation Party, stated, "we protest against the violation of the political and civil rights of Azeris living in Iran. We demand that cultural autonomy be granted to the Azerbaijanis in Iran."[152]

Amirali Lakhrudi, chairman of the Democratic Party of Azerbaijan, remarked that:

In 1992, we adopted a new platform. Our goal is national and cultural autonomy for Azerbaijan. We believe that Iran must become a federal state modeled after the USA, present-day Russia, India, Switzerland, etc. We are in favor of a federate Iran. The desire for full independence for South Azerbaijan and its separation from Iran will not gain support within the country. That is clear. We should consider the fact that not only the Persians but the Azerbaijan, Kurdish, and Baluchi elites thrive on the dreams of a "Great Iran."[153]

In December 1997, the United Azerbaijan Movement was established in Baku to promote the rights of Azerbaijanis in Iran and the unification of the Republic of Azerbaijan and Iranian Azerbaijan. Many youth organizations became part of this movement. It was headed by former president Elchibey. Other Baku-based organizations whose chief goals included the struggle for rights or independence of the Azerbaijanis in Iran were the Movement for the National Independence of South Azerbaijan and the Political Center of Azerbaijan. These organizations often organ-

---

149. Azadinform, December 11, 2000.

150. Radio Baku Network in Azerbaijani, March 1, 1993 (FBIS-SOV-93-039).

151. *Turan,* June 26, 1995.

152. *Turan* in English, July 5, 1995.

153. *Zerkalo,* December 2, 1995, p. 8.

ized protests in front of the Iranian Embassy in Baku, demanding rights for their co-ethnics in Iran.

Many organizations and parties in the Republic of Azerbaijan argued that the new republic needed unification with the south to preserve its independence and become a strong state. Asif Ata, founder of the Inam Movement, stated that

The problem of South Azerbaijan is the main political problem of Azerbaijan. Only after unification shall we be able to withstand the whole world. North Azerbaijan has backing, South Azerbaijan also. Our advantage is in our unity.[154]

Baku's interest in the cultural rights of the Azerbaijanis in Iran often complicated the state-to-state relations between Iran and the republic, no matter which regime was in power in Baku. Yet, many Azerbaijanis disagreed with the PFA policy of calling for unification, claiming that it was completely impractical. Many felt that it was imprudent to think about south Azerbaijan while the republic was engaged in a war with Armenia and its present borders were being threatened. Zardusht Alizade, former PFA activist and later a leader of the Social Democratic Party and editor of the newspaper *Istiqlal*, said that:

The fact that the PFA announced the struggle for the unification of the Southern and North Azerbaijan can become one more tragic page in the history of the Azeri people . . . If there is any disorder we will have a million refugees from the South, and I am sure that this time again, just like in January 1990, PFA will stand on the side and will blame everybody, except itself.[155]

The desire for political ties with the Azerbaijanis in Iran was not widely reciprocated. Though many groups and individuals in the republic declared their interest in unity with "south Azerbaijan," few from the south have openly articulated an interest in unification. Hence, there is a limited irredentist movement in the north, but no visible partner in the south. Of course any activity of this type would be severely curtailed by Tehran.

VIEWS OF ONE ANOTHER

The massive exchange of visits between the Azerbaijanis in Iran and in the Republic of Azerbaijan dispelled many myths formed during the time

154. *Hurriyet*, May 26, 1996.
155. *Turan* in English, July 5, 1995.

of separation. Many Azerbaijanis from both sides who were interviewed expressed curiosity about the Azerbaijanis on the other side, and many of them traveled there. Many Azerbaijanis sought their relatives on the other side in this period, and Azerbaijanis on both sides were excited by the meetings and renewal of family ties. In interviews, many of them were pleased by the establishment of professional contacts with co-ethnic colleagues from the other side. During visits to the north, some Azerbaijanis from Iran were moved when they saw schools, press, and cultural life operating in the Azerbaijani language, and this seems to have triggered them to intensify their demands for cultural freedom.

Nonetheless, after a "honeymoon" period, Azerbaijanis from both sides of the border seemed disappointed, having discovered many differences in the prevailing attitudes and cultural norms on the opposite side. Many northerners commented that the Azerbaijanis in Iran were too religious and conservative, while many southerners viewed the Azerbaijanis in the republic as very "Russified" and as having lost Azerbaijani or Muslim culture. In the interviews, many of the Azerbaijanis expressed a sense of "superiority" over their co-ethnics from other side: the northerners tended to view themselves as more cosmopolitan than the southerners, whereas the southerners tended to view themselves as culturally richer and more "civilized" than their co-ethnics from the north. A sense of rivalry was detected in many of the interviews, with each group seeing itself as the center and the other group as the periphery.[156] Many people interviewed from both the Republic of Azerbaijan and from Iran used the metaphor of East and West Germany. Yet, even those who perceived vast differences declared that they view all the Azerbaijanis as part of one people. Nevertheless, it was not clear whether they meant that they were all members of the same ethnic group or of the same nation.

Conclusions

The independence of the Republic of Azerbaijan paved the way to renewed intensive interaction between the Azerbaijanis on both sides of the Araz River. In the republic the impact of the interaction has been twofold. It gave some people a sense of strength as members of a larger and stronger people. But for most people the interaction seems to have had a so-

---

156.   Such rivalry is common in the relations of many centers with their diasporas. For a discussion of the rivalry between Israel and the Jewish diaspora, and among the Palestinians, see Sheffer, "A New Field of Study: Modern Diasporas in International Politics," pp. 10–11.

bering effect; they saw the great differences in identity and values between the two Azerbaijani populations.

The interaction and the existence of an Azerbaijani state spurred a process of identity exploration among many of the Azerbaijanis in Iran. Some affirmed their identity as Iranians, while others felt a heightened pride as Azerbaijanis, motivating them to demand more cultural rights and rebuff attempts to humiliate them. While many Azerbaijanis in Iran desire expanded rights to use their language and develop their culture, few are calling for the separation of the Azerbaijani provinces from Iran. The desire for more cultural rights as Azerbaijanis is not viewed by most as contradicting their identity as Iranians. However, Tehran finds it difficult to accept this premise. It generally views most attempts at asserting Azerbaijani identity and language, and related demands such as the rejection of the forced use of Persian, as disloyalty to Iran. Thus, it is the government in Iran, like the Pahlavi regime before it, that often forces the ethnic minorities to choose between their ethnic identity and their Iranian identity. This has strengthened the Azerbaijani identity of some, and has led others to assimilate into the Persian majority.

Many researchers have portrayed Baku's "longing" for renewal of ties with the Azerbaijanis in Iran during the Soviet period as a propaganda ploy to increase the Soviet Union's influence in north Iran, possibly with the ultimate goal of taking over this territory.[157] However, the north's interest in relations with the Azerbaijanis in Iran and its feeling of common nationhood with the south persisted and even increased after the fall of the Soviet Union. This shows that these ties were not simply a Soviet fiction; they arose from a local Azerbaijani perception of a common identity. Of course, Moscow used these yearnings for its own interests.

The developments of the identities in the two communities in this period were significantly different. The primary ethnic and national identity of a clear majority of the Azerbaijanis in the republic is as Azerbaijanis. Additional identities as Muslims and Turks are seen by most as a component of Azerbaijani identity, not as competing forms of identity. However, the extent to which Turkic identity is a component of Azerbaijani identity has not been resolved. For most north Azerbaijanis, the Turkic identity is secondary to distinctive Azerbaijani identity. In the Republic of Azerbaijan, the residents are concentrating on the development of state

---

157. For example, Bennigsen and Wimbush, *Muslims of the Soviet Empire: A Guide*, p. 144.

identity and determining the place of Azerbaijani identity within that new state.

In contrast, among the Azerbaijanis in Iran, Azerbaijani identity is focused on the ethnic level. There is great diversity in their national identities. Most Azerbaijanis in Iran who have two Azerbaijani parents are aware of their separate ethnic identity as Azerbaijani Turks. For most raised in the Azerbaijani provinces, Azerbaijani is the primary spoken language. There seems to be a correlation between the amount of time spent in the Azerbaijani provinces and the extent of Azerbaijani national identity. Those who grew up in these regions seemed much more attached to their Azerbaijani identity than those living in the Persian-dominated center of Iran. Tehran has become a multi-ethnic city; about half of its inhabitants are non-Persians and a high percentage of its residents are immigrants from outlying provinces. A multi-cultural Iranian identity is emerging among many of the capital's intellectuals, and many Azerbaijanis there identify with it.

Among the less educated classes in Tehran, there seems to be a greater degree of ethnic cohesiveness. Azerbaijanis tend to work in certain sectors, such as the construction industry, and they own most of the bakeries in the city. Within these sectors, they usually continue to speak Azerbaijani among themselves. Yet, those who are rooted in Tehran, especially those with successful businesses, tend to oppose autonomy of the Azerbaijani provinces because they are more deeply involved in Iranian society, especially in the economic sphere. In Tehran, there are far more interethnic marriages involving Azerbaijanis than in the provinces, leading to the birth of many ethnically mixed children. It appears that, when the mother is Azerbaijani, the children are more likely to identify as Azerbaijanis than when an Azerbaijani father is married to a non-Azerbaijani woman. This point is very interesting: formally, among Muslims, identity is passed on to the children through the father.

Chapter 6

Lessons on Iran and Identity Theory

Resting joyfully in the arms of the old ocean, a young wave jumped up and asked: "Will we ever know, mother, what's going on in the heart of the old Savalan?"

"It's not possible for us to know the inside of a mountain just by looking at the surface," said the ocean. "Just as it's not possible for a mountain to know the secrets of the heart of an ocean. One should learn to be patient and to wait. All will be revealed in due time!"

–From an Azerbaijani folk tale

A distinct Azerbaijani identity was the prominent collective self-identification of the Azerbaijanis in Soviet Azerbaijan and its successor, the Republic of Azerbaijan, for the greater part of the twentieth century. In Iran, vast numbers of Azerbaijanis have maintained Azerbaijani identity throughout the century despite intensive efforts to eradicate their culture. Now that there is an independent Azerbaijan, the ethnic or national Azerbaijani identity contains tensions between the territorial aspects of Azerbaijan and the civic identity of the independent Republic of Azerbaijan. Azerbaijanis in the Republic of Azerbaijan share special ties with other citizens of the state, while they also identify strongly with ethnic Azerbaijanis beyond its borders. Many Azerbaijanis in Iran, as well, identify strongly as Azerbaijanis and identify with the Azerbaijanis outside Iran. Many feel that they also live in Azerbaijan (though not the Republic of Azerbaijan). In addition, many identify also as Iranians. However, the establishment of the Republic of Azerbaijan unleashed an exploration of collective identity among the Azerbaijanis in Iran, and for some this has resulted in an increased Azerbaijani self-identification. This conclusion—that a distinctive Azerbaijani identity exists on a meaningful level in Iran—challenges many of the common academic assessments on Iran. Moreover, there are indications that ethnic politics will play a role in the continued developments in Iran.

A second conclusion of this book is that Azerbaijani political activity was a facet of the Islamic Revolution in Iran, and that the failure of the revolution to meet many of the Azerbaijanis' expectations for language and cultural rights affected their support for the regime and their identity as Iranians. A third conclusion of this work is that the Azerbaijani political awakening in the Soviet Union predated the emergence of the Nagorno-Karabagh conflict. This work disputes the idea that glasnost and the Nagorno-Karabagh conflict were instrumental in the birth of the contemporary Azerbaijani national movement; it disagrees with works which have claimed that the Azerbaijanis only began to openly articulate their national identity in the late 1980s and that this assertion was chiefly a response to the struggle with Armenia for control over Nagorno-Karabagh.[1] Expressions of Azerbaijani national identity were clearly present in the Soviet Union before the inauguration of glasnost in the mid-1980s. While glasnost certainly affected the Azerbaijani national movement's timing, intensity, and success in achieving statehood, it did not create an ideological "vacuum" that was filled by ethnic identity; rather, it revealed the identities that had been competing with the state identity demanded by the Soviet Union and it created the conditions for open political activity among those who espoused different identities. Outside challenges and threats from Armenia and Moscow unleashed by glasnost helped transform the Azerbaijani collective identity into an active political movement. However, that identity did not emerge in response to these outside challenges.

The different regimes and nationality policies that the two groups of Azerbaijanis lived under for more than 150 years has affected the development of their collective identities. Soviet policy unintentionally fostered the development of Azerbaijani collective identity, and that of many other ethnic groups in the Soviet Union; however, and in contrast to official Soviet ideology, full assimilation of non-Slavs into mainstream Soviet or Russian society was quite rare, further eroding the possibility that Azerbaijanis would adopt a Soviet identity. In Iran, on the other hand, little expression of collective ethnic or especially national identity was allowed for any group except the Persians, but full assimilation into Persian culture was encouraged. A higher proportion of Azerbaijanis adopted an Iranian primary identity in the south than a Soviet or Russian

---

1. See, for instance, Saroyan, "The Karabagh Syndrome and Azerbaijani Politics," pp. 14–29; and Carrere d' Encausse, *The End of the Soviet Empire*, p. 59.

primary identity in the north. This book concludes that separation under two fundamentally different regimes (the Soviet Union and later the independent Republic of Azerbaijan, on the one hand, and Pahlavi Iran and later the Islamic Republic, on the other hand) produced some cultural differences between the Azerbaijanis in the north and the south. Nevertheless, a large number of Azerbaijanis in both the north and south consider themselves one people and ethnic group. In the north, the overwhelming majority see their primary collective identity as something they have in common with the southern Azerbaijanis. However, a large portion of the southern Azerbaijanis do not maintain a primary identity with the north.

The Azerbaijanis provide an excellent example of how the role of contiguous populations must be studied to understand the development of collective identity and national movements on either side of a border. The establishment of the independent Republic of Azerbaijan in 1991 challenged the identity of the Azerbaijanis in Iran, and caused many of them to redefine it, either reaffirming their identity as Iranians or augmenting their self-perception as Azerbaijanis. This rising identity has generated few calls for the Azerbaijani provinces to secede from Iran and join the new republic, but rather more calls for increased rights within Iran. Following the establishment of the Republic of Azerbaijan and the subsequent reduction of restrictions on direct ties, family and commercial ties were renewed and much intellectual and academic exchange took place. Within a short period after the renewal of ties, expressions of rising Azerbaijani assertiveness and self-pride were observed in Iran. Azerbaijanis began to take offense at remarks about their accents and ethnic origin, and to feel a sense of legitimacy in their Azerbaijani culture. Azerbaijani students formed organizations and coordinated efforts throughout Iran to demand and exercise their cultural rights more fully. Many of these demands focused on the symbolic and abstract level more than the concrete—such as ending their "humiliation" or retaining the name "Azerbaijan" in the name of the new province—indicating that a change occurred in their self-perception. Many of the students' statements and the platforms of the new organizations reflected how the establishment of the Republic of Azerbaijan had provoked this change of consciousness.

Azerbaijanis in the new state were also affected by the renewal of ties with the south. Most of the activists in the north who stress Azerbaijani identity and culture are also committed to the renewal of ties with the south and often view the "liberation" of the south as critical to the prosperity of the north. The status and rights of the Azerbaijanis in Iran became an important issue in the internal politics in Baku, and the relationship with this population beyond its borders is a major part of the self-identity of the new state, even affecting its foreign policy and relations.

Themes in Azerbaijani Identity

This book analyzed trends in Azerbaijani identity, focusing on the period since the emergence of the Islamic Revolution in Iran in the late 1970s, and showed that many had precedents in earlier periods in Azerbaijani history. Among the recurring themes in Azerbaijani identity development, this study showed that formal delineation of borders does not necessarily delimit the cultural and human boundaries, and revealed the active role of the Azerbaijani provinces in trade outside of Iran; the prominence of secularism among Azerbaijanis; the emphasis placed by Azerbaijanis on their language; Tehran's continued regard of any articulation of demands for ethnic-based rights as an expression of separatism; and the diverse impact of technological developments on identity formation. Despite the formal separation of Azerbaijan in 1828 under the Treaty of Turkmenchay, commercial and cultural links between the two halves remained quite strong until the period of Stalin's consolidation of the Soviet regime. The Azerbaijanis on both sides of the border formed one intellectual sphere, and the political ideologies and ideas that evolved in Baku and in Tabriz (and were then passed on to Tehran) were fostered by the interaction among Azerbaijani intellectuals. Even under the repressive Soviet and Pahlavi regimes, limited ties between the Azerbaijanis endured; despite the great risk involved, many Azerbaijanis kept track of their relatives living on the other side of the Araz, and illegal crossings took place. As Moscow's power waned under Gorbachev and reprisal no longer appeared to be a threat, Azerbaijanis from both sides of the borders sought out relatives from the other side, as exemplified by the border meetings and the advertisements placed in newspapers in Baku and in Tehran.

Since the split of Azerbaijan in the first half of the nineteenth century, ties between the co-ethnics continually transcended the political borders separating them. Many mutual influences remained, and Azerbaijanis on both sides of the Araz share many common historical memories and many symbols. The Safavid regime is venerated by both groups as a symbol of Azerbaijani leadership in Iran, and the *Qizilbash* have been embraced as a symbol of Azerbaijani military prowess. Babak is a common symbol of independence and Azerbaijani resistance to foreign rule. Pictures of the Tabriz Ark and Mt. Savalan are found in Azerbaijani homes on both sides of the Araz. The Azerbaijani case illustrates that there are several types of borders—such as political, physical, and cultural—

that are not always congruent, and that political borders can have a smaller effect on the identity of the peoples than many researchers assume.

In the second half of the nineteenth century and the beginning of the twentieth, the Iranian provinces were Iran's gateway to Russia and Istanbul, and through them to the West. Since the Soviet breakup the provinces seek to reestablish this role, particularly in the areas of foreign ties and cooperation. Formerly, Tabriz's connections boosted the region's status within Iran. Tabriz is again using its reestablished ties with Baku as a basis to demand more resources from the center and greater freedom of action for direct cooperation. Unimpeded cooperation between the Azerbaijani provinces and Baku, often circumventing Tehran, has emerged. Encouraged by their direct ties with Baku, the Azerbaijani provinces in Iran have expanded their foreign cooperation with other Turkic peoples in Turkey and Tatarstan. In recognition of its historical role as a defender of democracy in Iran, Iranian President Khatami called Azerbaijan the birthplace of civil society in Iran during a 1998 visit to Tabriz.[2] The Iranian Azerbaijani provinces' expanding contacts with Baku and other groups outside Iran may have helped stimulate their more recent assertive political activity in Iran.

The Republic of Azerbaijan's declaration in its 1995 constitution of a clear separation between religion and state is consistent with the anti-clericalism and Muslim secularism found among both north and Iranian Azerbaijanis. While there are certainly religious Azerbaijanis, as the vast number of Azerbaijanis in Iran's clerical elite shows, since the second half of the nineteenth century Azerbaijanis have also been in the forefront of Muslims who advocate a secular Muslim identity. Under Russian Imperial rule the clerics were severely restricted and could not intimidate secular-oriented intellectuals, as they did elsewhere in the Muslim world. Furthermore, Azerbaijani subjects in the Russian Empire had access to secular education, which attracted many to secular ideas. Azerbaijani intellectuals in Iran could live among their co-ethnics in the Caucasus, escaping the threats of the Iranian *ulama*, and compose their secular treatises; few other ethnic groups had similar retreats. Thus, a disproportionate number of the Iranians who advocated secular ideologies in the late nineteenth and early twentieth centuries were actually Azerbaijani. In addition, Azerbaijanis, who are connected to both the Turkic and Shi'i worlds, have played a prominent role in advocating ideologies that bridge Shi'i and Sunni Islam, such as pan-Islam.

---

2. IRNA, November 22, 1998.

Throughout the twentieth century, the Azerbaijanis generally made political demands relating to Azerbaijani collective identity when the central government's power had eroded, thus incurring less risk. For example, the Azerbaijanis in the Russian Empire attempted to attain an independent state after the fall of the Romanov dynasty. In Iran, the Azerbaijanis were most aggressive in their political demands when Tehran's power was limited, such as during Khiyabani's revolt in 1920, which took place during the turmoil that characterized the end of Qajar rule, or when Iran was under Allied occupation and the Provincial Government of Azerbaijan was established in Tabriz in 1945. Since the late 1970s, Azerbaijanis were most assertive in their political demands when Moscow's and Tehran's power had abated: under glasnost in the Soviet Union (1987–91); during the turmoil surrounding the Islamic Revolution in Iran (1978–79); and in the period after the Iran-Iraq War, when an atmosphere of relative political liberalization emerged. The journal *Varliq* became progressively less assertive in demanding Azerbaijani rights as the Islamic Republic consolidated its rule and became more explicitly exposed to appeals of this type. Evidently, this decline was the result of the change in the sanctions threatened by the regime, not a shift in the contributors' beliefs. Similarly, declines in the centers' power did not cause the rise in articulation of Azerbaijani collective identity, but just made it more possible to express that identity and make related political demands. Since the regimes were restrictive, it can be assumed that Azerbaijani national identity was often present during periods of increased repression but that outward expressions were often curtailed; this explains the lack of continuous, clear external manifestations of that identity, and the surges in expressions of identity when sanctions were removed. Researchers must recognize that a lack of overt and especially political expressions of an identity may only indicate fear. It does not give conclusive evidence of the state of the identity.

The issue of the use and status of the Azerbaijani language was a focus of the Azerbaijanis both in the north and in Iran, including individuals who did not speak Azerbaijani for professional work. In periods of relative political ease, Azerbaijanis under both regimes were quick to raise the language issue. For instance, a plethora of publications in the Azerbaijani language frequently appeared during the periods of relative political liberalization in Iran, many evidently written during the periods of oppression. Immediately after the Shah's departure from Iran and in the early 1990s there were outpourings of writings in Azerbaijani. Throughout the 1980s and 1990s, Azerbaijani scholars in both Iran and Azerbaijan continued efforts to develop their language and spread the use of it among Azerbaijanis. After the Islamic Revolution, intellectuals in

Iran considered what would be the most appropriate alphabet for Azerbaijani, some suggesting the Latin script while others created revised versions of the Arabic script. Many Azerbaijani writers in Iran have added vowel markers to the Arabic script used to write Azerbaijani in Iran to better reflect a highly-vowel based Turkic language and make it accessible to a greater number of people. The status of the Azerbaijani language, and an appropriate name and alphabet, were the focus of debates in Azerbaijan just before and after it achieved independence. Like activists from many other national movements, many Azerbaijani activists in both Soviet Azerbaijan and Iran struggled to revitalize a language that was not their primary language, and to revive a culture that had been lost. Most Azerbaijanis do not see their language as inferior or less developed than Persian or Russian.

Throughout the twentieth century, observers in Tehran and researchers outside Iran generally interpreted any serious demands for expanded cultural and language rights by various Azerbaijani movements or other ethnic groups in Iran as attempts to secede or as the result of foreign meddling. This interpretation helps delegitimize the ethnic groups' claims and rally support for their suppression. Interestingly, scholars and politicians alike have consistently used terminology that the movements themselves never employed. For instance, they referred to the Provincial Government in Tabriz (1945–46) as the "Azerbaijan Democratic Republic." Similarly, researchers and government officials called Azerbaijani demands for expanded language rights "Pan-Turkist," and condemned them as threatening the territorial integrity of Iran. Yet many of the activists, including such prominent Azerbaijanis as Khiyabani, leaders of the Provincial Government in 1945, and Azerbaijani writer 'Ali Tabrizli, clearly explained that they possessed supra-ethnic Iranian identity, one that encompassed non-Persian ethnic groups. (For example, a Scotsman may be able to identify with Great Britain, although he does not identify himself as an Englishman.)

While many Azerbaijanis have been at the forefront of those espousing a strong Iran, and some even championed the adoption of Persian by all the ethnic minorities in order to unite the country, most Azerbaijanis with two Azerbaijani parents did not define themselves as "Persians," but as Iranians. Many Western observers believe that this articulation of Iranian identity by members of the ethnic minorities in Iran indicates identification or assimilation as Persians. This theme of supra-ethnic identity was frequently voiced in the period studied in this book, such as by the Azerbaijani students in their letter-writing campaigns. Many Azerbaijanis identified as Iranians when they did not feel that this was equated with Persian language or culture. Moreover, they saw the

Azerbaijanis as playing a major role in the history and development of Iran. Since Iran feels threatened by expressions of ethnic identity, it often forces the ethnic minorities to choose between their particular ethnic identity and their Iranian identity. This has strengthened the Azerbaijani identity of some, and led others to assimilate into the Persian majority.

Technological developments that facilitated contacts between Azerbaijanis and non-Azerbaijanis both encouraged and discouraged the coalescence of collective identity. As Abrahamian pointed out, technological advances during the early part of Reza Shah's rule promoted contacts with co-ethnics in contiguous regions, and so facilitated the emergence of ethnic identity in the peripheral provinces of Iran.[3] In addition, encounters with members of different groups often underscored the differences between them and thus augmented particularistic identity. In contrast, the modern infrastructure built during the first half of the twentieth century made the center more accessible, exposing many members of the country's various ethnic groups to the modern state and fostering identification with that state. In Iran, modernization has brought interethnic marriages and assimilation into Persian culture, and has fostered in some a belief in a strong, centralized Iran. In the north, in contrast, interaction with non-Azerbaijanis has usually augmented Azerbaijani identity, due to the profound differences between the Azerbaijanis and the Russian population and the lack of opportunity for social assimilation. Tehran seems to have become something of an Iranian "melting pot," which has enhanced the Iranian identity of many who live there. Television broadcasts from the Republic of Turkey have had a striking impact on Azerbaijani identity both in the north and in Iran. In Iran, they seem to have contributed to the rising trend of Turkic and Azerbaijani self-pride. In the north, they are rapidly making the Azerbaijani language more similar to Turkish, while expanding an awareness of greater Turkic identity.

The Fall of the Other Wall: Renewal of Ties

The impact of the collapse of the Soviet Union on the ensuing renewal of East-West ties is quite apparent. However, the Soviet fall led to the breakdown of an additional wall: between north and south. A significant consequence of the Soviet collapse was the development of direct ties and cooperation between residents of the new republics and their co-ethnics in adjoining regions in Iran, which has had significant impact on both sides of the former Soviet border. Following the independence of the Republic

---

3. Abrahamian, *Iran Between Two Revolutions*, p. 428.

of Azerbaijan, dramatic changes took place in the nature and the intensity of the contacts and relations between the Azerbaijanis on both sides of the border.

In light of the implications of the contacts emerging between populations in many of Iran's border areas, one may have to rethink the characteristics associated with a center of a state and with the periphery. Living in the periphery may be an asset, and Iran's provinces, especially in light of the difficult economic situation in Iran, are attempting to transform their location into an advantage by strengthening their ties to co-ethnics and to the bordering provinces and new states. Since the majority of the residents of Iran's border areas are non-Persians, this development will inevitably affect ethnic relations in Iran.

Lessons on Collective Identity

The results of this study suggest seven refinements to the theory of collective identity. First, family ties are an important factor in preserving the identity of peoples divided by a political border. Azerbaijanis from both sides of the Araz particularly valued family ties. These bonds helped preserve a sense of common peoplehood that survived the physical and political separation of the Azerbaijanis. Azerbaijanis with relatives on the other side of the border seem generally more interested in the renewal of ties with the other community, and identified more as a common people than those without these family ties.

Second, it is often suggested that the more access members of subgroups have to the state's means of power, the more they will be inclined to identify with that state. Many policies that give minorities special opportunities for access to jobs and education are based on this premise. Under the Islamic Republic, many Azerbaijanis in Iran have attained financial wealth, higher education, and positions of power in the state; nevertheless, they are still outsiders in many social circles in Iran, and many Iranians still consider their language inferior to Persian. The case of the Azerbaijanis in Iran demonstrates that gaps created between newly acquired professional and economic status and an established social status can actually stimulate identity with collectives that compete with state identity. In Iran, the higher the Azerbaijanis climbed professionally, economically, and into positions of power in the state, the more they have become interested in addressing past injustices and gaps and in raising the issue of Iran's treatment of sub-state groups. The first half of the 1990s was marked by many expressions of indignation over a low social status that contrasts with the Azerbaijanis' self-image based on their political and economic success in Iran. In the Pahlavi period, it seems that many

Azerbaijanis internalized the regime's message that "Turks" were inferior, and many attempted to assimilate into Persian society. During the period of the Islamic Republic, however, a number of factors, including the establishment of the Republic of Azerbaijan, raised Azerbaijani self-pride and increased the intensity of their collective demands. Since the late 1970s, many of the Iranian Azerbaijanis' demands center on intangible concepts such as ending the degradation of the Azerbaijanis and returning the name Azerbaijan to their province. The abstract nature of these demands indicates that their social status is as important to the Azerbaijanis as their economic, professional, and legal status. The widely implemented policies that promote economic and professional equality may do little to promote a primary state identity.

Third, the founding of a new state diversely impacts co-ethnics beyond its borders.[4] In most cases, it seems to catalyze an exploration by co-ethnics of their identity and relationship to the new state. The founding of the Republic of Azerbaijan challenged the identity of co-ethnics beyond the borders of the new state and stimulated some to identify with the group represented by that state, though not necessarily with the state itself. However, the establishment of a new state can also lead to a decline in the politicization of co-ethnics outside its borders, since the formation of the new state is viewed as a solution to the group's "national problem." The Azerbaijani example should be studied in attempts to understand, for instance, how the establishment of a Palestinian state might affect Palestinians or how Kurdish autonomy affects co-ethnics. The important question is whether the creation of political entities can attempt to quell ethnic strife. The most common response to ethnic-based demands is to establish a political entity, most often a state or autonomous region. When these entities do not include most of the lands that the ethnic group considers its traditional territory, or the majority of its co-ethnics, do they solve the ethnic conflict, or just lead to a new one in the future?

Fourth, the case of Iran demonstrates the need to differentiate between diaspora communities and contiguous populations of co-ethnics. Relations between a core state and adjoining co-ethnics are very different than those between an ethnic-based state and diaspora members abroad, especially if the co-ethnics have emigrated from the country. The idea that the territory of the co-ethnics is also often part of the traditional

---

4. The impact of the establishment of the State of Israel on various Jewish communities also illustrates this point; different Jewish communities and individuals within communities responded in varying ways to the establishment of a Jewish state in 1948.

homeland is an element to the relations between the ethnic state and the co-ethnics beyond its border, and can become an issue of contention in the state-to-state relations between two neighboring states. The overwhelming majority of the ethnic minorities in Iran did not immigrate to Iran, and they tend to view Iran as their own state, not a host state. Those who live in the Azerbaijani provinces in Iran do not feel that they live "abroad," but rather on Azerbaijani land that is also Iranian. In fact, many Azerbaijanis view Iran as an Azerbaijani state, and some political groups on both sides of the border claim that the Azerbaijanis are actually the largest ethnic group.[5] Moreover, most of the literature on the links between ethnic-based states and co-ethnics abroad seems to assume that the majority of the ethnic group always resides in the core state. However, in many of the states and autonomies that have been established since the early 1990s, at least half or more of the members of the ethnic group reside outside the new state, often in territories contiguous to it. Among the Azerbaijanis there is no consensus that the community inhabiting the Azerbaijani state is necessarily the center and that the community in Iran is its periphery. Most of Iran's Azerbaijanis do not view Baku as the capital, but instead consider Tabriz the historical center of their people. Moreover, within the Azerbaijani community in Iran, a center-diaspora relationship seems to exist between those who live in the Azerbaijani provinces and in Tehran, with Tehran serving as center.

Fifth, it is important to distinguish between Islamic religious identity and social conservatism. Many factors, such as social segregation and occupational differentialization between the sexes and modest dress and the covering of the hair among women, are interpreted by many researchers as external signs of Islamic religiosity and identity. However, in conducting this study, I observed that many Azerbaijanis, predominantly from the north, were secular in their outlook and did not observe many explicit Islamic laws (such as the prohibitions on alcoholic drinks and eating pork), but did observe many conservative social customs. The practitioners did not seem to associate this traditional behavior with the Islamic religion when observing them. Thus, in research on the identity of different Muslim peoples, it is important to separate social conservatism

---

5.   Azerbaijanis often illustrate this point by pointing to the fact that the Safavid dynasty in Iran, which was founded in 1501, was established in Azerbaijan and that the Safavids were predominately Azerbaijani-speaking. Moreover, in a 1998 letter to President Khatami, Iranian Azerbaijani intellectuals claimed that the Azerbaijani population comprises half of the population of Iran. See "Letter to President Khatami of Iran," May 5, 1998; printed in *Qurtulush* (Spring 1999) p. 54.

from Islamic belief and religious devoutness. Throughout Azerbaijani contemporary history, there is a strong secular tradition among large proportions of the population, especially in the north and among educated classes on both sides, while many conservative social norms persist.

Sixth, a choice of language is not always a reliable indicator of identity preference. A person's emotional attachment to a language may be a stronger indicator of primary identity than actual proficiency. Decisions to use Persian or Russian rather than Azerbaijani were often motivated by practical considerations, and were not always an emotional or ideological choice. An individual's primary language is a particularly poor indicator of primary identity, since in multi-ethnic states many citizens are truly multi-lingual. For instance, many Azerbaijanis in Iran view Azerbaijani as their primary spoken language, but Persian as their primary language for writing and reading. Even as a spoken language, people often have one "mother tongue" and a different "family tongue" because members of other ethnic groups have married into the family, changing the language spoken at family gatherings.[6] One can have one primary professional language and another primary home language. The means of communication can determine the primary language employed. For instance, two individuals who share a common primary language other than English may e-mail in English, yet on the phone speak to one another in a different common language. Many interviewees stated that it was common for Azerbaijani businesspeople in Tehran to take orders from Azerbaijani customers in the Azerbaijani language, while they write down the order in Persian because they do not know how to write in Azerbaijani or are not accustomed to it.

Seventh, the case of the Iranian Azerbaijanis demonstrates that primary identity is often unclear to many members of a group. Many Azerbaijanis in Iran who identify as both Azerbaijanis and Iranians have no clear idea which identity is primary. Most see these identities as coexistent and seem to hope that they will not become incompatible. Like the natural capability of children for multilingualism, the Azerbaijanis in both the north and in Iran have demonstrated their ability to be multilingual and multicultural. As the Azerbaijanis have shown, people have the ability to speak a number of languages and function in a number of cultural milieus simultaneously.

---

6.   Hobsbawm, *Nations and Nationalism Since 1780*, p. 99. Hobsbawm points out that in surveys conducted by the Habsburgs in their empire, the question of family tongue versus mother tongue was asked.

Implications for Iran

During the 1990s, Azerbaijanis in Iran expressed indignation over their low social status, which contrasts with their self-image based on their marked political and economic success in Iran. While the rise in Azerbaijani identity does not seem to be leading to calls for secession from Iran, it has placed additional demands on the regime for greater liberty and less centralization. Challenging the long-held assumption that Azerbaijanis in Iran have overwhelmingly assimilated into Persian culture and that little remains of their distinctive identity, this book suggests that the Azerbaijani ethnic factor must be considered in assessing the stability of Iran's regime, and should be seen as a potential element in future developments there. Members of ethnic minorities in Iran have compounded grievances against the regime; while all the citizens of Iran have been denied civil liberties, the cultural and linguistic rights of those groups have been violated as well. During the period of the Islamic Revolution and again in the first half of the 1990s, the Azerbaijanis demonstrated their ability to organize coordinated political activity throughout Iran. Their long-established ties traversing Iran facilitated this activity. Azerbaijani student groups were particularly active in campaigning for their group's cultural and linguistic rights in the 1990s, and their role in Iranian politics, like that of Iran's ethnic groups in general, should be explored in future research.

This study revealed a general, growing trend of regionalism in Iran.[7] A large number of the Majlis delegates' speeches dealt with attempts to obtain resources for their home provinces. Their statements and interviews reflect a sense of regional identity and show that many Azerbaijanis in Iran, including those who view themselves primarily as Iranians and are associated with the regime there, such as Majlis representatives, feel attachment to the area of Azerbaijan and are interested in its prosperity. Rising regionalism is developing as an added pressure and challenge to the central government. Tabriz's direct foreign cooperation and contacts may encourage other provinces to establish direct cooperation with groups beyond Iran's borders; this could prove an additional challenge to Tehran's centralized control.

Rising ethnic demands may renew interethnic strife within Iran if the groups dispute the demarcation of borders and resources within the

---

7. President Khatami seemed aware of this growing trend of regionalism and aspired to tap into it politically. This is illustrated by his leading role in the conducting of elections for the local government councils in February 1999.

state. A future adoption of some kind of confederate or federative relationship between Tehran and the ethnic minorities in Iran might provoke conflicts between the various minority groups. Clashes of this type are most likely to emerge between Azerbaijanis and Kurds, who throughout the twentieth century violently engaged each other in West Azerbaijan over disputed lands and control in the area.[8] This could affect other regional actors.

The sentiments and political demands that surfaced in the 1990s in Iran are locally rooted, but the fact that Iran's ethnic minorities have links to co-ethnics in neighboring states has complicated Tehran's ability to address some of the ethnic-based demands. Many neighboring states, such as the Soviet Union, retained ties with members of the ethnic minorities and often supported their autonomy or independence as a way to retain influence in Iran and to extract concessions from Tehran. This history, and the current links between co-ethnics, have made Iranians especially sensitive to any ethnic-based demands, and rarely open to accommodation. Tehran brands any of the organizations and movements that have campaigned for ethnic rights in Iran or for provincial autonomy as secessionist stooges and agents of foreign states in order to discredit them. While few of the ethnic-based movements have worked for secession, but rather for granting of autonomy or rights as part of Iran, Tehran's intransigence may actually encourage some of the ethnic organizations to escalate their demands.

The existence of a major Azerbaijani community in territories in Iran contiguous to the new Republic strongly affects relations between Baku and Tehran. Iran's fear that the establishment of a strong and attractive Republic of Azerbaijan could lead to a rise in identity of its own Azerbaijani minority led Iran to adopt a policy of de facto support of Armenia in its conflict with Azerbaijan over Nagorno-Karabagh. Baku often brings up the Iranian Azerbaijanis when it is pressuring Iran to change some of its policies toward the Republic of Azerbaijan, such as border closures.

It is not clear how democratization will affect the ethnic identity of Iran's citizens. Further relaxation of restrictions on the use of non-Persian languages and other expressions of ethnic culture could bring about an accommodation with various collectives within the state which would strengthen their attachment to the state and identification with it. However, democracy might also stimulate members of sub-collectives within the state (ethnic groups, regional groupings, etc.) to make greater de-

---

8. For instance, violence erupted between Kurds and Azerbaijanis in the area of Naqadeh in West Azerbaijan province in April 1979, evidently over land allocation.

mands and reinforce their belief in the legitimacy of such claims, thus weakening ties to the state. Iranians of Persian origin may have conflicting feelings about implementing full democracy, since it could require the granting of rights to ethnic minorities and ending the monopoly of the Persian language in Iran. Rising ethnic-based identity in Iran might induce the Persian majority to more actively advance their own nationalism, further exacerbating ethnic relations; this is a topic worthy of further study. Post–Islamic Revolution Iran will have to redefine its relations with the ethnic minorities, especially if it attempts to become a democratic system, and the United States and other states need to formulate policies in anticipation of the escalation of the demands by these ethnic groups.

Some of the political forces in Iran, such as President Mohammed Khatami, have capitalized on ethnic-based demands. For example, when Khatami was first elected in the 1997 presidential elections in Iran, supporters of Khatami distributed election materials in the Azerbaijani and Kurdish languages, breaking with the previous practices on non-Persian language use. During his campaign, Khatami promised voters that Articles Fifteen and Nineteen of the Iranian Constitution, which grant language rights to the non-Persian minorities, would be upheld, reflecting his assessment that this issue was important to the ethnic minorities. Khatami's lead in conducting the 1999 local government elections indicates his willingness to tap into Iran's periphery, and consequently into the ethnic minority groups, as part of his struggle with the prevailing elite in Iran.[9]

President Khatami's policy of limited appeals to ethnic sentiments in Iran and to provincial sources of power may have long-term consequences. While this policy is useful in the short term in building his base of support, once these groups are empowered they may not again accept their secondary status at Khatami's command. The expressions of ethnic sentiments and ethnic-based political demands in Iran, and their challenge to center-periphery relations and official Persian linguistic and cultural dominance, will be an important issue in the political arena of Iran, and may affect the stability of the regime.

---

9. The holding of local elections appears in the Constitution of the Islamic Republic of Iran, but was not implemented until Khatami's presidency.

Appendix:
The Azerbaijani Population

In the Republic of Azerbaijan, ethnic Azerbaijanis account for close to 91 percent of the population of 8.1 million.[1] In the neighboring Republic of Georgia, there are approximately 300,000 Azerbaijanis. Estimates of the number of Azerbaijanis in Turkey range between 500,000 and 2 million. This group is concentrated in northeast Turkey, predominantly in the area of Kars and Igdir.[2] In Iraq, there are an estimated 300,000–900,000 Turkic speakers whom Baku considers Azerbaijanis. No data has been obtained on their self-identity.

Approximately half of the population of Iran is non-Persian. In the Pahlavi period and under the Islamic Republic, the Iranian governments have not published census information regarding the primary language or ethnic identity of citizens, so the ethnic breakdown cannot be precisely determined. Moreover, the subjective self-identification of the population of Iran is inherently fluid. The approximate ethnic breakdown of non-Persians in Iran is: Azerbaijanis and tribal Turks (20–30 percent); Kurds (9 percent), Baluchis (3 percent), Arabs (2.5 percent), Turkmen (1.5 percent).[3] Many of the ethnic minorities are concentrated in specific prov-

---

1.   State Statistics Committee of Azerbaijan, 2001.

2.   The author observed pictures of Imam 'Ali in a number of shops in this area, illustrating the Shi'i identity of many of the residents. For more information on the Azerbaijanis in Turkey, see Peter Andrews, *Ethnic Groups in the Republic of Turkey* (Wiesbaden: Dr. Lutwig Reichert Verlag, 1989), pp. 73–77.

3.   Shahrzad Mojab and Amir Hassanpour, "The Politics of Nationality and Ethnic Diversity," Saeed Rahnema and Sohrab Behdad, eds., *Iran After the Revolution: Crises of an Islamic State* (London: I.B. Tauris, 1995), pp. 229–230.

inces. The Azerbaijanis, for instance, are the predominant population in three provinces: East Azerbaijan, West Azerbaijan, and Ardebil Province. Tehran itself is a multi-ethnic capital, and non-Persians comprise the majority of the city's population.

There is a considerable lack of consensus regarding the number of Azerbaijanis in Iran; most researchers who quote an exact number are usually quoting one of their colleague's studies, which are generally based on estimates and not field research. Furthermore, many parties with vested interests manipulate figures and information to suit their political agendas. Official Iranian sources tend to deflate the number of Azerbaijanis in order to project a clear Persian majority in Iran, and thus preserve their claim to linguistic and cultural predominance.[4] Azerbaijani political groups, on the other hand, tend to inflate the numbers to project the image of a large people and reinforce their claims for Azerbaijani rights in Iran. In this book, both official Iranian sources and claims by Azerbaijani activists outside of Iran have been excluded from the calculation. However, assertions by Azerbaijani groups operating in Iran today have been included in this analysis.

Most mainstream estimates on the number of ethnic minorities in Iran claim that the Persians account for approximately 50 percent of the country's population, the remaining half being comprised of various minorities, of which the Azerbaijani is the largest.[5] Most conventional estimates on Azerbaijani population range between one-fifth to

---

4. The *Area Handbook for Iran* (Washington, D.C.: Government Printing Office, 1971), p. 81, states that "the US government affirms that both the censuses of 1956 and 1966 were underreported, partly because of census-taking methods and the government's efforts to minimize the significance of ethnic and linguistic diversity." Nikki Keddie pointed out that the Iranian "official figures greatly underestimate the size particularly of the largest groups, the Azerbaijanis and the Kurds, while some recent estimates of these groups somewhat overestimate their numbers." See Nikki R. Keddie, *Iran and the Muslim World: Resistance and Revolution* (New York: New York University Press, 1995), p. 134.

5. Among those claiming that the Persian-speaking population is approximately 50 percent of the total population of Iran is Patricia J. Higgins, "Minority-State Relations in Contemporary Iran," *Iranian Studies*, Vol. 17, No. 1 (Winter 1984), p. 47. Some researchers on Iran have even estimated the Persian population of Iran as comprising less than 50 percent of the general population. For instance, Ervand Abrahamian has claimed that the Persians are only 45 percent of the population in "Communism and Communalism in Iran: the Tudah and Firqah-i Dimukrat," *International Journal of Middle East Studies*, Vol. 1, No. 4 (1970), p. 292. See also S. Aliyev, "The Problem of Nationalities in Contemporary Iran," English summary of the Russian text in *The Central Asian Review*, Vol. 16 (1966), p. 64.

one-third of the general population of Iran, the majority claiming one-fourth.[6]

Azerbaijani groups in Iran have published higher estimates of the number of Azerbaijanis living in Iran. Azerbaijani student groups in Iran claim that there are 27 million Azerbaijanis residing in Iran.[7] The editor of *Varliq*, Javad Heyat, published the claim that one-third of Iran's populace is Turkic.[8]

A number of factors affect the varying estimates on the number of Azerbaijanis in Iran. The first is the determination of who is Azerbaijani. Some estimates include all the Turkic-speaking peoples in Iran in this category, while others preclude certain Turkic-speaking groups, such as many of the tribal groups and the Turkmen. Many estimates do not include those who reside outside the Azerbaijani provinces.[9] By failing to count as Azerbaijanis many of the residents of Tehran who emigrated to the capital, and the Turkic population living in the area between the Azerbaijani provinces and Tehran in places such as Hamadan and Zenjan, many of the population estimates are faulty.[10] Estimates of the

---

6.   Those claiming that Azerbaijanis comprise about one-third of the population of Iran include George Thomas Kurian, ed., *Encyclopedia of the Third World* (New York: Facts on File, 1992), Vol. 2, p. 869; Farhad Kazemi, "Ethnicity and the Iranian Peasantry," in Milton J. Esman and Itamar Rabinovich, eds., *Ethnicity, Pluralism, and the State in the Middle East* (London: Cornell University Press, 1988), p. 213. In a conversation with the author, a senior demographer in Iran estimated the Azerbaijani population as one-third of the country's general populace. Those claiming that the Azerbaijani population is approximately one-fourth of the total population of Iran include: Erhard Franz, *Minderheiten in Iran* (Hamburg: German Orient Institute, Middle East Documentation, 1981), p. 23; Shahrzad Mojab and Amir Hassanpour, "The Politics of Ethnic Diversity," p. 229; Pierre Oberlang, "Iran," in Margaret Bainbridge, ed., *The Turkic Peoples of the World* (London: Kegan Paul International Ltd., 1993), p. 148; Keddie, *Iran and the Muslim World: Resistance and Revolution*, p. 131; and Abrahamian, "Communism and Communalism in Iran," p. 292.

7.   "Letter of the Azerbaijani Students Studying in the Tehran Universities to the Azerbaijani Deputies of the Iranian Majlis"; and "Letter of the Meshkinshahr Students Studying in the Universities of the Country to the Government of the Islamic Republic of Iran."

8.   Heyat, "Regression of Azeri Language and Literature," p. 9.

9.   See, for example, Amirahmadi, "A Theory of Ethnic Collective Movements and its Application to Iran," p. 374.

10.   Heyat, "Regression of Azeri Language and Literature," p. 1. Many estimates claim that the Azerbaijani-Persian linguistic border falls somewhere near the bilingual town of Qazvin, near Tehran. See, Wimbush, "Divided Azerbaijan: Nation Building, Assimilation, and Mobilization Between Three States," p. 75.

Turkic composition of Tehran range from one-third to over half of the city's residents.[11]

In this study, members of Turkic tribal groups in Iran are counted as Azerbaijanis. Many of the tribal Turks also possess additional specific tribal identities. In an interview, an Azerbaijani of tribal origin claimed that tribal Turks identify with the Azerbaijanis and are among the least assimilated into Persian culture of all the Turks living in Iran, and that they are quite tenacious about preserving Azerbaijani Turkic culture, which forms a more central part of their lives than among the urbanized Turks. The primary language of most of the tribal Turks in Iran is Azerbaijani, and compared with non-tribal origin Turkic counterparts, far fewer have adopted Persian as a primary language.[12] Moreover, some of these Turkic tribes, such as the Shahsevens, have co-tribesmen in north Azerbaijan.[13]

In contrast, in this study the Turkmen are considered a separate ethnic category, since they seem to consider themselves as such. Moreover, unlike many of the Turkic tribal groups in Iran, the Turkmen do not have relatives in north Azerbaijan, thus they are not linked in mutual identity with it.

Taking into account the significant Azerbaijani population that lives outside the Azerbaijani provinces, especially in Tehran, as well as the tribal Turkic population, it seems that the Azerbaijanis comprise between one-fourth and one-third of the population of Iran, or approximately 20 million. This estimate is reinforced by the fact that most pre-Pahlavi surveys that related to the ethnic makeup of Iran estimated that the Turkic groups comprised at least one-third of Iran's population.[14] Considering that, relative to the Persian population, many more of them live in agricultural settings and thus tend to have large families, there is no reason to believe that their proportion of the population has declined. If anything, their relative percentage of the population would have been expected to

---

11.   The estimate of one third is from U.S. Government (as represented by the Secretary of the Army), *Iran: A Country Study* (Washington, D.C: U.S. Government, 1989), p. 92.

12.   The Qashqai speak a Turkic dialect, which is very close to Azerbaijani, while the Shahsevens speak Azerbaijani. In "Persia-Part II," *Central Asia Review*, No. 2 (1956), p. 419, it is claimed that the language of the Afshars is Azerbaijani.

13.   Chantal Lemercier-Quelquejay, "Islam and Identity in Azerbaijan," *Central Asian Survey*, Vol. 3, No. 2 (1984), p. 42.

14.   Ervand Abrahamian estimates that the Azerbaijani and tribal Turkic population in Iran in 1850 was 29 percent of the population. Abrahamian, *Iran Between Two Revolutions*, p. 12.

increase. An additional indication that the Azerbaijanis comprise one-third of the country is found in Michael Fischer's analysis of the students at Qom, assuming that the student body at Qom is fairly representative of the general population in Iran. Fisher found that one-third of the *madrasa* students in Qom were Azerbaijani.[15]

---

15.   Michael Fischer, *Iran: From Religious Dispute to Revolution* (Cambridge, Mass: Harvard University Press, 1980), p. 78.

Selected Bibliography

Periodicals and Newspapers

Ädäbiyyat vä Injäsänät (Baku). Writers' Union and Ministry of Culture, Azerbaijan SSR, literary weekly.

Azärbayjan (Baku). Writers' Union monthly.

Khalq-e Musulman (Tehran), journal of the Muslim People's Republican Party (MPRP).

Kommunist (Baku), Azerbaijan Communist Party daily (in Azerbaijani).

Varliq (Tehran) initially the organ of the Anjuman-i Azerbayjan.

Yol (Tehran).

Primary Sources

Äfändiyev, Rasim. *Azärbayjan Khalg Sänäti* (Baku: Ishïk, 1984).

Akhundov, Ä. *Azärbayjan Khalg Dastanlari* (Baku: Yazïchï, 1980).

Aliyev, Heydar. *Bakinskii rabochii*, June 14, 1981.

Aliyev, Heydar. *Bakinskii rabochii*, December 12, 1981.

Aliyev, Kemal. *Antichnaia Kavkazskaia Albaniya* (Baku: Izdatelstro Azerbaidzhan, 1992).

Alkarim, 'Abed, and Khamena, Manzuri. *Mukalemat-e Ruzmarah-e Turki-Farsi* (Türkche-Farsche Me'amuli Danishiqlar) (Tehran, 1993).

Ashurbeyli, Sara. *Gosudarstvo Shirvanshakhov* (Baku: Elm, 1983).

"Azerbayjan Jumhuriyat Reis: Dunyanin Butun Azerbayjanlari Birlash-mehlidirler," *Kayhan Havai* (Azerbaijani section), January 20, 1993.

Azärbayjan Mahabbat Dastanlari (Baku: Elm, 1979).

Azärbayjan Respublikasïnïn Konstitusiyasï (Baku: Azärbayjan Press, 1996).

Azärbayjan Sovet Ensiklopediyasï.

Azärbayjan Tarikhi: Än Gädim Dövrlärdän XX Äsrin Ävvällärinä Gädär (Baku: Elm, 1993).

Azäroghlu, "Häyat Yolu," *Azärbayjan* 8 (1987).

Baghcheban, Samineh. *Galin Turkja Danishaq* (Tehran: Offset Publishing House, 1981).

Bairamzade, S. Z. "Osnovnye izmeneniia sotsial'no-klassovoi struktury Iranskogo Azerbaidzhana v 1947-1962 gg," *Aktual'nye Problemy Stran Vlizhnego i Srednego Vostoka* (Moscow: USSR Academy of Sciences, 1986), pp. 80–88.

Bakhïsh, Eldar. "Balïg Ölümü," *Azärbayjan* 7 (1988).

Bala, Mirzä. "Azärbayjan Tarikhinde Türk Albaniya," *Azärbayjan* 10 (1989).

Baraheni, Reza. *The Crowned Cannibals: Writings on Repression in Iran* (New York: Vintage Books, 1977).

Behrengi, Samad. "Agha-ye Cox Bakhtiar" (A Very Lucky Man), unpublished poem.

Behrengi, Samad. *Afsanaha-ye Azarbayjan* (Tales of Azerbaijan), translated from Azerbaijani into Persian. vol. 1, (Tabriz, 1965), vol. 2, Tehran (1968).

Behrangi, Samad. "A Look at Today's Literature: A Study of (Gholam Hosayn Sa'edi's) the Mourners of Bayal," in Thomas M. Ricks, ed., *Critical Perspectives on Modern Persian Literature* (Washington, D.C.: Three Continents Press, 1984).

Behrangi, Samad. *The Black Fish and Other Modern Persian Stories* (Washington, D.C.: Three Continents Press, 1987).

Behzadi, Behzad. *Azarbayjani-Farcha Sözlük* (Tehran, 1990).

Büniatov, Ziya. *Azärbayjan Tarikhi Khäritäläri* (Baku: Azärbayjan Ensiklopediyasï, 1994).

"Chand Pishnahad Bara-ye Taqviyat-e Zaban-e Azeri," *Keyhan*, June 15, 1988.

Constitution of the Azärbayjan Qurtulush Teshkilatï (Azerbaijani) (unpublished).

Constitution of the Islamic Republic of Iran, Keyhan, November 17, 1979.

Doktor Javad Hey'ät (Baku: Azärbayjan Publishers, 1995).

Farzanah, Muhammad 'Ali. *Dastur-e Zaban-e Azarbayjani* (1979).

Firuz, 'Ali Isma'il. *Azeri Türkcensinde Benzer Sözcukler* (Tehran, 1989).

GAMIC Announcement Regarding Azerbaijani Students' Demonstration, May 1995 (unpublished).

Guluzade, Zümrüd. "Elmi Tädgigatlarïn Näshri," *Ädäbiyyat vä Injäsänät*, November 7, 1986.

Güney Azärbaycan Milli Istiqlal Jäbhäsi (The South Azerbaijan National Front for Independence) founding statement, 1995 (Azerbaijani, unpublished).

Hafizzadah, Muhammad. *Aras dar Guzargah-e Tarikh* (Aztasharatniye, 1995).

Hajïyev, Magsud. "Sämäd Behränqinin Häyat vä Yapadïjïghïna Dair," Azerbaijan SSR Academy of Sciences *Khäbärli* (Literature, Language and Art Series) No. 3, (1988).

Hariri-Akbari, Mohammad and Aazbdaftari, Behrooz. "A Brief Review of Contemporary Azerbaijani Poetry," *Critique* (Fall 1997, No. 11).

Hasanov, Qasam, Aliyov, Kamil, and Khalilov, Faridun. *Azärbayjan Dilinin Grameri* (Tabriz, 1992).

Heyat, Javad. "Regression of Azeri Language and Literature under the Oppressive Period of Pahlavi and Its Renaissance after the Islamic Revolution," *First International Conference of Turkic Studies*, Bloomington, Indiana, May 19–22, 1983).

—— *Türklärin Tarikh vä Mädäniyyätinä Bir Bakhïsh* (Baku: Azerbaijan State Publishers, 1993).

——*Azärbayjan Ädäbiyyatïna Bir Bakhïsh* (Baku: Yazïchï, 1993).

——"Origins of the Name and Boundaries of Azerbaijan," *Reform*, Vol. 1, No. 1 (March 1995).

Huseynov, Nazim. "Täbriz," *Azärbayjan Muällimi*, August 2, 1985.

Ibrahimov, Mirzä (Mirza). *Azerbaijanian Poetry: Classic, Modern and Traditional* (Moscow: Progress Publishers, 1969).

——"Jänubda Dirchälish," *Azärbayjan* 1 (1980).

—— *Mirzä Ibrahimov: Äsärläri On Jilddä* (Baku: Yazïchï, 1980, 1981).

—— *Jänubi Azärbayjan Ädäbiyyatï Antoloqiyasï*, Vol. 1 (Baku: Elm Publishers, 1981).

—— *Jänubi Azärbayjan Ädäbiyyatï Antoloqiyasï*, Vol. 2 (Baku: Elm Publishers, 1983).

—— *Jänubi Azärbayjan Ädäbiyyatï Antoloqiyasï*, Vol. 4 (Baku: Elm, 1994).

Institute of Art and Architecture in Baku, letter printed in "Samizdat Armenia-Azerbaijan Conflict," *Central Asian Survey*, Vol. 7, No. 4 (1988).

Ismayïl, Mahmud. *Azärbayjan Tarikhi* (Baku: Azerbaijan State Government Publishers, 1993).

Iunusova, Leila. "Pestraya palitra neformal'nykh dvizhenii v Azerbaidzhane," *Russkaia mysl'*, September 22, 1989.

—— "End of the Ice Age: Azerbaijan, August–September 1989," *CACC*, Vol. 8, No. 6 (1989).

Jänubi Azärbayjan Tarikhi Mäsäläläri (Baku: Elm, 1989).

Kärimov, Lätif. *Azärbayjan Khalchasï* (Baku: Yazïchï, 1985), Part II (Baku: Gyandzhlik, 1983), Part III (Baku: Gyandzhlik, 1983).

Kasravi, Ahmad. *al-'Irfan*, Tishrin I, 1922, pp. 121–123. (Evan Siegal, translation).

Khalilov, Aydin. *Ilk Azärbayjan Kitabï* (Baku: Sharq-Qärb, 1995).

Khamachi, Behruz. *Tavaf-e Saha* (Tabriz, 1991).

Khäzri, Näbi. "Dokkuz Qün, Dokkuz Qeje-Iran Täässuratï," *Azärbayjan* 9 (1983).

"Latïn Grafikalï Azärbayjan Älifbasï," (Baku: Azärnäshr, January 28, 1992).

"Letter of the Azerbaijani Students Studying in Tehran Universities to the Azerbaijani Deputies of the Iranian Majles" (Persian), June 1994 (unpublished).

"Letter of the Meshkinshar Students Studying in the Universities of the Country to the Government of the Islamic Republic of Iran," Varliq (April–June, 1994), pp. 93–96. (originally published in the weekly *Omid-e Zenjan*).

Mämmädli, Allahverdi. "Sän Yolsan, Män Yolchu," *Azärbayjan* 3 (1985).

Mohseni, Eziz. *Azerbayjan Edebiyyat Tarikhinden Qizil Yarpaqlar* (Tehran: Neshar, 1995).

Muhammad Chehregani's election platform, 1996 (unpublished).

Muhsini, Aziz. *Dinlah Mani* (1991).

Mustafaev, V.K. "Nekotorye aspekty kontseptsii natsii v obshchectvennoi mysli Irana (konets XIX – I polovina XX v.)," (Baku: Academy of Sciences, Azerbaijan SSR, History, Philosophy and Legal Series, 1989, No. 2).

Mustafeyeva, Nisä. *Jänubi Azärbayjan Khanlïglarï* (Baku: Azerbaijan Government Publishers, 1993).

Naseri, Halil. "Farhang-e Ma Huiyat-e Mast," *Ülker*, Esfand, 1359 (February–March 1981).

Näsibzadä, Näsib. (Nasib Nasibzade), "Täbriz Universiteti," *Ulduz* 9 (1983).

——"K ekonomicheskoi politike shakhskogo pravitel'stva v Azerbaizhane v 60-70-kh godakh," *Problemy ekonomicheskogo razvitiia stran Azii i Severnoi Afriki* (Moscow: Nauka, 1983).

——"Puti i formy ideologicheskogo vozdeistviia shakhskogo rezhima na Azerbaidzhanckoe naselenie Irana (60-70-e gody)," *Ideologiia i Politika* (Part II) (Moscow: Oriental Institute, 1986).

—— "Territoriia rasseleniia i vopros o chislennosti Azerbaidzhantsev v Irane," *Aktual'nye Problemy Stran Vlizhnego i Srednego Vostoka* (Moscow: USSR Academy of Sciences, 1986).

—— "A. R. Nabdel' i A. Tabrizli: Dva uklona v ideologii natsional'no-osvoboditel'nogo dvizheniia Azerbaidzhantsev v Irane," AnAz.SSR *Izvestiia*, Ser. Ist. Fil. No. 2 (1988).

—— *Azärbayjan Demokratik Respublikasï* (Baku: Elm, 1990).

—— *Yeni Musavat*, April 17, 1995.

Orujovun, Ä.Ä. *Azärbayjan Dilinin Izahlï Lüghäti* (Baku: Elm Publishers, 1983).

Pashayev, Hafiz. *Shäkilli Sözlük* (Ushaq Kitabï, Baku: Azärbayjan Publishers, 1992).

Payfun, Muhammad. *Farhang-i Azerbayjani* (Tehran: Danishneye Publishing, 1983).

Programme of the People's Front of Azerbaijan, *Rafsanjani Dar Azerbayjan Bedumbale Che Bud?* Teshkilat-e Feda'iyin-e Azerbayjan (Azerbaijan Feda'iyin Organization), July 13, 1995 (Persian, unpublished).

"Report of the Patriotic Muslim Students of Tabriz on the Tabriz Uprising," *RIPEH/The Review of Iranian Political Economy and History*, Vol. 2, No. 2 (June 1978).

Sabri Tabrizi, Gholam-Reza. *Iran: a Child's Story, a Man's Experience* (Edinburgh: Mainstream Publishing Company, Ltd., 1989).

Saläddin, Äli. *Azärbayjan She'ri ve Folklor XIX–XX Äsrlär* (Baku: Elm Publishers, 1982).

Samed Vurgun 1906-1956: Bibliografiya (Baku: Azerbaijan SSR Academy of Sciences Publishing, 1965).

Shabistari, Vahdat. *Dadli Sözler* (Tabriz, 1992).

Shaida, Yayda. *Edabbiyat Ujaghi* (Tabriz, 1987).

Shähriyar, Mähämmäd Hüseyn. "Heydar Babaya Salam," (1954), in *Yalan Dünya* (Baku: Azärbayjan Ensiklopediyasï, 1993).

Shukur, Muzäffär, ed. *Ashïk Shämshir* (Baku: Azerbaijan State Publishers, 1973).

Sumbatzade, A. S. *Azerbaidzhantsy-Etnogenez i Formirovanie Naroda* (Baku: Elm, 1990).

Täbrizdän Dörd Däftär (Baku: Azerbaijan State Publishers, 1994).

Taghïyeva, Sh. Ä. "Azadlig vä Mäsläk Fädaisi," Azerbaijan SSR Academy of Sciences, *Khäbärläri* (History, philosophy and law series) Vol. 1 (1983) (Baku: Elm Publishers).

Taqizadeh, Hasan. "The Background of the Constitutional Movement in Azerbaijan," *Middle East Journal* 14 (1960).

Vafasi, Zahareh. *Folklor Ganjinahsi, Oyunlar* (Entesharat-e yaran).

Vahabzade, Bakhtiyar. *Mugham* (Baku: Azerbaijan SSR Government Publications, Yazïchï, 1982).

——(Hadi Sultan-Qurraie, ed.) *Selected Works of Bakhtiyar Vahabzade* (Bloomington, Indiana: Indiana University Turkish Studies Publications, 1998).

Zafarkhah, 'A. *Ata babalar Diyiblar* (Tabriz: Entesharat-e yaran, 1991–1992).

Zeyhalov, Färhad. *Türkoloqiyanïn Äsaslarï* (Baku: Maarif Publishing, 1981).

Secondary Sources

BOOKS

Abrahamian, Ervand. *Iran Between Two Revolutions* (Princeton: Princeton University Press, 1982).

—— *Radical Islam: The Iranian Mojahedin* (London: I.B. Tauris & Co. Ltd., 1989).

—— *Khomeinism: Essays on Islamic Law* (Berkeley and Los Angeles: University of California Press, 1993).

Akzin, Benjamin. *States and Nations* (Garden City, N.Y.: Anchor Books, 1964).

Alstadt, Audrey. *The Azerbaijani Turks* (Stanford: Hoover Institute, 1992).

Anderson, Benedict, *Imagined Communities* (N.Y.: Verso, 1991).

Andrews, Peter Alford. *Ethnic Groups in the Republic of Turkey* (Wiesbaden: Dr. Lutwig Reichert Verlag, 1989).

Area Handbook for Iran (Washington, D.C.: U.S. Government Printing Office [GPO], 1971).

Atabaki, Touraj. *Azerbaijan: Ethnicity and Autonomy in Twentieth-Century Iran* (London: British Academic Press, 1993).

Atkin, Muriel. *Russia and Iran 1780-1828* (Minneapolis: University of Minneapolis, 1980).

Browne, E.G. *A Literary History of Persia*, Vol. 4: Modern Times (1500–1924) (London, 1924).

—— *A Year Amongst the Persians* (London: Adam and Charles Black, 1959).

Bayat, Mongol. *Mysticism and Dissent: Socioreligious Thought in Qajar Iran* (Syracuse: Syracuse University Press, 1982).

——*Iran's First Revolution: Shi'ism and the Constitutional Revolution of 1905-1909* (N.Y.: Oxford University Press, 1991).

Bennigsen, Alexandre and Wimbush, S. Enders. *Muslim National Communism in the Soviet Union: A Revolutionary Strategy for the Colonial World* (Chicago: The University of Chicago Press, 1979).

——*Muslims of the Soviet Empire: A Guide* (Bloomington, Indiana: Indiana University Press, 1986).

Berengian, Sakina. *Azeri and Persian Literary Works in Twentieth-Century Iranian Azerbaijan* (Berlin: Klaus Schwarz Verlag, 1988).

Brubaker, Rogers. *Nationalism Reframed: Nationhood and the National Question in the New Europe*, (Cambridge: Cambridge University Press, 1996).

Carrere d' Encausse, Helene. *The End of the Soviet Empire* (New York: Basic Books, 1993).

Cottam, Richard W. *Nationalism in Iran: Updated Through 1978* (Pittsburgh: University of Pittsburgh Press, 1979).

Deutsch, Karl. *Nationalism and Social Communication* (Cambridge: MIT Press, 1953).

Franz, Erhard. *Minderheiten in Iran* (Hamburg: German Orient Institute, Middle East Documentation, 1981).

Gellner, Ernest. *Nations and Nationalism* (Oxford: Basil Blackwell, 1983).

Ghods, M. Reza. *A Comparative Study of the Causes, Development, and Effects of the Revolutionary Movements in Northern Iran in 1920–21 and 1945–46* (Ann Arbor, Michigan: University Microfilms, 1991).

Halliday, Fred. *Iran: Dictatorship and Development*, 2d. ed., (London: Penguin Books, 1979).

Hiro, Dilip. *Iran Under the Ayatollahs* (London: Routledge and Kegan Paul, 1985).

Hobsbawm, Eric. *Nations and Nationalism Since 1780* (Cambridge: Cambridge University Press, 1990).

Hunter, Shireen T. *The Transcaucasus in Transition: Nation Building and Conflict* (Washington, D.C.: Center for Strategic and International Studies, 1994).

Javadi, Hasan. *Satire in Persian Literature* (London: Associated University Press, 1988).

Katouzian, Homayoun. *The Political Economy of Modern Iran* (London: Macmillan, 1981).

Kazemi, Farhad. *Poverty and Revolution in Iran: the Migrant Poor, Urban Marginality and Politics* (New York: New York University Press, 1980)

Kecmanovic, Dusan. *The Mass Psychology of Ethnonationalism* (New York and London: Plenum Press, 1996).

Keddie, Nikki R. *Iran and the Muslim World: Resistance and Revolution* (New York: New York University Press, 1995).

Kurian, George Thomas, ed. *Encyclopedia of the Third World* (New York: Facts on File, 1992), Vol. 2.

Lapidus, Ira M. *A History of Islamic Societies* (Cambridge: Cambridge University Press, 1988).

Litvak, Meir. *Shi'i Scholars of Nineteenth-Century Iraq: The 'Ulama' of Najaf and Karbala* (Cambridge: Cambridge University Press, 1998).

Menashri, David. *Education and the Making of Modern Iran* (Ithaca: Cornell University Press, 1992).

Nahaylo, Bohdan and Swoboda, Victor. *Soviet Disunion: A History of the Nationalities Problem in the USSR* (New York: The Free Press, 1990).

Nissman, David. *The Soviet Union and Iranian Azerbaijan: The Uses of Nationalism for Political Penetration* (Boulder: Westview, 1987).

Parsa, Misagh. *Social Origins of the Iranian Revolution* (New Brunswick: Rutgers University Press, 1989).

Savory, Roger. *Iran Under the Safavids* (London: Cambridge University Press, 1980).

Schahgaldian, Nikola B. *The Iranian Military Under the Islamic Republic* (Santa Monica: RAND Corp., 1987).

Seton-Watson, Hugh. *Nations and States: An Enquiry into the Origins of Nations and the Politics of Nationalism* (Boulder, Colo.: Westview Press, 1977).

Sheffer, Gabriel, ed. *Modern Diasporas in International Politics* (London: Croom Helm, 1986).

Smith, Anthony D. *National Identity* (Reno: University of Nevada Press, 1991).

Spector, Ivar. *The Soviet Union and the Muslim World 1917–1958* (Seattle and London: University of Washington Press, 1959).

Suny, Ronald Grigor. *The Revenge of the Past: Nationalism, Revolution and the Collapse of the Soviet Union* (Stanford, California: Stanford University Press, 1993).

Swietochowski, Tadeuz. *Russian Azerbaijan, 1905-1920: the Shaping of National Identity in a Muslim Community* (Cambridge: Cambridge University Press, 1985).

———*Russia and Azerbaijan: A Borderland in Transition* (New York: Columbia University Press, 1995).

Taheri, Amir. *The Spirit of Allah: Khomeini and the Islamic Revolution* (London: Hutchinson, 1985).

U.S. Government (as represented by the Secretary of the Army), *Iran: A Country Study* (Washington, D.C.: U.S. Government, 1989).

Vostokovednye Tsentry v SSR, Vol. I (Azerbaijan, Armenia, Georgia, Ukraine) (Moscow: Main Editor of Eastern Literature, 1988).

Zabih, Sepehr. *The Iranian Military in Revolution and War* (London and New York: Routledge, 1988).

ARTICLES

Abrahamian, Ervand. "Communism and Communalism in Iran: the Tudah and the Firqah-i Dimukrat," *International Journal of Middle East Studies*, Vol. 1, No. 4 (1970).

———"Kasravi: The Integrative Nationalist of Iran," in Elie Kedourie and Sylvia G. Haim (eds.), *Towards a Modern Iran: Studies in Thought, Politics and Society* (London: Frank Cass, 1980).

Afary, Janet. "Peasant Rebellion of the Caspian Region during the Iranian Constitutional Revolution 1906-1909," *International Journal of Middle East Studies*, Vol. 23 (May 1991).

Aghajanian, Akbar. "Ethnic Inequality in Iran: an Overview," *International Journal of Middle East Studies* Vol. 15, No. 2 (1983), pp. 211–224.

Al-e Ahmad, Jalal. "Samad and the Folk Legend," in Michael C. Hillmann (ed.), *Iranian Society: An Anthology of Writings by Jalal Al-e Ahmad* (Lexington, Kentucky: Mazda Press, 1982).

Aliyev, S. "The Problem of Nationalities in Contemporary Iran," English summary of the Russian text in *The Central Asian Review*, Vol. 16 (1966).

Amirahmadi, Hooshang. "A Theory of Ethnic Collective Movements and its Application to Iran," *Ethnic and Racial Studies*, Vol. 10, No. 4 (1987).

Aslan, Yasin. "Azerbaijani Intellectuals Discuss Legacy of Alphabet Reforms," *Report on the USSR* (RFE/RL), No. 71 (February 1, 1989).

Azerbaijan-Iranian Relations (Baku: FAR Centre for Economic and Political Research), May 1996.

Babayev, E. Ch. "Iuzhnyi Azerbaidzhan v Iranskoi Revoliutsii 1978-1979 gg," *Jänubi Azärbayjan Tarikhi Mäsälaläri* (Baku: Elm, 1989).

Bakhash, Shaul. "Center-Periphery Relations in Nineteenth-Century Iran," *Iranian Studies* Vol. 14, No1–2 (Winter–Spring 1981).

Bayatly, Tamam. "Alphabet Transitions: The Latin Script: A Chronology, Symbol of a New Azerbaijan," *Azerbaijan International*, Vol. 5, No. 2 (Summer 1997).

Bennigsen, Alexandre. *Azerbaijan* (paper prepared for conference of the Kennan Institute for Advanced Russian Studies, The Wilson Center, May 1979).

Bilinsky, Yaroslav. "The Soviet Education Laws of 1958-59 and Soviet Nationalities Policy," *Soviet Studies*, Vol. 14, No. 2 (October 1962).

Bohr, Annette and Aslan, Yasin. "Independent Azerbaijan, 1918-1920: Call to Reevaluate History of Former Nation-State," *RFE/RL* 377/88 (August 18, 1988).

Chehabi, H. E. "Ardabil Becomes a Province: Center-Periphery Relations in Iran," *International Journal of Middle East Studies*, Vol. 29, No. 2 (1997), pp. 235–253.

Connor, Walker. "Nation-Building or Nation-Destroying?", *World Politics* 24 (April 1972).

——— "Ethnonationalism: Looking Backward," in Myron Weiner and Samuel Huntington (eds.), *Understanding Political Development* (Glenview, Illinois: Scott, Foresman/Little, Brown Higher Education, 1987).

Ememi-Yeganeh, Jody. "Iran vs. Azerbaijan (1945–46: Divorce, Separation or Reconciliation?)," *Central Asian Survey*, Vol. 3, No. 2 (1984).

Fischer, Michael. *Iran: From Religious Dispute to Revolution* (Cambridge: Harvard University Press, 1980).

Fuller, Elizabeth. "The Nemat Panakhov Phenomenon—As Reflected in the Azerbaijani Press," *Report on the USSR*, No. 70 (January 31, 1989).

Hanson, Brad. "The 'Westoxication' of Iran: Depictions and Reactions of Behrengi, Al-e Ahmad, and Shari'ati," *International Journal of Middle East Studies*, Vol. 15, No. 1 (1983).

Higgins, Patricia J. "Minority-State Relations in Contemporary Iran," *Iranian Studies*, Vol. 17, No. 1 (Winter 1984).

Hyman, Anthony. "Soviet-Iranian Relations and the Two Azerbaijans," *Report on the USSR*, No. 19 (1990).

Javadi, Hasan. "Research Note: Azeri Publications in Iran," *Critique*, No. 8 (Spring 1996).

Kazemi, Farhad. "Ethnicity and the Iranian Peasantry," in Milton J. Esman and Itamar Rabinovich (eds.), *Ethnicity, Pluralism, and the State in the Middle East* (London and Ithaca: Cornell University Press, 1988).

Keddie, Nikki R. "The Iranian Power Structure and Social Change 1800-1969: An Overview," *International Journal of Middle East Studies*, Vol. 2, No. 1 (1971).

Hunter, Shireen T. "Great Azerbaijan: Myth or Reality?", in M.R. Djalili (ed.), *Le Caucase Postsovietique: La Transition Dans Le Conflit* (Paris: L.G.D.J., 1995).

Law, Henry D.G. "Modern Persian Prose (1920s-1940s), in Thomas M. Ricks (ed.), *Critical Perspectives on Modern Persian Literature* (Washington, D.C.: Three Continents Press, 1984).

Lazzerini, Edward J. "Sayyid Jamal al-Din al-Afghani from the Perspective of a Russian Muslim," in Elie Kedourie and Sylvia G. Haim (eds.), *Towards a Modern Iran: Studies in Thought, Politics and Society* (London: Frank Cass, 1980).

Lemercier-Quelquejay, Chantal. "Islam and Identity in Azerbaijan," *Central Asian Survey*, Vol. 3, No. 2 (1984).

Menashri, David. "Shi'ite Leadership: In the Shadow of Conflicting Ideologies," *Iranian Studies*, Vol. 13 (1980).

Michaeli, Mirza. "Formation of Popular Front in Azerbaijan," *RFE/RL* 558/88 (December 9, 1988).

——"Azerbaijan Notebook," *Report on the USSR* (RFE/RL) 155/1989 (March 15, 1989).

Minorsky, Vladimir. "The Poetry of Shah Isma'il I," *Bulletin of the School of Oriental and African Studies*, Vol. 10, No. 4 (1942).

Mojab, Shahrzad and Hassanpour, Amir. "The Politics of Nationality and Ethnic Diversity," in Saeed Rahnema and Sorab Behdad, *Iran after the Revolution: Crises of an Islamic State* (London: I.B. Tauris and Co. Ltd, 1996).

Morton, A.H. *The Early Years of Shah Isma'il in the Afzal al-tavarikh and Elsewhere*, Pembroke Papers 4 (1996).

Nikazmerad, Nicholas M. "A Chronological Survey of the Iranian Revolution," *Iranian Studies*, Vol. 13, Nos. 1–4 (1980).

Nissman, David. "The Origins and Development of the Literature of 'Longing,'" *Journal of Turkish Studies*, Vol. 8 (1984), pp. 199–207.

Oberlang, Pierre. "Iran," in Margaret Bainbridge (ed.), *The Turkic Peoples of the World* (London: Kegan Paul International Ltd., 1993).

Öztopchu, Kurtulush. "A Comparison of Modern Azeri with Modern Turkish," *Azerbaijan International* (September 1993).

Perry, John R. *Persian in the Safavid Period: Sketch for an Etat de Langue*, Pembroke Papers 4 (1996).

"Persia-Part II," *Central Asia Review*, No. 2 (1956).

Reese, William. "The Role of the Religious Revival and Nationalism in Transcaucasia," *RFE/RL* 535/88 (December 5, 1988).

Renan, Ernest. "What Is a Nation?" in Omar Dahbour and Micheline R. Ishay, *The Nationalism Reader* (Atlantic Highlands, New Jersey: Humanities Press, 1995). Originally appeared in *Oeuvres Complètes* (Paris, 1947-61), Vol. 1, pp. 887–907.

Ross, E. Denison. "The Early Years of Shah Isma'il," *Journal of the Royal Asiatic Society* (1896).

Rossow, Robert Jr. "The Battle of Azerbaijan, 1946," *The Middle East Journal*, Vol. 10 (Winter 1956), pp. 17–56.

Saroyan, Mark. "The Karabagh Syndrome and Azerbaijani Politics," *Problems of Communism*, Vol. 39, No. 5 (September/October 1990).

Slezkine, Yuri. "The USSR as a Communal Apartment, or How a Socialist State Promoted Ethnic Particularism," in Geoff Eley and Ronald G. Suny (eds.), *Becoming National* (New York: Oxford University Press, 1996).

Suny, Ronald Grigor. "Nationalism and Social Class in the Russian Revolution: the Cases of Baku and Tiflis," in R.G. Suny (ed.), *Transcaucasia: Nationalism and Social Change* (Ann Arbor: University of Michigan Press, 1983).

Vatanabi Shouleh. (ed.), "Azerbaijan," *World Literature Today*, Vol. 70, No. 3 (Summer 1996).

Wimbush, S. Enders. "Divided Azerbaijan: Nation Building, Assimilation, and Mobilization Between Three States," in William O. McCagg, Jr. and Brian D. Silver (eds.), *Soviet Asian Ethnic Frontiers*, (New York: Pergamon Press, 1979).

About the Author

Brenda Shaffer is the Research Director of the Caspian Studies Program at Harvard University's Kennedy School of Government. Shaffer is a specialist on Central Asia, the Caucasus, Iran's policies in the Caspian region, Russian-Iranian relations, ethnic politics in Iran, and the Nagorno-Karabagh conflict. She lectures at the Hebrew University of Jerusalem and is the recipient of the "Young Truman Scholars" Award in the field of Middle East studies at the Harry S. Truman Research Institute for the Advancement of Peace at the Hebrew University. She received her Ph.D. from Tel Aviv University, and has served in the Israel Defense Forces.

Shaffer is the author of the book *Partners in Need: The Strategic Relationship Of Russia and Iran* (Washington Institute for Near East Policy, 2001). She has published a major policy recommendation paper for the Bush Administration on U.S. policy in the Caspian region, and is researching a book on the connection between culture and foreign policy, *The Limits of Culture: Foreign Policy, Islam and the Caspian* (The MIT Press, forthcoming 2003).

Index

BCSIA Studies in International Security

Published by The MIT Press

Sean M. Lynn-Jones and Steven E. Miller, series editors
Karen Motley, executive editor
Belfer Center for Science and International Affairs (BCSIA)
John F. Kennedy School of Government, Harvard University

Allison, Graham T., Owen R. Coté, Jr., Richard A. Falkenrath, and Steven E. Miller, *Avoiding Nuclear Anarchy: Containing the Threat of Loose Russian Nuclear Weapons and Fissile Material* (1996)

Allison, Graham T., and Kalypso Nicolaïdis, eds., *The Greek Paradox: Promise vs. Performance* (1996)

Arbatov, Alexei, Abram Chayes, Antonia Handler Chayes, and Lara Olson, eds., *Managing Conflict in the Former Soviet Union: Russian and American Perspectives* (1997)

Bennett, Andrew, *Condemned to Repetition? The Rise, Fall, and Reprise of Soviet-Russian Military Interventionism, 1973–1996* (1999)

Blackwill, Robert D., and Michael Stürmer, eds., *Allies Divided: Transatlantic Policies for the Greater Middle East* (1997)

Blackwill, Robert D., and Paul Dibb, eds., *America's Asian Alliances* (2000)

Brom, Shlomo, and Yiftah Shapir, eds., *The Middle East Military Balance 1999–2000* (1999)

Brom, Shlomo, and Yiftah Shapir, eds., *The Middle East Military Balance 2001–2002* (2002)

Brown, Michael E., ed., *The International Dimensions of Internal Conflict* (1996)

Brown, Michael E., and Šumit Ganguly, eds., *Government Policies and Ethnic Relations in Asia and the Pacific* (1997)

Carter, Ashton B., and John P. White, eds., *Keeping the Edge: Managing Defense for the Future* (2001)

Elman, Colin, and Miriam Fendius Elman, eds., *Bridges and Boundaries: Historians, Political Scientists, and the Study of International Relations* (2000)

Elman, Miriam Fendius, ed., *Paths to Peace: Is Democracy the Answer?* (1997)

Falkenrath, Richard A., *Shaping Europe's Military Order: The Origins and Consequences of the CFE Treaty* (1994)

Falkenrath, Richard A., Robert D. Newman, and Bradley A. Thayer, *America's Achilles' Heel: Nuclear, Biological, and Chemical Terrorism and Covert Attack* (1998)

Feaver, Peter D., and Richard H. Kohn, eds., *Soldiers and Civilians: The Civil-Military Gap and American National Security* (2001)

Feldman, Shai, *Nuclear Weapons and Arms Control in the Middle East* (1996)

Feldman, Shai, and Yiftah Shapir, eds., *The Middle East Military Balance 2000–2001* (2001)

Forsberg, Randall, ed., *The Arms Production Dilemma: Contraction and Restraint in the World Combat Aircraft Industry* (1994)

Hagerty, Devin T., *The Consequences of Nuclear Proliferation: Lessons from South Asia* (1998)

Heymann, Philip B., *Terrorism and America: A Commonsense Strategy for a Democratic Society* (1998)

Kokoshin, Andrei A., *Soviet Strategic Thought, 1917–91* (1998)

Lederberg, Joshua, *Biological Weapons: Limiting the Threat* (1999)

Shaffer, Brenda, *Borders and Brethren: Iran and the Challenge of Azerbaijani Identity* (2002)

Shields, John M., and William C. Potter, eds., *Dismantling the Cold War: U.S. and NIS Perspectives on the Nunn-Lugar Cooperative Threat Reduction Program* (1997)

Tucker, Jonathan B., ed., *Toxic Terror: Assessing Terrorist Use of Chemical and Biological Weapons* (2000)

Utgoff, Victor A., ed., *The Coming Crisis: Nuclear Proliferation, U.S. Interests, and World Order* (2000)

Williams, Cindy, ed., *Holding the Line: U.S. Defense Alternatives for the Early 21st Century* (2001)

The Robert and Renée Belfer Center for Science and International Affairs

Graham T. Allison, Director
John F. Kennedy School of Government
Harvard University
79 JFK Street, Cambridge, MA 02138
Tel: (617) 495-1400; Fax: (617) 495-8963
http://www.ksg.harvard.edu/bcsia bcsia_ksg@harvard.edu

The Belfer Center for Science and International Affairs (BCSIA) is the hub of research, teaching and training in international security affairs, environmental and resource issues, science and technology policy, human rights, and conflict studies at Harvard's John F. Kennedy School of Government. The Center's mission is to provide leadership in advancing policy-relevant knowledge about the most important challenges of international security and other critical issues where science, technology and international affairs intersect.

BCSIA's leadership begins with the recognition of science and technology as driving forces transforming international affairs. The Center integrates insights of social scientists, natural scientists, technologists, and practitioners with experience in government, diplomacy, the military, and business to address these challenges. The Center pursues its mission in four complementary research programs:

- The **International Security Program** (ISP) addresses the most pressing threats to U.S. national interests and international security.

- The **Environment and Natural Resources Program** (ENRP) is the locus of Harvard's interdisciplinary research on resource and environmental problems and policy responses.

- The **Science, Technology and Public Policy Program** (STPP) analyzes ways in which science and technology policy influence international security, resources, environment, and development, and such cross-cutting issues as technological innovation and information infrastructure.

- The **WPF Program on Intrastate Conflict, Conflict Prevention and Conflict Resolution** analyzes the causes of ethnic, religious, and other conflicts, and seeks to identify practical ways to prevent and limit such conflicts.

The heart of the Center is its resident research community of more than 140 scholars: Harvard faculty, analysts, practitioners, and each year a new, interdisciplinary group of research fellows. BCSIA sponsors frequent seminars, workshops and conferences, maintains a substantial specialized library, and publishes books, monographs and discussion papers.

The Center's International Security Program, directed by Steven E. Miller, publishes the BCSIA Studies in International Security, and sponsors and edits the quarterly journal *International Security*.

The Center is supported by an endowment established with funds from Robert and Renée Belfer, the Ford Foundation and Harvard University, by foundation grants, by individual gifts, and by occasional government contracts.